THE HUTT ADAPTATION OF
THE BENDER-GESTALT TEST

THE HUTT ADAPTATION OF THE BENDER-GESTALT TEST

Rapid Screening and Intensive Diagnosis

FOURTH EDITION

MAX L. HUTT, Litt. D.

Professor (retired), University of Detroit
and
Consultant in Clinical Psychology

Grune & Stratton, Inc.
(Harcourt Brace Jovanovich, Publishers)
Orlando   San Diego   New York
London   Toronto   Montreal   Sydney   Tokyo

Library of Congress Cataloging in Publication Data

Hutt, Max L.
  The Hutt adaptation of the Bender-gestalt test.

  Bibliography: p.
  Includes indexes.
  1. Bender gestalt test. I. Title. [DNLM: 1. Bender-
Gestalt Test. WM 145 H982c]
  BF698.8.B4H8   1985   155.2'84   85-7656
  ISBN 0-8089-1718-8

*Acknowledgment is made to Dr. Lauretta Bender
and the American Orthopsychiatric Association,
Inc., for permission to adapt and use the
test figures used in the Bender-Gestalt Test. Dr.
Bender and the American Orthopsychiatric
Association of course do not assume any responsibility
for the contents of this book.*

Grune & Stratton, Inc.
Orlando, FL 32887

Distributed in the United Kingdom by
Grune & Stratton, Ltd.
24/28 Oval Road, London NW 1

Library of Congress Catalog Number 85-7656
International Standard Book Number 0-8089-1718-8
Printed in the United States of America
85 86 87 88 89 10 9 8 7 6 5 4 3 2 1

CONTENTS

TABLE OF PLATES

TABLE OF CHARTS

PREFACE

The HABGT has become well established in the clinical psychology community over the past 40 years or so. Many psychologists use it as a preferred psychological tool, although they vary considerably in the ways in which they administer and interpret the "findings." Some prefer to "scan" the protocol, for example, while others prefer to score it and conduct an "inferential analysis" in depth. Perhaps its most frequent use is as a screening device for cases suspected of organic brain damage.

At the same time research studies have proliferated over the years. Findings to-date suggest that Configurational Analysis of the test protocol, a fairly rapid procedure, yields highly effective discrimination between groups of organics and nonorganics. Although such procedures are highly valuable, they are only a first step in clinical diagnosis. Other research studies attest the power of the HABGT in uncovering various types of psychopathology or in evaluating certain personality characteristics. Continuing research confirms the validity of certain test indices in discriminating between well-adjusted and poorly adjusted children and adolescents.

Our purpose in this 4th edition of the HABGT is to make these clinical and research findings more readily available to the clinician. Toward this end, the entire work has been reorganized. Part I deals with the various roles in which the test has been employed and presents a brief history of its use and clinical/research findings. The varied and ingenious methods of test administration are also described in detail. Part II presents the major test factors, the objective scales and configurational patterns, and normative data. The research findings related to these aspects are discussed simulatenously so that the reader may be able to integrate applications with values and limitations. This section of the book offers the clinician rapid and effective methods of screening patients and deriving nosological findings. Part III then goes into further and more intensive detail, offering evidence concerning other test factors and methods of intensive and/or projective analysis of the HABGT. The last chapter, for the first time, presents rationale and principles, with case illustrations, of the application of the test in clinical practice and in therapeutic work, in particular. It is hoped that this reorganization of the text, together with the summaries of recent research, will make the HABGT more useful to both researcher and clinician. Although there has already been extensive research, much remains to be done, particularly in the area of projective testing and analysis.

If I may be permitted the luxury of speculating on the virility of the HABGT, I would offer the following comments. In the first place, the test has a strong appeal to many because of its simplicity: ease of administration and simple methods of scoring/evaluation. And then, it provides a sample of nonverbal, perceptual-motoric behavior that is lacking in most other test procedures. This second advantage provides access to behavior that clinicians recognize as highly important in gaining a broad perspective of the patient. In the third place, the HABGT enables the clinician to "test-out" various hypotheses about the patient by procedures I have called, variously, "testing-the-limits," "experimental-clinical procedures," and most recently, "microdiagnosis." Such procedures not only permit the testing of relevant hypotheses, but also stimulate the uncovering of assets and potentials, not otherwise readily discernible. Of course, such procedures may take valuable clinical time and require sophistication and ingenuity on the part of the clinician, but the "pay-off" can be considerable. This is why many clinicians prefer the HABGT to other tests of perception and perceptual-motoric skills. They consciously or unconsciously wish to make clinical sense and use of the test data, rather than simply obtain a measure of perceptual-motoric maturity.

I am deeply indebted to the many colleagues, too numerous to mention, who, in workshops I have given, in research they have published, or in personal discussions, have challenged my views, offered alternative explanations, or supplemented my, sometimes, myopic or obstinate position. Most of all, I am indebted to my patients who have taken the test, have shared their reactions with me, and have occasionally "seen" aspects of the test that I had been unable to see. Through their reactions and their movement during the therapeutic experience, they have made me a wiser and more "open" clinician.

Max L. Hutt
Ann Arbor, Michigan

THE HUTT ADAPTATION OF
THE BENDER-GESTALT TEST

PART I

Test Forms, History, and Administration

1
The Many Faces of the HABGT

When Wertheimer published his classic study of perception in 1923 (Wertheimer, 1923), his interest was in Gestalt principles governing perception. He did not indicate that his test designs could be utilized for psychodiagnostic purposes. It remained for Schilder, who was familiar with both the work of Gestaltists in Germany and the particular work of Wertheimer, to recognize that visual perception involved the personality operating in a given situation and not simply the mechanical act of perceiving (Schilder, 1934) and he encouraged others (including this writer) to explore the inter-relationships of personality and perception. One of those who took up his challenge was his wife, Lauretta Bender, who explored the relationships between the reproduction of some of Wertheimer's original visual designs and various types of psychopathology (Bender, 1938). Her work remained largely unknown to psychologists and psychiatrists, except to those who worked with her at the Bellevue Hospital in New York City, mainly because her test cards were not published until many years later and she did not conceive of the use of her test cards as useful for personality diagnosis.

The impetus for utilization of the Bender Gestalt Test (BGT) as a *personality test* came from the exigencies of World War II. There was an urgent need for personality tests to diagnose a vast number of soldiers from greatly diverse cultural backgrounds. Many of these soldiers were illiterate, some suffered from organic brain damage, and still others suffered from a variety of psychopathological disorders. The writer, who was the senior instuctor in an Officers' Course in Clinical Psychology in the U.S. Army, decided to utilize his own clinical experience with the

3

BGT and his, then, limited research data with the test, and to instruct these psychologists in the varied ways that the instrument could be used. As part of this program he wrote and published a tentative manual (Hutt, 1945a). He also published an article describing how this procedure might be utilized, along with others, for purposes of diagnostic screening and therapeutic planning (Hutt, 1945b).

Largely as a consequence of this teaching and writing program, the BGT became widely known and widely used. Whereas prior to 1945 only a handful of psychologists knew or used this test, in the years immediately following the war, the test gained widespread clinical use and research studies began to proliferate. In one early study of the use of the test (Korner, 1962), it was found that the test ranked sixth in 1950 and fourth in 1958. Various other surveys of the usage of the test indicated that it maintained or increased its popularity (Lapointe, 1974; Lubin, Wallis, & Paine, 1971; Mills, 1965). By 1974 the BGT ranked second in frequency of use (Brown & McGuire, 1976). Moreover, research studies on the test or with the test also proliferated. Prior to 1945 no research on the test had been published. By 1960 almost 300 research studies were available (Hutt, 1977), and by 1965 Crenshaw, et al, (1968) reported that this test was the fifth most frequently used projective test in research in this area. Research studies using the BGT have continued to appear regularly since that time (Tolor & Brannigan, 1980). Moreover, Brown and McGuire (1976) reported that the BGT had maintained its position over a 15-year period.

But the BGT *is not a single test,* but the basis for a variety of "tests." The original test procedures developed by Wertheimer involved asking his experimental subjects to describe his large sample of designs. Bender (1938) selected nine of these designs and asked her patients to draw them on a single sheet of paper (see also, Bender, 1946). The designs on Bender's cards were originally drawn freehand and later reproduced by means of a mimeograph procedure. Because they contained many irregularities and were discrepant, in some respects, from Wertheimer's designs, Hutt (1945a), with the assistance of F. L. Wells, had accurate reproductions of the nine designs prepared and printed for use in army medical installations. In 1960, with the publication of the first edition of the Hutt Adaptation of the Bender-Gestalt Test (Hutt, 1960), these test cards became widely available. Various researchers and clinicians (see Chapter 2) introduced other methods of administering and scoring the "test" and some introduced modified test materials.

We shall, therefore, present an overview of our own methods in utilizing this procedure, entitled the HABGT, so that the reader may be alert to its multiple possibilities and utilize it most effectively.

THE HABGT AS A SCREENING DEVICE

Over the years since its introduction, despite its presentation as a projective test by Hutt, the HABGT, as well as the BGT, have been most frequently used for screening purposes. And, among such screening objectives, the most frequent use has been, and remains, the screening for organic brain dysfunction (Sipola, 1984). However, the HABGT is also useful in screening for other psychiatric conditions, notably for psychosis and for mental retardation.

In using this test for such purposes only the *Copy Phase* need be administered (see Chapter 3). Such administration only takes some 10 minutes, although this may vary widely depending on the condition of the subject. Not only is little time required for administration, but "scoring" requires only checking or counting for the designated pathological signs in the configuration (see Chapter 4). Research findings with this procedure indicate that such screening is from 80 to 85% accurate for most organic brain syndrome (OBS) conditions (Tolor & Brannigan, 1980; Lacks, 1984).

It should be strongly emphasized that screening for OBS is not equivalent to diagnosing for OBS. Screening, no matter how high the probability that S falls in a given category, needs to be checked for both false positive and false negative findings. Moreover, the conscientious clinician will wish to test both for alternative explanations of the findings as well as for indications of modifiability, concurrent conditions, and the like. We shall have much more to say about such matters in later chapters.

THE HABGT AS A DIAGNOSTIC TEST

We use the term *diagnosis* to distinguish this procedure both from *screening* and *psychodiagnosis*. In diagnosis the objective is to establish with relative certainty the particular nosological category (or categories) into which a given individual is most likely to be placed as well as to establish the probability that he *does not fall into some other category*. Diagnosis is thus understood as *differential diagnosis*. Moreover, the course (development) and degree of pathology are also determined. Usually, the objective of diagnosis requires the administration of more than one diagnostic procedure as well as consideration of the history and special circumstances that might affect the finding. We employ the term *psychodiagnosis* to denote a more complete and detailed evaluation of the individual, including such factors as an evaluation of other personality characteristics, psychological defenses, and coping strategies that are employed, and probable behavioral consequences of the condition. Psychodiagnosis is, thus, a more complete evaluative procedure and provides for some indication of the strengths and weaknesses of the individual.

In diagnosis, therefore, the examiner will aim to learn more than whether an individual is likely to fall into a particular nosological category; more evidence is needed to describe and evaluate him. The aim is to determine with greater probability that he falls into a particular category (or categories) as well as to determine the peculiar characteristics of his adjustment.

In using the HABGT for diagnosis only the Copy Phase of the test needs to be administered. The examiner may also wish to use other procedures (see Chapter 3) to increase the fund of test information available. The Copy Phase will yield not only a Configuration Score, as indicated in the Screening procedure, but also a *Psychopathology Score*. The latter can be utilized to determine the probability that S belongs in a particular psychopathological category. Not only will this score increase the validity of the diagnosis, but the several factors comprising the score may be utilized to scrutinize the subject's performance and thus provide for differential diagnosis. As will be learned later, the Psychopathology Score consists of 17 test factors, each of which yields psychological information concerning the subject's performance. The examiner may also scrutinize the separate scores on these factors to investigate and evaluate the specific nature of the subject's particular psychopathology; i.e., such as contact with reality; degree of impulsivity; nature of affective behavior; and the like.

The Copy Phase of the test can also yield an *Adience-Abience* score that provides still additional information (see chapters 3 and 6). The most pertinent contribution is an assessment with respect to the subject's potential for improvement.

Other phases of the test may also be employed to enrich the diagnostic evaluation. These will be discussed and illustrated in later chapters of this work.

THE HABGT IN PSYCHODIAGNOSIS
AND MICRODIAGNOSIS

It is in the areas of intensive psychodiagnosis that the potential of the HABGT may be fully realized. Too often, in routine clinical work, the clinician who prefers to utilize a battery of psychological tests and limits the use of the HABGT to casual inspection of the results of the Copy Phase, or simply scores for Configuration and Psychopathology scores, neglects the rich harvest of data provided by this perceptual-motoric task. We shall explore the nature of this "harvest" in later chapters, but wish to note the outlines of this field so as to increase awareness of the rich lode.

We have already defined the problem of psychodiagnosis in the preceding section. The writer has developed special procedures to maximize the depth and extent of clinical data that the test can provide. In addition to asking the subject to copy the designs from the test cards (leaving "unstructured" the number of pages he can employ in completing this task, the Copy Phase), the subject is asked to engage in two other basic tasks. First, in the *Elaboration Phase,* the subject is shown the test cards again (or a sample of them) and is asked "to modify the drawings, or to change them in any way you wish, so as to make them more pleasing to you." The major objective of this additional procedure is to maximize the projective aspects of the test situation (see Chapter 3). Following this, the examiner conducts the *Association Phase* of the test, asking the subject to offer associations to *both* the test cards and the drawings produced in the Elaboration Phase. These procedures offer an extensive set of data for developing and confirming hypotheses related to the subject's performance; i.e., the basic personality characteristics.

We shall see later how these procedures produce significant data about both motoric and perceptual performance, provide better access to the subject's fantasy life, highlight motivational and restitutional aspects of performance, and allow for an exploration of conflicts, defenses, and coping strategies.

In some cases, especially when the examiner wishes to explore alternative explanations of the subject's performance or when leads for therapeutic management and strategy are desired, an experimental-clinical procedure, which this writer has called *microdiagnosis* (Hutt, 1980) to distinguish it from *macrodiagnosis* (or nomothetic diagnosis), may be employed to test out and check not only alternative explanations for the subject's performance but to explore the "idiosyncratic routes" that led to the subject's performance as well as possibilities for modification/improvement of the subject's performance.

We shall reserve for later exposition and clinical illustration the extensive possibilities of microdiagnostic methods. At that time we shall also present methods of inferential diagnosis (see chapter 9). These varied uses of the HABGT demonstrate that it is, in fact, more than "one test" and that is also more than a simple test of perceptual-motoric maturity.

THE HABGT AND PSYCHOTHERAPY

Our preceding discussion has suggested that the data derived from the HABGT may be used for more than screening and diagnostic purposes and has alluded to its potential for use in therapy. At this point, some general possibilities in this respect may be indicated briefly, to be explored more fully in later chapters.

Aside from the general guidelines that any psychodiagnostic evaluation provides—such as knowing the type and depth of psychopathology and recognizing the defenses and coping strategies that the subject employs—the subject's productions on the HABGT may prove useful in a number of specific ways:

1. E may question the subject, after the testing has been completed, with respect to his awareness of problems that the subject experienced while taking the test. This may lead to more complete understanding of how the subject experiences tensions such as the test situation stimulates.
2. The examiner may ask the subject to elaborate on the associations that have been prompted by the subject's test drawings. Often the subject will elaborate his own awareness of particular conflicts and concerns as well as reveal how he attempts to deal with them.
3. The examiner may ask the subject to note certain discrepancies between the test designs and the subject's modification of them and ask for the subject's comments about these. Often the subject will become aware, or increasingly aware, that he has special concerns that the subject has attempted to deny or has partially repressed.
4. In some instances, the symbolic meaning of the designs for the subject or the associations stimulated by the subject's associations, will lead to further, significant exploration of the subject's conflicts and defenses. These can then be investigated in the course of therapy.
5. During therapy the examiner may call attention to the subject's performance and associations during the previously administered HABGT. Because the HABGT is a perceptual-motoric task, the drawings by the subject and the associations evoked by them will sometimes lead to the conscious recall of previously repressed or "defended" personal experiences. In our later discussions of this topic we shall present evidence to support the view that many conflictful experiences during the early formative years are "released" during such activities as motoric representation, role playing, and the like. Such experiences are encoded in motor activities accompanying the conflict-laden situation before language has become the primary cognitive tool. Repeating such motoric (or perceptual-motoric) expe-

riences, or engaging in experiences that contain some of these affectively loaded memories can lead to their being reexperienced during test performance. In some instances, as we shall illustrate, the recovery of such experiences can be quite dramatic.

OTHER FACES OF BENDER-GESTALT TESTS

Our focus thus far has been on the HABGT. These test materials, the BGT materials, and methods of administering and scoring them have been used by clinicians and researchers in many innovative ways. In Chapter 2 we shall review some of these alternative materials and methods in some detail. At this point, we shall refer to some of them to help the reader become more fully aware of many ramifications.

The BGT and the HABGT are sometimes administered as a multiple-choice test (Spraings, 1966). Sometimes a tachistoscopic method of administration has been employed (Rosenberg & Rosenberg, 1965). Some investigators have used a "recall method" in which the subject is asked to reproduce the designs after a suitable interval of time (Bender, Curran, & Schilder, 1938; Hanvik & Andersen, 1950; Holland & Wadsworth, 1979; Olin & Reznikoff, 1957).

Attempts to increase the validity of the test in screening for organicity have been varied and ingenious. Among these, the work of Canter (1966; 1971; 1976), involving the use of test paper with curved intersecting lines as distractors, is noteworthy.

Other investigators have changed the presenting position of either test cards or test paper in order to investigate possible effects (Hannah, 1958; Verms, 1974). Still others have studied the effects of group administration (Becker & Sabatino, 1971; Hutt, 1945a; McCarthy, 1975; Suczek and Klopfer, 1952; Tolor, 1960).

There have also been various modifications of the test designs. Aside from the differences between the test cards furnished by Bender and by Hutt, some workers have simplified the designs (Shapiro, Post, Löfving, et al, 1956) and others have attempted to change the card's kinesthetic quality (Barker, 1949). The issue of the effect of changes in test designs will be dealt with in Chapter 3.

It is clear that the Bender-Gestalt is not one test or one procedure. Even methods of scoring vary among workers. Both the clinician and researcher will therefore be well advised to consider the effects of any of these variations upon results that are obtained.

2
The Roles and History of a Visual-Motor Test

As we have seen, the HABGT consists of a single administration or several administrations of a particular set of test designs. The HABGT designs, presented on Plate 1, are distinctively different in several respects from those presented by Bender, and it is recommended that these designs be employed when using our scoring procedures and our normative data. The performance by a subject on these designs can be evaluated in several ways, the most notable being: counting of pathological signs (or configurational analysis); obtaining an objective score or scores (Psychopathology Scale Score or Adience-Abience Score); inferential analysis; and microdiagnositic procedures. To understand the basis of such procedures, let us first consider how these roles of a "test" are developed.

THE ROLES OF A VISUAL-MOTOR TEST

The Hutt Adaptation of the Bender-Gestalt Test can provide a unique contribution to the assessment process in clinical evaluation: it requires visual-motor functions, and so can offer data for analysis of perceptual and motor maturation; it is essentially nonverbal, and so can provide samples of behavior that do not depend on linguistic development and are not easily influenced by many cultural factors; and it is a "malleable" procedure—it can be adapted to the specific requirement of the individual, clinical case. It can and does have some of the properties of the usual standardized test (see Chapter 4), and it is unusually appropriate for projective analysis (see Chapters 9, 10, and 11), but it is particularly useful for intensive clinical adaptation and analysis.

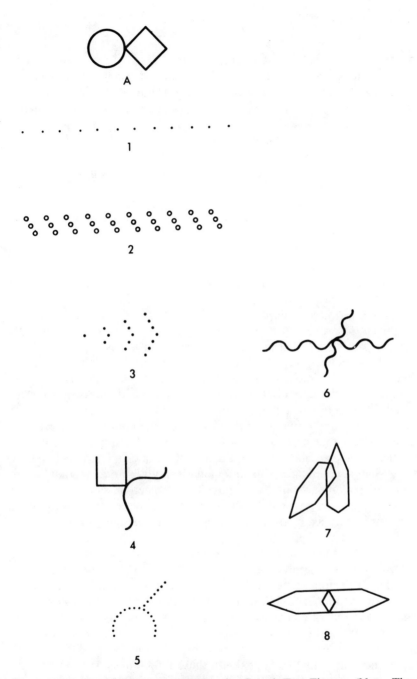

Plate 1. The Hutt Adaptation of the Bender-Gestalt Test Figures. (Note: These designs are significantly different from those used by Bender, and are the basis for our normative data. This and other illustrations in the book have been reduced by about 45% from original size. Figures are numbered for identification only.)

We have come, in this country, to rely excessively on assessment methods that can be objectified and standardized. Such approaches have value, but they are also burdened with serious limitations. We shall delay a more complete discussion of these values and limitations until Chapter 3, for now, but let us point out that they are most pertinent for purposes of group comparisons or comparison of an individual with a group (or group norm). Moreover, objective scores and norms—no matter how sophisticated their derivation and no matter how adequate the population sample—essentially rely on the assumptions of a nomothetic conception of personality. These assumptions include the following. (1) All individuals derive their scores on the standardized test by the accumulation of the same or equivalent elements of the test. (2) Motivational factors in the performance on the test that lead to certain successes or failures are equivalent for all subjects. (3) Previous experience (educational, cultural, and social) is held to be equivalent for all subjects or is held to be insignificant.

None of these assumptions may hold in an individual case and they may be entirely invalid in a great many, if not most, cases that come to the clinician's attention. Perhaps the most relevant is assumption 2. Cases referred for clinical evaluation are likely to be ones in which motivation is abnormal, aspiration level is low, self-concepts are confused or conflicted, and such factors as capacity for attending and for persistent effort have been affected. The nomothetic approach to assessment masks these factors, and many others, and thus obscures from our scrutiny precisely those matters that need to be considered in evaluating the test product and the test score. The core question that the clinician attempts to answer is: "What accounts for this individual's atypical or aberrant performance?" A comparison of the individual's objective score with a group norm only tells us how much difference there may be, but it does not aid us in our inquiry as to how this discrepancy came about and how to effect an improvement, if possible.

In contrast with nomothetic approaches to assessment are two other general diagnostic approaches: *inferential diagnosis* and *process diagnosis*. These two approaches are discussed in detail in Chapters 3 and 9, but some brief comments about their nature and their function may be noted here. In inferential diagnosis the psychologist attempts to follow the sequential steps and notes the productions of the subject as he carries out his successive test tasks, noting how he performs, what difficulties are experienced and how he copes with these difficulties. At the same time the examiner is attempting to infer what is contributing to the ongoing and successive productions. During this process he raises as many relevant hypotheses (or even speculations) as are possible about the test productions, discarding some as they prove fruitless or inadequate, integrating relevant hypotheses, and refining them until the most parsimonious and pertinent explanation(s) is achieved. In this process of attempting to empathize with the subject, the psychologist notes discrepancies in performance level (i.e., whether particular tasks cause difficulty, if there is consistently poorer performance as tasks become more difficult, if there is cumulative effect of failure experience, etc.). The inferential approach involves many hazards and does not, by itself, lead to any firm conclusions. However, it provides rich sources of data and often enables one to explain test phenomena in ways that uniquely fit the subject and that lead to appropriate efforts at rehabilitation and improvement in the subject's functioning. (See Chapters 9 and 11 for more detailed discussion.)

Process diagnosis overlaps with methods of inferential diagnosis but addresses itself more explicitly to the component aspects leading to the final product in performance. It attempts to determine *under what conditions the subject fails and under what conditions he succeeds*. In short, it is the adoption of an experimental method to test performance. For instance, suppose we ask the subject to copy design A from the Hutt Adaptation of the Bender-Gestalt Test (HABGT). As will be seen in Plate 1, this design involves a circle and a diamond that are tangential to each other. Suppose the subject draws this as two separate designs, a circle and a diamond. After the test has been completed, the examiner may pursue, for example, the following experimental process procedure to attempt to determine what led to the failure on this design, i.e., the separation of the two parts. First he may again show the test card to the subject, placing it alongside the design the subject made, and he may ask, "Are these two, the one on the card and the one you made, exactly alike?" If the subject indicates that they are not, the examiner may ask, "And what's different about them?" If the answer indicates the subject perceives what is wrong, he may then be told, "I'd like you to do this one again, making sure to draw it just like the one on the card." This time the subject may draw two tangential circles or he may draw the circle accurately but in trying to make the diamond tangential to the circle, he may distort the shape of the diamond. The examiner may note that the task appears to be too complex perceptually for the subject since he could draw the circle and the diamond accurately only when they were separated. He may then test this hypothesis by asking the subject to copy two tangential diamonds and/or two tangential circles.

By these and other similar procedures, the examiner (experimenter, now) tries to tease out the specific factor or factors that led to the error in the first place. He questions, he observes, he tries out the same or similar tasks under differing conditions until he learns precisely what has caused the difficulty. Suppose the subject said, when asked why he drew the two parts of this design separately (after he acknowledged that he was aware of the error), that he did it "the easier way." In the discussion that follows, the examiner might learn that the subject characteristically did not attempt to work hard at tasks that he regarded as too difficult for him, that he had a low aspiration level, that he was hostile to the examiner (or the examining situation), that he disliked drawing, or that he was fearful in entering new (test) situations. There might be many other explanations for the failure. In any event, process diagnosis attempts to elucidate the cause(s) of the difficulty by experimentally varying the conditions of the test (experiment) until it becomes clear what the problem is. Such procedures are especially valuable in testing for possible organic brain damage, as we shall see when we discuss that problem. They are also valuable in testing for malingering, for cultural deprivation, and for capacity to improve in functioning under certain conditions of encouragement or support. In short, process diagnosis attempts to gain a more complete understanding of the test performance by testing out the conditions that lead to success or failure.

Now let us consider the nature of the HABGT as we have developed it. It is based on the original work of Wertheimer (1923), who explored Gestalt phenomena by means of many experimental visual designs. His major concern was the confirmation of certain Gestalt principles of behavior as opposed to the then prevalent stimulus-response analysis of behavior. Perception was seen as involving the recognition of *basic Gestalten* rather than as the integration of disparate parts or segments into a total visual interpretation. His focus was on the total complex response and the conditions that explained how and why experiences were responded to in terms of primary configurations rather than in terms of successive steps, which, he believed, could not explain the total, immediate configurational characteristics of the stimulus.

Some years later, Bender became interested in using some of the experimental test designs as a means of studying certain forms of psychopathology (1938). The nine test designs employed by Bender in her clinical study of various pathognomonic groups were designs she had selected from the figures developed by Wertheimer and had adapated in order "to simplify them or to accentuate some basic Gestalt feature" (Tolor & Schulberg, 1963). Because he believed that these adaptations contained some undesirable features, Hutt developed another set of figures that seemed to him to be more similar to those used by Wertheimer and that did not contain any drafting irregularities that might influence the response. The usual task given a subject requires that he reproduce these designs freehand without the use of any mechanical aids. This seemingly simple task is far more complex than might at first be suspected. It involves both visual and motor behavior, not only in the reproduction of the designs, but also in the perception of them on the stimulus card. It further requires both visual and motor adaptations in the placement of the repro- ductions on the page or pages used by the subject as he engages in the "task of the test." In short, the behavior that is elicited is an *integrated whole* and is determined by many factors. As Schilder puts it in his Pref- ace to Bender's monograph (Bender, 1938): "It approaches the funda- mental problems of perception and action from a new angle. . . . It shows the continuous interplay between motor and sensory factors." He adds, ". . . gestalt patterns are *experiences* [italics mine] of an individual who has problems and . . . the final configuration of experience is not merely a problem in perception but a problem of personality. This becomes par- ticularly clear when one studies the Gestalt function in neurotics."

The HABGT is an attempt to utilize this procedure as a *projective* device. It goes beyond the classical Gestalt laws of perception (namely, pregnanz, closure, nearness, and the like) and tries to understand both the *process* of responding and the *final product* in such ways as to maximize the understanding of the behaving individual: his idiosyncratic personality style; his needs, conflicts, and defenses; his level of maturation; and his coping methods and ego strengths. Such an approach can make use of both objective scores and complex clinical judgments. It utilizes the large body of evidence that has been acquired concerning the general nature of perceptual and motoric development, the nature of projective phenom- ena, and the effects of psychological and intracranial damage upon behav- ioral functions. It attempts to understand the individual's global function- ing in the most parsimonious terms that will enable us to describe him and to predict some significant aspects of his behavior under defined circum- stances. In subsequent chapters we shall provide a rationale for various methods of analysis of test findings and relate each of these methods to clinical experience, research findings, and experimental evidence when- ever possible. However, many aspects of the methods of analysis that are proposed are frankly based on hypotheses that will require considerable research study and further clinical investigation.

First let us consider some propostitions that we hold to be axiomatic, even though there is considerable evidence to support them. All behav- ior—from the most simple to the complex—is a result of the interplay of conscious and unconscious factors. Of course, it is also much more than this; it involves the physical condition of the organism, its state of matura- tion; its prior experience, and its immediate state of expectancy at the time of the emergent behavior. In some kinds of behavior, conscious factors may play the decisive, in fact, almost the all-inclusive role. The distinguishing feature of such behavior is deliberate choice, in contrast to automatic functioning in situations of conflict-free spheres of operation. Such behaviors "of choice" most likely lie in the realm of simple, short-term performances, but they may occur in more complicated performances as well. We assume that as civilized human beings we are capable of and usually make deliberate choices in most of our behavior, but in fact far more frequently factors of unknown origin play a decisive role. Clinical and experimental evidence strongly suggests that unconscious motivational factors play a significant role in our general style of adjustment, in our postural and motoric style of behavior, in our level of aspiration, in our perception and understanding of situations that confront us, and in the specific ways we go about adapting our behaviors to the ongoing problems before us. Not only slips of the tongue, acts of forgetting, distortions of reality, and prejudicial attitudes, but even styles of speaking, facial expression, tempo and movement, and affective tone are, in part, influenced by factors of which we are utterly unaware or only partially aware. Often we can "explain" such behaviors after the fact, but frequently our explanation is of the order "that's the way we are."

Although it is problematic how decisive unconscious factors are in a great many aspects of our everyday behavior, the role of such factors becomes clearer when we examine dream material or when we evaluate neurotic behavior. It is widely accepted that the substance of psychopathologic behavior is largely determined by unconscious motivations that find expression in symptomatic acts or in characterologic traits. Yet, some workers prefer to dismiss the concept of the unconscious, suggesting instead that we view behavior entirely from a phenomenonologic stance. Such an orientation is possible, but I believe that if one takes this stance the very essence of the quality of being human is thereby eliminated and the meaning of motivation in human behavior is entirely neglected. Our problems of analysis of behavior are, in fact, not simplified but only compounded by this outlook, for we are omitting the crucial and meaningful characteristic of the human organism—its striving, actualizing, and self-determining characteristics. Instead, it would seem that although overt phenomena are resultants of the interplay of many factors, unconscious factors often play a central role. Even in so-called normal individuals there is evidence that factors of which the individual is unaware exert a considerable, and often central, influence on the direction and nature of adjustment (Solley & Murphy, 1960).

From a clinical viewpoint, the assumption of unconscious motivation seems highly profitable. Although it is possible to alter overt behavior without understanding the role of conscious and unconscious motivational factors, existing conflicts that gave rise to the behavior may persist or may even become reinforced, and other, ancillary behaviors may develop that may be even more objectionable. An example is the devastating consequences that occur when strong anxiety drives are suppressed or no outlet for them is provided and severely disorganized or psychotic behavior develops. However, when both conscious and unconscious motivations are carefully evaluated and the dynamics of an individual's behavior are understood—even approximately—more effective methods for dealing with pathologic behavior can be devised and outcomes can be more accurately predicted. The methods of dealing with conflicts may themselves be quite diverse, but at least they will tend to be more congruent with the individual's total adjustmental status and more effective in securing some enduring consequences.

Hence, we view it as of great and even crucial importance that the clinician understand the individual's conflicts and their unconscious derivation. A great many methods are available for the evaluation of these problems: structured and unstructured interviews, free associations, dream material, role playing sessions, objective personality tests, verbal projective tests, the use of drawings as projective devices, cartoon-like test devices, and the like. All of these have their place, and sometimes one or another may be most helpful in an individual instance. We suggest, however, that the visual-motor assessment of behavior and underlying dynamics has some unique as well as some common advantages.

As already noted, the use of a visual-motor task in testing personality reactions provides a sample of behavior involving complex functions. Like other projective procedures for assessing personality, such complex examples of behavior offer clues to the general style of adaptation, cognitive methods of behaving, affective types of responses, areas of conflict, specific defensive methods, and maturational characteristics. Unlike many other projective methods, especially those emphasizing verbal comprehension and verbal response, perceptual-motoric functioning has some special characteristics and possible advantages. Perhaps central to such special characteristics is the probability that styles of perceptual, motoric, and perceptual-motoric functioning become established, or tendencies toward such styles are established, very early in life—before language comprehension and usage have developed (Solley & Murphy, 1960; Werner, 1957). Space does not permit a summary of observational and experimental studies of early perception, motoric behavior, and the "integrated" perceptual-motoric behaviors that develop during infancy and very early childhood. Instead we shall note some principles that have emerged and their implications.

The infant has some individual and some general characteristic ways in which, based on constitutional factors, he perceives his immediate world. He is able to make some rudimentary figure-ground differentiation before learning takes place (Hebb, 1949). But his response potential is quite limited because of his immaturity and, more precisely, because he has not yet learned how to mediate incoming stimuli. As Gesell, Ilg, and Bulliss (1949) have shown, the infant soon learns to mediate some of these stimuli by perceptual and tactual responses. Deprivation or frustration experiences tend to disrupt these early integrated response patterns just as they tend to disrupt acts of visual attention (Drever, 1967). The infant's mind grows by the successive laying down of memoric traces that are closely dependent upon immediate experiences (Koffka, 1931). Moreover, probably a great deal of classical conditioning (and imprinting) may occur because of the infant's low level of awareness and high level of affective need.

When motoric behavior is insufficient to reduce the tension level that internal need and perceptual experience have generated, autistic perception tends to result (Helson, 1953). As Helson puts it, the tendency to autistic perception (or perception that is more determined by inner needs than by outer reality) may result from "memories, residual traces from previously experienced dangers, excessive anticipatory reactions before danger actually threatens, or the result of magnified feed-back mechanisms wherein awareness of one's own bodily process figures prominently." Then, affective needs reinforce autistic perception and only further maturation and differentiation of needs and response patterns can alter this trend; otherwise hallucinatory substitutes for need satisfaction or motoric discharge can provide some partial tension reduction (Rapaport, 1951). With further development, unless traumatic experience is overwhelming, the child learns to utilize improved perceptual-motoric responses to meet his needs and to mediate his experience. Only very gradually does greater "field independence" develop (Witkin, Dyk, Faterson, Goodenough, & Karp, 1967) and does a greater repertoire of coping behaviors emerge.

One implication of these findings is that some important aspects of conflictful experiences are expressed early in life through perceptual-motoric modes or styles of behavior—in fact so early in life that language has played little or no part in them. Even in later years of early childhood, perceptual-motoric modes may be greatly influenced by significant emotional and conflictful experiences. Such experiences and the "memories" of them may, in fact, be "bound" in the motoric style. Sometimes one can infer from the style what the general nature of these experiences might have been. Sometimes *the repetition of the perceptual-motoric act may redintegrate the repressed emotional experience.* As we shall see later, the subject who performs on both the copy phase and the elaboration phase of the HABGT often expresses, knowingly or unknowingly, many facets of his hitherto "covered over" experiences. In any case, his perceptual-motoric behavior may reveal much of his characteristic ways of defending and coping, which his verbal behavior may conceal.

Two other special values of a nonverbal, perceptual-motoric projective test of personality reactions should be noted. Since the conventions of what is "good" and what is "bad" behavior are not known to the subject who performs such a task, he is less likely to conceal from the examiner those aspects of himself that he fears to reveal, whereas on a verbal task such conventions are more widely known and can be used to avoid such confrontations. Even when the subject has no conscious intent to conceal, the cultural overlay of language itself may becloud the meaning of the test response. Another way of stating this is that perceptual-motoric behavior is more likely to be idiosyncratic, whereas verbal behavior is more likely to be "culture bound."

In summary, perceptual-motoric test behavior offers a sampling of aspects of behavior not readily available in verbal tests, it may tap earlier levels of meaningful and conflictful experience, and it may be less consciously distorted because its meaning is not so obviously meaningful.

To whom might the HABGT test be profitably administered? The answer depends, in part, upon one's philosophy of testing. In the author's view, psychological testing should be undertaken only when there is a clear, functional use for such testing—first of all, in terms of the patient's or subject's interests; second, in terms of research or administrative interests. Considering the first of these uses, testing with a particular instrument should involve the probability that the findings will better enable us to serve the patient: enabling him to make more effective use of his capacities; enabling him to understand himself more deeply and fully; or enabling us to understand and assist him toward these objectives. From such a viewpoint, the following categories or classes of people for whom the HABGT would be most profitable should be considered.

Category I. This category consists of patients whose verbal behavior does not afford an adequate sampling of their personality strengths and deficits *even though they are able to use verbal means of communication quite effectively.* Although it may be true that words "conceal as well as reveal" in all cases, it is especially true for persons in this group, and they are the ones from whom the HABGT is especially useful. Who are these people? First of all, this category includes those whose verbal defenses are so strong or ingrained that their communication acts as a facade—e.g., the obsessive intellectualizer or the verbally facile rationalizer. They may appear on the surface to be far better integrated than is actually the case. Such people may use language consciously to distort the picture of their underlying problems or they may unconsciously present a picture of themselves as different from what is actually the case. In addition to defensive use of intellectualization, such individuals may be detected by their glibness, their inability to express affect spontaneously, or their preoccupation with a fantasy life. In all such instances, samples of behavior derived exclusively from verbal tests can yield distorted findings. They may sometimes show a pseudo ego control in their verbal beahvior, as to obsessive people who are able to conceal from themselves and others the disintegration of ego controls that may lie behind such verbal behavior.

A special subgroup of individuals falling within Category I consists of malingeres. Such persons may, for either conscious or unconscious reasons, attempt to convey an impression of greater pathology than actually exists. Or they may attempt to convey an impression of meeting the norms of behavior that they believe are expected of them. In any case, even when the clinician is aware that malingering is occurring, it is difficult to make an accurate assessment and valid differential diagnosis. However, when such people are asked to take a nonverbal test such as the HABGT, they are deprived of their usual verbal-intellectual defenses and are more likely to reveal aspects of themselves—superior or inferior—which might otherwise be obscured. They do not know what various perceptual-motoric kinds of behavior reveal about them and are therefore less competent in concealing or distorting. In later chapters we shall discuss various procedures that may be employed in further clarifying the meaning of test behavior that is engaged in malingerers.

Category II. This category consists of individuals who are unable or unwilling to produce an adequate sample of verbal behavior for diagnostic purposes. There are several subgroups in this category, with quite different characteristics. There are those whose verbal behavior is significantly impaired. They may have come from culturally deprived backgrounds, or from a culture in which they had little opportunity to master our language. They may show significant inhibition in verbal behavior, which limits the usefulness of their verbal test behavior. For example, they may be severely depressed and unable to verbalize freely. Or they may be markedly withdrawn in all of their interpersonal behavior, including language, as are catatonics or individuals with schizoid inhibition. Sometimes, in cases involving intense, acute, or chronic anxiety, verbal behavior may become markedly disturbed. In these cases not only is the sample of verbal behavior insufficient for evaluative purposes, but even this sample may be nonrepresentative of many aspects of the personality—especially of those healthy aspects that could make for effective growth or recovery. In many instances, the sample of behavior that is obtained with verbal tests is so meager that it is difficult to assess its meaning properly with respect to either the severity of the pathology or areas of conflict. Persons who fall in Category II confront us, then, with two related types of clinical problems: the problem of the representativeness of the sample of behavior which has been elicited, and the problem of identifying the underlying pathology or the areas of most intense conflict.

Category III. This category consists of individuals who suffer from some form of intracranial pathology. Except in certain circumstances, patients who are suspected of having such damage cannot be easily evaluated as having brain damage by means of samples of verbal behavior. Verbal behavior may be least affected by such damage or may reveal such damage only when the condition has deteriorated severely. Moreover, there are many cases of brain damage that are not readily discoverable by routine neurologic diagnostic procedures. In these, tests such as the HABGT can be highly useful in pointing up the possibility of damage that might otherwise be overlooked. In addition, such tests are useful in assessing the type or degree of change that may occur as a result of treatment or surgery, as our later survey of the literature will indicate. Perceptual-motoric tests are routinely useful for both diagnostic and treatment purposes in all instances in which brain damage is present or suspected. Moreover, since the way in which a person reacts to intracranial pathology is a function of both his personality and the type of organic damage, a technique that reflects both of these, such as the HABGT, is useful in the clinical management of such people.

Category IV. We should like to reserve this category for the so-called mentally retarded individuals. The diagnosis of mental retardation presents many special problems. As has now been abundantly demonstrated (Hutt & Gibby, 1976), this group of individuals is frequently characterized by moderate to severe cultural deprivation. The usual verbal intelligence tests, which have a high degree of correlation with verbal skills and with scholastic achievement, are not particularly valid as predictors of intellectual potential or of academic growth in such cases. It is probably true that many children who come from deprived cultural backgrounds obtain scores on such tests that are not necessarily indicative of their mental status or their academic potential if proper and intensive remedial assistance were to be provided, especially in the early stages of their school careers. In order to prevent the inappropriate classification of those in this group who are not truly retarded in the intellectual sphere but are largely or only retarded linguistically and culturally, some measure of intellectual potential that is not so closely bound to cultural experience is needed. Tests of perceptual maturity, in general, and perceptual-motoric tests such as the HABGT are particularly useful in such cases.

Hutt and Gibby (1976) have also shown that many individuals who are classified as mentally retarded may function below average in the intellectual sphere because of severe emotional handicaps that interfere with their intellectual functioning and may produce cognitive inhibition and lower their aspiration and motivation for academic and other achievements. It has been demonstrated that the complex interaction between cultural deprivation and emotional frustration may, temporarily or more enduringly, interfere with intellectual growth and functioning (Hunt, 1961). In order to assess such individuals better, the diagnostic battery should include personality tests that, on the one hand, are not unduly biased by linguistic and cultural factors and, on the other hand, provide some basis for assessing the degree of interference of emotional factors with intellectual functioning. The HABGT and other versions of the Bender-Gestalt Test, as well as other nonverbal tests of intelligence and of personality, are especially useful for such purposes. Tests of perceptual-motoric maturity have been shown to provide useful information in predicting about and in guiding individuals who are handicapped by factors such as those just discussed.

Moreover, many retarded individuals may have some organic brain damage, even if slight, or some special personality problems that contribute to mental malfunctioning. The HABGT is a useful device in evaluating the possible contribution of these factors to functional mental retardation and in differentiating those for whom such factors are not particularly relevant.

Category V. The last group contains a miscellaneous population of individuals. Here we would group the illiterates, the uneducated, and the foreign born unskilled in English—all of the individuals who are handicapped in verbal communication. Such persons are likely to give atypical test protocols on instruments designed for individuals with normal linguistic skills and who meet the "normal" conditions of the usual standardization population employed in developing such tests and their norms. Tests such as the HABGT, which rely upon more universal background experiences and do not emphasize culture-bound symbol development to so great an extent, do not place such persons at an even greater disadvantage in the attempt to assess their intelligence and personality functioning. Moreover, to the extent that perceptual-motoric performance reveals basic aspects of the personality, particularly those aspects dependent upon very early experiences, the HABGT has uncommon advantages for persons who fall in Category V.

The foregoing discussion has attempted to highlight the general categories of individuals for whom tests such as the HABGT are particularly useful. Our emphasis in this discussion was our concern with the individual, and reflects our desire to employ tests in the diagnostic battery that will be most useful in evaluating and providing remedial help when needed. In addition to these considerations, many clinicians have employed the test for other purposes, as later discussion will illustrate. The following listing of the more frequently mentioned uses of the HABGT may help the reader to see the broader vista of the clinical potential of this test.

1. The HABGT has been found useful as a *buffer* test. Every clinicain tries to develop good rapport with his subject. Among the ap-

proaches used in developing such a relationship, the use of a seemingly simple, nonthreatening test as the first test in the schedule may be helpful in many cases. Not only is the test not likely to be experienced as threatening, but it is enjoyed by most subjects and lends itself to discussion about the function of the diagnostic battery. In some instances, patients who are covertly hostile to testing find it easy to express their anger by externalizing it upon a test procedure that they see as childish or silly. The skillful clinician will utilize this cathartic expression of feeling to explore the patient's attitudes in order to help him accept the testing situation in his own personal terms.

2. The HABGT is useful as a supplementary devise in rounding out the assessment procedures so that verbal behavior is not overemphasized in the total evaluation.

3. The HABGT is useful when tests involving *minimal examiner-patient interaction* are required. It has been demonstrated that some patients are significantly influenced by such interactions, so that valid assessment is difficult. The HABGT can be administered so as to minimize such "interfering" factors.

4. The HABGT has special value in assessing the illiterate, the uneducated, and the culturally deprived. Such individuals present special problems in assessment. Although no test can be entirely "fair" in such cases, those relying upon perceptual-motoric performance and involving very little verbal skill are an important part of the test battery in such instances.

5. The HABGT may be useful in the differential diagnosis of mental retardation. In cases of suspected retardation it is extremely important to evaluate or to de-emphasize the contributing roles of prior cultural experience, emotional interference with intellectual functioning, and possible intracranial damage.

6. The HABGT is useful for patients whose verbal behavior provides a screen that conceals aspects of personality functioning.

7. The HABGT is especially useful in cases in which malingering is suspected.

8. The HABGT is useful in the differential diagnosis of intracranial pathology. Although all psychological manifestations of brain damage are influenced not only by the type and amount of damage, they are also influenced by the subject's personality functioning. The HABGT has been found in both clinical and experimental studies to be quite successful in differentiating some types of brain damage.

9. The HABGT is often useful in differentiating psychotic process phenomena that are sometimes concealed in verbal projective tests. Perceptual-motoric behavior can reveal evidence of such psychotic

processes, especially when they are not otherwise flagrantly apparent.

10. The HABGT is useful in delineating aspects of conflict areas and defense styles. Among these, problems in identity, sexual identification, general patterns of interpersonal relations, and approach-withdrawal tendencies are prominent.

11. The HABGT is sometimes useful in determining the degree of psychological regression and intellectual impairment. Among other features of the test, comparisons of performance on the designs that differ in level of maturity can lead to important inferences along these lines.

12. The HABGT is helpful in predicting some aspects of school achievement. It has been studied extensively in relation to the prediction of the early phases of reading.

13. The HABGT may be found useful in the study of intercultural differences. Although this device is not entirely free of cultural influences, it taps some important levels of personality functioning that intercultural investigations have been concerned with.

14. The HABGT may be used in the study of the effects of various forms of chemical and physiological therapy, such as the use of pharmacologic agents and the use of electroconvulsive therapy.

15. The HABGT may be used in connection with studies investigating the possible effects of psychotherapy.

16. The HABGT may be useful in research studies involving relationships between perceptual-motoric behavior and various personality dimensions.

As we have noted, the above list summarizes some of the more frequent uses of the HABGT. Not all of these uses are equally pertinent for this test and some uses may, finally, be found to be less significant than was at first hoped. And, of course, further research and ingenuity may lead to significant uses for the test that have thus far not been recognized. The listing should be regarded as suggestive. Each user of the test, in this or in other forms, has the final obligation of evaluating for himself the validity and significance of any alleged claims, and each user of the test must decide whether and how to use it in clinical study or in research.

A BRIEF HISTORY OF THE HABGT

The HABGT constitutes one general method for the clinical use of selected designs from the original Wertheimer experimental designs. Its chief characteristic is the projective features of the test protocol that result from the interplay of the method of administration, the methods of work by the subject, and the test product that is analyzed and scored for evidences of projection. Even our objective scales (Psychopathology Scale and Adience-Abience Scale), described in detail in Chapter 4 and 6 are based on assumptions germane to the projective approach. It is desirable to keep these considerations clearly in mind when evaluating this approach and when comparing it with other approaches using this or similar test material.

It is inaccurate to speak of the "Bender-Gestalt Test" as if this were a single test instrument. Not only do test cards differ from one version to another, but methods of administration, scoring, analysis, and evaluation also differ significantly. Each of these approaches may have its own particular values and limitations. Thus, we do not have one Bender-Gestalt Test, but rather many procedures for eliciting test behavior and for analyzing test products. This proliferation of test materials and test analyses is welcomed by this writer since it leads to exploration and evaluation that, in the long run, can help us to establish the precise value that each has. Our own interest in the Wertheimer figures is in the special clinical usefulness they have, under certain conditions, in delineating personality problems, in more accurately assessing evidence of mental impoverishment, and in analyzing possible consequences of neurological impairment or deficit. Out attempt has been *to mazimize projective features of the test performance and to provide both clinical and objective methods for its analysis.*

Taken together, the various forms of the Bender-Gestalt Test now constitute one of the most widely utilized methods in clinical assessment in this country. They are also widely used throughout the world. The clinical and research literature has burgeoned over the past few decades and several summaries of the findings from these studies are available (e.g., Billingslea, 1963; Koppitz, 1965, 1975a; Landmark & Grinde, 1964; Lubin, Wallis, & Paine, 1971; Sonoda, 1968; Tolor, 1968; Tolor & Schulberg, 1963; Tolor & Brannigan, 1980). We shall not attempt to describe each of the studies that have been published; that would deserve another volume in its own right. Rather, we shall refer to those studies that are most pertinent to the development of our own approach and that offer evidence concerning the validity of certain test indicators and scores.

As noted in the preceding chapter, the nine figures comprising the usual set of stimuli that are in both the HABGT and the Bender-Gestalt Test were selected from those used by Wertheimer in his studies of Gestalt functions (Wertheimer, 1923). Using a much larger sample of designs, Wertheimer investigated the patterns of visual perception by asking his "apparently" normal subjects to describe what they saw. Bender became interested in the use of some of these designs as a means of exploring deviations in the maturational process in perceptual-motoric functions that were associated with certain pathologic conditions, among which were mental retardation, schizophrenia, organic brain damage, aphasia, manic-depressive psychosis, and certain toxic conditions. For these purposes, she used nine designs, labeling the first one "A," since she conceived of this one essentially as an introductory or practice design (at least in the beginning), and the others from "1" to "8." As she stated: "Only test figures A, 3, 7, and 8 closely resemble the designs used by Wertheimer. The others have been modified usually to simplify them or to accentuate some basic Gestalt feature" (Tolor & Schulberg, 1963).

During the 1930s almost all of the work done with these figures consisted of clinical investigation by Bender, herself, of the clinical groups in which she was interested. A major innovation in using these figures was that subjects were asked to *copy* them, and *not* to describe them. Her position with regard to this test procedure's possible value in assessing personality disturbances was, at first, abmiguous. In her first general summary of her clinical work, speaking of the characteristics of the drawings of her subjects, she maintained, "The final product is a visual motor pattern which reveals modifications in the original pattern by the integrating mechanism of the individual who has experienced it" (Bender, 1938). She also offered little hope that the procedure would be useful in studying personality disturbances in psychoneurotics, stating: "We do not expect to find disturbances in perception or in the visual motor Gestalt function in the psychoneuroses." Yet, in the same paragraph she notes, " . . . it would not be surprising to find that some such Gestalten might become the symbol of the individual's unsatisfied infantile drives." Her general position, nevertheless, seemed to indicate little faith that the test could be used effectively in studying personality disturbances. This is all the more surprising in that her husband, Paul Schilder, who interested her in this work and who wrote the preface to this monograph, states: "Dr. Bender does not forget that Gestalt patterns are experiences of an individual who had problems and that the final configuration of experience is *not merely a problem of perception but a problem of personality* [italics mine]. This becomes particularly clear when one studies the Gestalt function in neurotics."

Our review of the pertinent literature since the introduction of the HABGT in World War II will focus selectively on several aspects of administration, scoring, and differential value in diagnosis and personality evaluation. We shall reserve for Chapters 4 and 8 the research on specific test factors.

METHODS OF ADMINISTRATION

As will be noted in Chapter 3, administration of the HABGT involves three phases (*Copy, Elaboration,* and *Association*) in order to maximize the projective features of the test. Some research has been done on the effects of this approach and on other methods of administration.

Hutt (1945a) suggested that tachistoscopic presentation of the test designs, using a five second exposure, would increase the test's effectiveness in screening for organic brain damage. Others (Korchin & Basowitz, 1954; Lindsay, 1954) suggested that tachistoscopc exposure might be useful in assessing ego strength and in differentiating neurotics from normals. A few studies have explored the value of tachistoscopic presentation. Rosenberg and Rosenberg (1965) explored the effect of administering the copy phase, followed by the tachistoscopic method, followed in turn by a memory phase versus a sequence with the tachistoscopic, then copy, and then memory phase. Subjects were patients from psychiatric and neurological wards and "normals." Test protocols were scored using the Hutt and Briskin scoring method (1960). They found that the latter sequence reduced the discriminatory power of the copy phase findings.

Snortum (1965), using the Pascal and Suttell scoring system (1951), studied the relative discriminatory ability of the copy and tachistoscopic methods (they administered the copy phase first and the tachistoscopic phase second to all subjects) with normals, neurotics, alcoholics, and brain injured individuals. Both methods were found to discriminate well among the several groups (at the .01 level of significance), although the copy phase did not produce as much differentiation among the pathological groups. The tachistoscopic method did discriminate effectively (p = .02) between organics and neurotics. In another study (Bernstein, 1963), the relative effectiveness of copy and tachistoscopic presentations in differentiating schizophrenics from nonschizophrenic subjects was investigated. The schizophrenic population performed more poorly under both conditions, but the tachistioscopic method did not significantly differentiate the two groups more effectively. In this study, scoring was done with the Pascal-Suttell method.

The findings on the relative merits of copy (or standard) administration and tachistoscopic administration are far from conclusive due both to limitations in research design and in definition of criterion groups. They are suggestive that tachistoscopic presentation may increase discrimination of organics from nonorganics.

Other investigations have focused on the effects of: the position of the test paper (see Chapter 3); size of the test paper; and position of the test cards. We refer the reader who is interested in these test factors to the pertinent studies (Allen, 1968; Allen & Frank, 1963; Freed & Hastings,

1965; Hasazki, Allen, & Wohlford, 1971; Weiss, 1971b). In general it has been found that these differences in administrative procedure do produce differences (greater frequency of "errors") when the "standard method of administration" is employed as compared with the modified procedures. They suggest that (1) Etaminer should be aware of the effect of any change in test administration upon test performance; and (2) the standard procedure for administration of the test tends to maximize differentiation among the several diagnostic categories.

One of the most promising innovations in administration of the BGT, developed in the hope of improving the test's capacity to screen for organic brain damage, is the Canter Background Interference Procedure (BIP). Introduced in 1963 (Canter, 1963) and subjected to various research studies (Canter, 1966; 1968; 1971), this procedure involves administering the test in the standard manner followed by an administration utilizing specially prepared test paper with background, wavy lines. Both test protocols are scored by a modified Pascal-Suttel method and the difference in errors on the two performances is then calculated. The aim of this modification in administration is to maximize disruptive effects in perceptual-motor performance as a result of the distractions produced by the wavy line background. Interjudge reliability in scoring is satisfactory (Canter, 1968) and differentiation of organics from normals and other psychiatric groups has been reported as satisfactory (Canter, 1968; Yulis, 1970), although one researcher found that the BIP difference scores showed relatively low reliability (Boake & Adams, 1982). Canter has also reported (1971) that both short-term and long-term hospitalized schizophrenics did not reveal any significant loss on this test although organics did. It is also worth noting that Heaton, Baade, and Johnson (1978), after reviewing the findings from 94 studies on neuropsychological tests, concluded that there was no consistent evidence to favor the use of the BIP over the standard BGT.

The BIP, of course, takes more time to administer and to score than the standard (or Copy Phase) of the HABGT. This might not seem important if it produced significant improvement in screening for organicity. As we have seen, that may not be the case. It would seem worthwhile to evaluate the possible improvement in detecting organicity (roughly 80% accuracy) if the BIP were evaluated by means of Hutt's Configuration Score for Organicity (see Chapter 5), which can be scored quite rapidly.

McCann and Plunkett (1984) investigated the relative efficiency of four methods of administration of the BGT in differentiating 30 patients with Korsakoff's psychosis from 30 paranoid schizophrenics and 30 normal controls. The four methods were: recall (10 second exposure of each card); standard (copy) presentation; drawing with the nonpreferred hand; and, a so-called "perfect" method (subject was asked to compare his drawings with the test designs and to eliminate any errors he saw. All four methods of administration significantly differentiated the three diagnostic groups. Scoring utilized the Pascal-Suttell method. The perfect method yielded very slightly better "hit" (or success) rates for the organic group than the other three methods. From a practical viewpoint (that of the clinician who wishes to confirm an individual diagnosis) the differences are insignificant. However, as we shall indicate in our later discussion of the *clinical use of the HABGT,* this study confirms the value of experimental-clinical methods of evaluation (the microdiagnostic method) in ascertaining with greater certainty in an individual case the meaning of the performance on the test.

Another innovation in BGT administration involves group administration. Such administration could save considerable time and could be especially useful for screening purposes. (For clinical work, however, most, if not all, of the observational data would be lost.) Keogh and Smith (1961) first explored group administration utilizing large stimulus cards (11 × 16 ¾ inches). Dibner and Korn (1969) used individual decks of cards and were able to examine 2 to 4 children at a time. Keogh and Smith (1961) report the use of "copying booklets" and slides for group administration. Most of this work has been done with children and most studies have employed the Koppitz (1975a) scoring method. Becker and Sabatino (1971) report an r of .85 between scores obtained under individual and group administration. They and others (Caskey & Larson, 1977; Howard, 1970; McCarthy, 1975) report that group administration does not produce any significant loss in reliability of the scores.

Finally, a word should be said concerning the administration of the BGT in mutiple choice form. The most notable of these are the methods of Labentz, Linkenhoker, and Aaron (1976) and of Friedman et al (1977). The approach, however, offers little over the standard method.

SCORING SYSTEMS

As has been indicated, the writer believes that scores on tests (and the normative data that illustrate how such scores are distributed in selected populations) have value in screening and initial diagnostic formulations. He believes, however, that both research and clinical evidence clearly indicate that scores are insufficient for *individual diagnosis* and are frequently misused (Hutt, 1980). American psychology has long been enthralled by scores that can be utilized in empirical research studies, which have an "air" of objectivity (often mistaken for validity) and that are readily manipulable with the assistance of computers and computer programs.

In introducing his version of the Bender-Gestalt Test (Hutt, 1945a), Hutt provided an inspection method for evaluating test protocols and offered some tentative "configurations" that seemed to characterize three types of clinical syndromes. Later, with the pressure of critics for "objective criteria" and for "objective scores," he proposed "patterns" that were statistically and significantly related to various diagnostic categories. During the ensuing years, as his own research data warranted, Hutt provided "objective" criteria for scoring test factors and he developed a comprehensive Psychopathology Scale for use *in conjunction with clinical observations and evaluations* (Hutt, 1953; 1960; 1969; 1977). It is interesting to note that Tolor and Schulberg (1963) shifted their evaluation of Hutt's work from" . . . it is felt that Hutt and Briskin's work provides the most promising approach for the development of a system which potentially permits creative interpretation based upon valid research", to their more recent position (Tolor & Brannigan, 1980), in which it is said ". . . it would appear that these new (sic) scales which measure adience-abience and psychopathology have considerable validity of the construct, concurrent, and predictive types; that they are highly reliable instruments."

It is not surprising that clinicians, despite psychology's clamor for well-validated and objective scoring methods, overwhelmingly utilize clinical judgment rather than scoring methods in their work with individual clients (Scholberg & Tolor, 1961). In this survey it was found that only 5% of experienced clinicians relied exclusively on any scoring system in evaluating Bender-Gestalt test protocols; some 31 percent used a combination of scores and clinical judgments. The basic reason for this phenomenon is that scores (and normative data) offer nomothetic data that describe statistically how a designated group of individuals perform, while the clinician's task is to evaluate how a particular individual's test performance sheds light on the specific nature of his personality adjustment. Thus an obtained score may be regarded as a signpost that the clinician still has to interpret in the light of all available data about that individual.

Over the years, many scoring systems have been proposed for evaluating Bender-Gestalt protocols, but only a few have survived the tests of time and research evaluation. Among these, the system developed by Pascal and Suttell (1951) is the most widely used, and was an attempt to provide a global measure of functioning. It can be regarded as a measure of the degree of general psychopathology, or, alternatively, as Pascal and Suttell themselves regard it, as a measure of ego strength. As they state: "If, for the purposes of this discussion, we limit our definition of ego functioning to the ability to reproduce faithfully the B-G drawings as presented, then we may say that ego strength lies on a continuum from very low to very high B-G scores." Clearly, such a definition of ego strength leaves undefined what ego strength really involves. In most of the research work that the Pascal-Suttell measure has stimulated, the objective was to investigate the scale's ability to differentiate different types of psychopathology. It is clear that interjudge reliability in scoring this scale is quite good, the reliability correlations generally ranging from .90 (Pascal & Suttell, 1951) to .99 (Story, 1960). In support of their contention that the score may be used as a measure of degree of psychopathology, Pascall and Suttell present data to show that there are progressive and significant differences in mean score between the normal group and the neurotic and the psychotic. Although some contradictory findings have been published, these conclusions by Pascal and Suttell have stood the test of research quite well: as a rough measure of severity of general psychopathology the scale has demonstrated validity. It is far more questionable whether the scale has demonstrated validity. It is far more questionable whether the scale can be used to differentiate brain-damaged cases from either neurotics or psychotics, and probably other measures should be used for such purposes. Organics may vary considerably in degree of psychopathology and need to be assessed specifically in terms of organic pathology, although the Pascal-Suttell score probably reflects some aspects of each type of phenomenon.

A study using very carefully matched groups of patients clearly showed that the Pascal-Suttell scale was very poor in discriminating organics from functionally disturbed individuals (Stoer, Corotto, & Curnutt, 1965). Two reservations concerning the value of the Pascal-Suttell scale in measuring the degree of psychopathology should be indicated. (1) Although it can reliably discriminate between *groups* of normals, neurotics, and psychotics, it does not predict very effectively in *individual* cases. Hence, its clinical utility is somewhat limited. (2) It does not, nor does it pretend to, make available specific predictive discriminations with respect to individual personality characteristics, such as areas of conflict or types of defense mechanisms, and is therefore of no value *in this sense* as a clinical instrument. Pascal and Suttell present norms for adults as well as tentative norms for children.

Hutt has developed a Psychopathology Scale (discussed in detail in Chapter 4) based on the 17 test factors that have proved to be most valid and discriminating. Beginning in 1960 (Hutt & Briskin, 1960), clinical and statistical evaluations were conducted on 26 potentially useful factors. Nineteen of these were subjected to further statistical analysis. Interjudge reliability (two raters) was reported as ranging from .51 to .96, with an obtained reliability of .91 for the total score (Pearson r's). Based upon the reported research of others (see next section of this chapter), and additional analysis by Hutt (1969), a revised Psychopathology Scale was developed. This scale comprised 17 test factors, some redefined, and yielded a reliability coefficient of .96 for the total scale, using two experienced judges on a population of 100 schizophrenic patients. This time the reliabilities for the several items ranged from .79 to 1.00, indicating improved objectivity in directions for scoring the items. Further study led to another revision of the Psychopathology Scale (Hutt, 1977), this time with 17 items. Not only was this scale shown to have adequate interjudge reliability, but the Psychopathology Score differentiated among several populations (normals, emotionally disturbed children, adult neurotics, unipolar depressives, schizophrenics, and cases with organic brain damage) showing mean differences in scores above the .01 level of probability except in the difference between chronic schizophrenics and organic brain damage cases (close to the .05 level). The specific research studies will be presented in succeeding chapters. Scoring of the 17 factors is facilitated by the use of a Scoring Template furnished by the publisher (Grune & Stratton).

The Hain scoring system has had fairly wide use and been employed in significant research (Hain, 1964). This investigator selected 31 "signs" on the Bender-Gestalt, and 15 of these were given differential weightings on the basis of their effectiveness in discriminating among brain-damaged, psychiatric, and control groups. Using the 15 "signs" and their weights, a score was derived for each individual. The score differed significantly (at the .01 level) for the organic group and each of the other groups. It identified 80% of the organic group. It was felt that the index was most effective for cases of *diffuse* brain damage and was likely to miss cases of *localized lesions and tumors*. In a more rigorous test of this index and of other scores and configurations, a later study compared the performance of 142 brain-damaged patients (76 cases of traumatic encephalopathy, 66 cases of miscellaneous neurologic disorder) with the performance of 120 control patients (28 cases of neurologic disturbance without brain lesions, 92 cases of acute schizophrenics) (Mosher & Smith, 1965). These workers found that both the Hain score and the Peek-Quast score differentiated the brain damage cases from the controls at the .001 level, but they also found that the cutting scores on both scales identified correctly only a relatively small percentage of the cases. In general, they conclude pessimistically that their study " . . . does not provide evidence that the BGT is at all useful in diagnosing these truly questionable cases." They felt that it was best in identifying the severely injured cases requiring surgery or involving skull fractures. Not only is this kind of generalization unwarranted on the basis of the evidence presented—since the composition of the groups, particularly of the control group, poses more problems than it solves—it is also in direct conflict with many other studies that will be referred to in discussing brain damage diagnosis (see especially Chapter 5 and 9). However, the study did highlight the relative efficacy of several perceptual-motoric factors: distortion, angulation difficulty, and poor, coarse coordination. In passing it should be noted that they tested five of the Hutt-Briskin signs and found three of these significant (two signs at the .01 level and one sign at the .05 level). The significant signs, *for this type of discrimination*, were: poor, coarse coordination; perseveration; and, collision. As an example of a study that reported results that indicated that the Bender-Gestalt was significant in predicting minimal neurologic damage (in children), there is the report by Wiener (1966), who found the following significant signs: curvature difficulty, angulation difficulty, and a tendency to gross perceptual-motoric distortion.

Hain's scoring method for detecting possible cerebral dysfunction has been tested in a number of additional studies, and has usually been found to be valuable. A recent study by Pardue (1975) is typical. She compared three groups of patients—brain damaged, schizophrenics, and nonorganic and non-brain damaged—with 20 in each group. She found, using Background Interference Procedures (discussed later), that the Hain scoring method differentiated these groups. Utilization of the Pascal-Suttell scoring led to individually reliable discrimination.

A number of scoring scales have been developed for work with children. As in the case of the scales developed for adults, the objective usually has been to develop a global measure of some kind. In most instances the predictive criterion considered was that of achievement in school work. Keller (1955) was one of the first to report on such efforts. Working with high-level mentally retarded children, and utilizing three categories of factors presumably related to maturity of visual-motor functions, Keller was able to demonstrate significant relationships between test scores and teachers' and psychologists' ratings. This study showed promise in the use of this type of score for predicting school achievement, but was limited in terms of its generalizability (only 36 mentally retarded boys were used as subjects) and in terms of an underlying rationale.

A simply rated score, based on "discriminated degrees of quality of production," was developed by a group of workers for application to the kindergarten population (Keogh & Smith, 1961). They found that their method yielded scores that offered considerable promise in predicting school functioning. It was simpler than the Pascal-Suttell scoring scheme, with which it correlated .80, and had fairly good interjudge and rerating reliabilities.

Koppitz has done extensive research with the Bender-Gestalt Test in developing a measure of developmental visual-motor maturity for children between the ages of 5 and 10 years, and has published two books dealing specifically with her method (1958; 1960; 1963; 1965; 1975a). As noted previously, she has also developed a score based on "emotional indicators" in which ten factors are involved. Although in her 1975 volume she suggests the value of specific emotional indicators as predictive of specific personality traits or problems, she does not believe that it is "possible to make a differential diagnosis between neurotic, psychotic, and brain-damaged patients on the basis of EI's [emotional indicators] on a Bender Test record" (Koppitz, 1975a). We might say that this finding is not at all surprising since the EI was not developed for this purpose; but her conclusion should not be taken to mean that other methods of scoring and analyzing Bender test protocols cannot yield such information! Her developmental score is of some value in predicting school achievement in the primary grades, although many other factors need to be taken into consideration. In a recent research report she finds that her developmental score differentiates, in an 8- to 9-year old group, between those with learning disability and a control group, but it did not differentiate between readers and nonreaders (Koppitz, 1975b). She has found that her developmental score is a better predictor of achievement in arithmetic in the primary grades than it is of reading achievement.

Norms for school children in the age range of 6 to 12 years have been provided by other workers (Armstrong & Hauch, 1960).

It should be added that the strong possibility exists that different factors operate in the performance of very young children, say, below 8 years of age, than in that of older children and adults. There is considerable evidence that perceptual and motoric maturity have different developmental curves and enter in differential manner into the performance of individuals at these differing age levels.

STUDIES OF TEST FACTORS AND PERSONALITY CHARACTERISTICS

Another area of investigation explored the possible presence of primary factors in the Gestalt reproductions of subjects. In a series of studies conducted by Guertin with hospitalized patients, including organics and schizophrenics, an attempt was made to isolate statistically independent factors by means of a factor analytic method (Guertin, 1952; 1954a; 1954b; 1954c; 1955). His first analysis resulted in five general factors: poor reality contact, propensity toward curvilinear movements, constriction, careless execution, and poor spatial contiguity. It was found that paranoids had the highest "loading" on "poor reality contact," for example, and that nonparanoid schizophrenics had the highest "loading" on "propensity toward curvilinear movements." Various meanings were assigned to each of these factors. In one of the later studies, further analysis was conducted on the phenomenon of curvilinear distortions, and this phenomenon was broken down to five subfactors. These studies were limited to specific types of patient subgroups, and therefore the generalizability to other psychiatric subgroups of patients and to nonhospitalized patients may be questioned; however, they mark a highly significant step toward classification and analysis of underlying processes, on the basis of which further progress in understanding the phenomena may be obtained eventually.

A more recent factor analytic study, which employed a number of tests (Bender-Gestalt, Frostig, and Benton Visual Retention Test) with 34 boys between the ages of 8 and 12 years, found 97% of the variance on these tests to be accounted for by the following, extracted factors: global figure-ground discrimination; perceptual differentiation; ability to discriminate positions and size relationships; perseveration; and visuomotor components (Wurst, 1974). Studies such as this one help to delineate primary factors in the total visual-motor performance, but of course they tell us nothing about personality and other correlates.

Still another line of study has been undertaken in investigating the possible meaning of basic perceptual-motoric processes. In some ingenious experiments, Fabian (1945, 1951) attempted to explore the meaning of "rotations" in the performance of school children and the relationship to reading difficulties. First, the frequency of the phenomenon of rotation was checked. It was found that rotation of the figures was very common in kindergarten children, but as children advanced in age the frequency of rotations diminished sharply. More than half of the very young children rotated the designs, but only 7% of those who were between 7½ and 9 years of age continued to do so. Then, using modified horizontal lines, it was found that 51% of 6-years-olds but only 22% of 6½-year-olds rotated either one or two of the figures. Children were also asked to draw straight lines, without any instruction relating to direction, and almost 70% drew vertical lines. These findings led Fabian to conclude that "verticalization" (or rotation toward the upright from the horizontal orientation) was a maturational or developmental process in young children and that the persistence of this tendency indicated a lag in such development or a regression. This lag was found to be related to poor learning in reading. It is interesting that the possible contributions to this lag of emotional factors were not considered, and that the lag was thought to be due to genetic factors, much as Bender had proposed earlier.

Lachman (1960) decided that it was important to explore the possible contribution of emotional factors to the developmental lag in both perceptual-motoric and reading ability. The research design permitted an evaluation of the contribution of each of these factors. A comparison of emotionally disturbed but normal readers showed that such readers also showed visual-motor distortions. It was concluded that the hypothesis of the developmental lag in percepual-motoric behavior could not account, by itself, for the reading difficulty. We might add that it is also quite possible that emotional factors can produce "rotations" and other distortions and that regressive signs of visual-motoric behavior can result from either anomalies in development or from psychological disturbances. In a later chapter of this book we shall comment on the finding, in Fabian's and in others' studies, that certain figures are more likely to be rotated than are others (see Chapter 4).

One intriguing problem concerns the relative contribution of perceptual and motoric processes to perceptual-motoric tasks such as the HABGT. We shall summarize the findings of three studies bearing directly on this problem. In the first (McPherson & Pepin, 1955), subjects were asked to reproduce the designs in the usual way (by drawing them) as well as by placing pieces of felt in the appropriate position to construct the designs. Their evidence seemed to indicate that motor ability is not, by itself, primarily responsible for correct reproduction, and that covert perceptual processes are primarily responsible for accurate performance. In another study (Niebuhr & Cohen, 1956), 40 subjects were administered the Bender-Gestalt under 4 different experimental conditions. The subjects were divided into 4 subgroups of 10 persons each: nurses, acute schizophrenics, chronic schizophrenics, and neurologic cases. The results indicated that both perceptual and motoric factors *were* correlated with the severity of the group's psychopathology so that the group with the most severe pathology scored poorest on *both* factors. However, this study does not answer a number of relevant issues: (1) Aside from the nurses, how sure can one be that the other groups differed significantly in degree of psychopathology? (2) Since these workers reported that age and severity of psychopathology, as it was evaluated, were highly correlated, could not the results have been attributed, at least in part, to the age factor? Nevertheless, the findings are suggestive that both perceptual and motoric factors do contribute to performance on the Bender, *as scored.*

A more sophisticated research design sheds some additional light on this problem (Stoer et al, 1965). In this study, discussed above in another connection, four groups of subjects (controls, organics, acute schizophrenics) were matched for age, sex, and intelligence. These adults were then asked to reproduce each of the Gestalt designs on a card exactly the same size as the test card. They were also asked to compare the stimulus with eight other designs (one of which was their own reproduction of that design), and to rank these in terms of a continuum from least like to most like the stimulus. Both the subjects' reproductions of the designs and the designs used in the comparison series were scored by the Pascal-Suttell method. No significant differences were found in the matching task. For the reproductions, variance in the four groups was significant at the .05 level. Stoer et al. concluded that deviant performance reflects "defects in motor and/or integrative functions." They believe that such a position ". . . is in good agreement with clinical experience concerning the usefulness of the test for the detection of both neurological and functional pathology." Once again the reader is cautioned not to generalize these findings and conclusions to other methods of scoring, to other nosologic groups, or to other methods of administration.

It should also be noted that, when there is severe motoric impairment, performance on the Bender-Gestalt procedures can be grossly affected. A study of motor-impaired children by Newcomer and Hammill (1973) clearly indicates this effect. Utilizing the Motor Free Test of Visual Perception and the Bender-Gestalt Test, they examined 90 children ranging in age from 5 to 12 years. They found that there was progressive deterioration on the Bender-Gestalt performance with increasing motoric impairment. Nevertheless, all of the findings to date, taken together, do suggest the essential nature of the integrative function tapped by perceptual-motoric tasks and indicate one possible reason why such a task, rather than a "purely perceptual" or a "purely motoric" task, is likely to prove more useful in many aspects of clinical work.

One of the most active areas of research has been in the differential diagnosis of organic brain damage. Such damage can of course take many different forms, involve "critical" or "noncritical" regions of the brain, be of moderate to great severity, be in the dominant or nondominant side of the brain, or involve small or localized portions of the brain or large or diffuse sections of the brain. Not only are these different conditions likely to influence performance on a perceptual-motoric task in quite different ways and to quite different degrees, but even the same condition may produce diverse psychological effects in different individuals, depending on such other factors as their prior physical and personality histories and the nature of the recovery or compensatory process that may be involved. It would be inconceivable, therefore, to expect *any single scoring system or any single method of analysis with any psychological test to be able to produce anything like near-perfect prediction of the whole gamut of organic deficits.* The aim should, of course, be much more modest: to predict with *reasonable accuracy* some types of organic defect under some types of conditions.

In their review of the literature on this subject prior to 1961, Tolor and Schulberg (1963) stated: "There is overwhelming evidence in these studies for the concurrent validity of the Bender-Gestalt Test. Consistently one notes that the Bender performance of cerebrally impaired groups can be distinguished from diverse psychiatric groups, either by means of objective scoring criteria or by more global evaluations." Yet in a subsequent review of the literature, Garron and Cheifetz (1965) stated that this test is relatively inefficient in differentiating *individuals* with severe psychological disturbance from those with organic brain disease. Nevertheless, they agreed that the various scoring methods did significantly differentiate the *means of groups* of various types of disorders. A sampling of the findings of relatively recent research on this problem may shed some light.

It should be noted that of the two studies referred to earlier [Mosher and Smith (1965) and Wiener (1966), which seemingly gave contradictory results], with patients showing minimal neurologic damage, the one which utilized *a scale of degree of neurologic deficit* based on perinatal data and early neurologic facts, and which also *controlled carefully* for race, sex, social, and maternal variables in a large group of subjects (822), did obtain results with the Bender-Gestalt that significantly predicted neurologic impairment in children. Although Wiener's positive findings need to be replicated, they are highly suggestive of the value of the "test" when appropriate factors are carefully taken into consideration. A related study (McConnell, 1967), conducted with children, also found that the "test," this time scored in terms of Koppitz' developmental norms, significantly differentiated 120 children who were divided into three levels *in terms of severity of organicity.*

An intriguing study, in this respect, is that reported by Landis, Baxter, Patterson, and Tauber (1974). They evaluated the use of the Bender-Gestalt Test, employing the Pascal-Suttell scoring method, in the detection of neurological damage following open heart surgery. In the usual surgical procedures extracorporeal blood circulation can create microemboli in the blood and thus lead to neurological damage. A new filter, designed to remove such emboli, was assessed by preoperative and postoperative Bender-Gestalt records. The patients, 28 in all, were between 38 and 66 years of age. It was found that (1) postoperative impairment in the Bender-Gestalt performance was consistent with ultrasonic counts of microemboli, and that (2) under conditions of the use of the new filter, there was less visual-motor damage that is associated with neurological defects. Corroborative evidence of the sensitivity of the Bender-Gestalt to the effects of brain damage was obtained in a study by Bravo (1973). The data on the test differentiated between patients with infantile minimal cerbral dysfunction and a control group.

Two recent books that report the results of intensive invesigations of Hutt's configurations for screening for organic brain damage contain a wealth of data on this subject. Marley (1982) reports the findings of 9 years of research on 640 acute stroke patients. She utilized the configuration proposed by Hutt and Briskin (1960) and added several test factors of her own, but finally settled on nine of Hutt and Briskin's criteria plus two of her own ("total time" taken to reproduce the figures, and "workover"). A so-called cross validation sample of 196 nonorganics and

200 organics (so-called because there was no matching for relevant variables) was also studied. Her scores consisted of the number of the presumed organic signs that were present in a record. Her results confirmed the power of this configuration in discriminating between organic and nonorganic patients. She states: "A one-way analysis of variance conducted on the Differential Diagnostic Scores of the four levels of organicity in the research group indicated there were significant differences between them . . . (p. .0001). Subsequent multiple comparison tests further indicated that each diagnostic group differed significantly from each of the other diagnostic groups." (p. 7) (The groups were: no organicity; mild organicity moderate organicity; and severe organicity.) She adds: "It is noteworthy that the findings indicated that there was no overlapping between the distributions of the Differential Diagnostic Scores for each of the four diagnostic levels" (p. 9), a conclusion that her presented results do not justify. She also found "that age and sex adjusted for level of organic deficit have little effect on the Differential Diagnostic Score. . . ." An interjudge reliability for the scoring (three judges) is reported as .99, an almost unbelievable finding.

This study has been reviewed in detail by Hutt (1983). The impressive findings are possibly marred by: (1) lack of published information concerning the test stimuli that were used (Marley reported in a personal letter to Hutt that she had used *modified* Orthopsychiatric designs because she had found these to be "defective and somewhat different from the original designs which Dr. Bender presented on Plate 1, Page 4 of her *Monograph*"; (2) insufficient data concerning possible contamination of the criteria with which organicity was evaluated; and, (3) extravagent claims for the specificity with which the precise localization and nature of the organic deficit are specified. Thus, although Marley's findings are highly impressive, the methodology and analysis of data may be questioned.

Lacks and coworkers have explored the utility of various scoring systems and test factors for a number of years, her work finally culminating in a book (Lacks, 1984) that describes the effectiveness of some of Hutt's "signs" of organic brain damage. Lacks, Colbert, Harrow, and Levine (1970) compared the Bender with the Halstead-Reitan battery of neuropsychological tests and found the latter more effective in screening organics but the former more effective for nonorganics. Lacks and Newport (1980) compared the Hutt-Briskin scoring system with other scoring systems and found the former more effective in differentiating among organics, psychotics, personality disorders, and chronic alcoholics. Further studies led to the development of a simplified scoring guide for Hutt's organic configuration and evaluation of its effectiveness in screening for organicity (Lacks, 1984).

In her final presentation, Lacks used her slightly redefined list of Hutt-Briskin's configurational factors for organic brain damage. She reports that this system achieved a diagnostic accuracy of 87% for organics and 80% for nonorganics, whereas other scoring systems using Bender protocols (Pauker, Hain and "Rotations") were considerably less accurate. She also reports her findings with respect to diagnostic accuracy in a comparison of the Bender with the Benton Visual Retention test and the Graham-Kendall Memory designs. She reports diagnostic accuracy, correcting for base rates, of 82% for the Hutt-Briskin scores, whereas it is 66% for the Benton and still lower for the Graham-Kendall. Interscorer reliability is also reported as very high. Based on results of two studies involving three scorers with widely varying levels of experience in one study (Lacks & Newport, 1980), interscorer reliability ranged from an r of .87 to an r of .90. Intrascorer reliability for one judge (an "expert" scorer) over a period of several years was .93.

Thus, Lack's work clearly supports the discriminating value of Hutt's configuration in differentiating between organic and nonorganic patients. It should be noted that his procedure is useful for *screening purposes,* but not for diagnosis. The latter requires not only the elimination of false positive or negative findings in an individual case, but further corroboration of possible alternative explanatory causes (see Chapter 9).

A particularly valuable study was conducted by Monheit (1983), evaluating the effectiveness of Hutt's 17-factor Psychopathology Scale in differentiating normal, emotionally disturbed, and delinquent male adolescents (ages 13–16). Utilizing the statistical method of discriminant analysis, she found that 16 of these signs effectively discriminated between normals, on the one hand, and emotionally disturbed and delinquent boys, on the other hand, the classification yielding 92.6% correctly placed normals. Only five of the normal adolescents out of ninety-five were incorrectly classified. The ability of the 16 factors to differentiate emotionally disturbed from delinquents was less satisfactory, only 68% of the former and 52% of the latter being properly placed. There are many possible explanations for this: (1) it is known that delinquents comprise a heterogeneous group, many of whom, on closer clinical evaluation turn out to be "normal" or "emotionally disturbed"; (2) many adolsecents who are characterized as "emotionally disturbed" are, in fact, only manifesting adolescent crises; and, (3) some of the test factors, as Monheit herself demonstrated, are influenced by differences in age (although our own studies indicate that *the total score on the Psychopathology Scale* does not show this effect).

Monheim did not explore the value of the total Psychopathology Score in this study, but she did investigate seven other test factors. Only one of these (central placement of the first figure), which Hutt discusses in his previous works but did not include in the Psychopathology Scale, was found to be significant. She also supplies intercorrelational data on the 17 factors. These findings will be discussed in connection with our later presentation of the current Psychopathology Scale.

This selective review of the uses of objective test indicators on the BGT and the HABGT demonstrates the vitality of this test and the possible values it may have in clinical work as well as in research on visual-motor phenomena.

3
The HABGT: Test Materials and Administration

There is considerable evidence that many factors can influence the results of testing. Among those that have received research documentation are: the expectancies of the examinee; the explicit test instructions; the "atmosphere" in which the examination is conducted; the personality of the examiner; the sex, race, and color of skin of examiner and examinee; and the point in the diagnostic sequence (or diagnostic-therapeutic sequence) in which the particular test or procedure is administered. Some tests are much more sensitive to such influences than others, and greater care is needed with such tests in interpreting results; both advantages and disadvantages accrue from such sensitivity. In addition to these general factors is the general problem of the effect upon test results of prior social–cultural–educational experiences of the individual.

It has been reported (Tolor & Schulberg, 1963) that, as suggested by this author (Hutt & Briskin, 1960), the HABGT or other variations of this test could be used as a buffer test due to its nonthreatening and nonverbal characteristics. Although such use of the test is helpful in many ways, this does not negate the importance of obtaining proper rapport *before* the test is administered. Developing such rapport would seem to have two highly important functions. First, it would induce maximal motivation on the part of the examinee, thus helping to insure that the product more accurately represents his present, full capacity. Second, it would enable the examiner to understand the examinee's expectancies and motivations and thus provide a more adequate basis for interpretation.

In order to develop proper rapport, the test procedure must be considered as a task governed by the examinee's needs. The examinee should be given an explanation of the test's purposes in terms of *his* needs, rather than those of the clinic, hospital, or diagnostician. In other words, the examinee should develop some conviction that taking the test will really be useful. In many cases, this will not require extended discussion; even when it does not, however, ample opportunity should be permitted for expression of feelings, fears and uncertainties. And when there is fear of reluctance to proceed with the testing, directly expressed or implied, great care should be taken to explore and discuss these issues—not in the spirit of conning the examinee into taking the test, but in the spirit of fully accepting his feelings as relevant and significant. Testing can proceed fruitfully only when such issues have been fully explored and accepted by the examinee in terms of his own needs and interests. If circumstances should arise when this is not feasible, and testing still has to be carried out, then this definition of the situation should be stated frankly and the results interpreted with considerably greater caution than would otherwise be necessary.

There is some evidence (see discussion in Chapter 2) that group administration does not, on the whole, significantly affect many aspects of the test results as compared with individual administration, but group administration cannot properly take into account the broad spectrum of the motivational factors we have been discussing and makes interpretation of individuals' results much more tenuous, to say the least.

TEST MATERIALS

The HABGT *test cards* are those published by Grune & Stratton. As has been noted previously, the designs on these nine test cards are those developed by Wertheimer (1923) so as to incorporate certain Gestalt features. Our statistical findings and normative data *are based on these designs,* presented on 3″ × 5″ white cards with the 5″ diameter as the base. Other test cards that are available, such as those furnished by the American Orthopsychiatric Association and utilized by Bender in her original work, are significantly different. These other cards are different in overall size, the designs vary in the several sets that have been furnished by the publishers, and some designs are *markedly different* in configuration, line quality, angulation of the figures, and curvature. There is no hard, research evidence indicating how much these differing features of the stimuli affect test results, although our own experience in using them indicates that certain test factors, such as number of perceptual rotations, closure, and spacing of the figures on the test protocol are *significantly different*. Hence, it is strongly advised that the HABGT test cards be employed if our norms and configuration findings are to be employed.

The other test materials consist of: a stack of white, unlined bond paper, 8½" × 11" in size; a number of medium soft pencils (2 to 3 in hardness); and, a pencil eraser.

The examinee should be seated in a comfortable position for drawing the designs and have a *smooth,* comfortable writing surface on which to execute the drawings.

ADMINISTRATION: FOR THE OBJECTIVE TEST SCALES

The maximal clinical utility of the HABGT involves the projective features incorporated in test procedures. Hence, for example, test cards and test paper are presented so as to maximize the effect of the *differing axes* of paper and cards. Similarly, test instructions, which emphasize the *unstructured* nature of the task, tend to facilitate projective features. Administrative features of test procedure, the so-called *Elaboration, Association,* and *Experimental-Clinical* phases, help to evoke significant idiosyncratic and projective responses. However, only the *Copy Phase* needs to be administered to utilize the *Objective Scales:* the Psychopathology Scale and the Adience-Abience Scale.

Copy Phase

The examiner places the stack of bond paper *near* the examinee and also places the pencils and the erasers in a conveniently accessible position. He then places the 9 HABGT cards in front of his own body, on the table, with the designs in a face-down position. The backs of the cards are thus exposed, in a pile, so that the examinee may see that there is a number of them, but he is *not* told how many cards there are. The following instructions are then offered. (The language may be varied so as to make the meaning clear, as may be necessary for some children and for adults who have language problems, but the essential content is kept constant.)

"I am going to show you these cards (pointing to the pile of cards), *one at a time. Each card has a simple drawing on it. I would like you to copy the drawing on the paper, as well as you can. Work in any way that is best for you. This is not a test of artistic ability, but try to copy the drawings as accurately as possible. Work as fast or as slowly as you wish."*

Any questions by the examinee are answered by paraphrasing the above, but *no suggestions are offered* as to methods of work, or the like. When such questions are raised, they should be answered with some such noncommital phrases as: *"Well, that's up to you.; Do it the way you think is best."* One question that is asked frequently is: "How many sheets of paper shall I use?" The response is: *"That's entirely up to you."* If one is asked: "May I erase or correct it?," the response is, again, *"That's up to you."*

The examiner then takes a *single sheet* of paper from the stack and places it directly in front of the subject, with the long (or vertical) axis of the paper at right angles to his body. The first test card, Card A, is then taken from the stack of cards, and is placed in front of the subject with the base of the card (as indicated by the letter A on the back) toward him. The instruction, *"Copy this as well as you can,"* is repeated.

Each of the pertinent features of this method of administration needs some comment.

1. *The stack of bond paper.* Presenting the examinee with a stack of bond paper gives him a choice: to use a single sheet, to use two sheets, or to use a number of sheets, possibly one for each drawing. For reasons that will be discussed in later chapters, it is believed that the way in which the examinee structures this aspect of the task for himself reveals important aspects of his life space in general. Although the forced use of a single sheet of paper for all of the drawings has other advantages, it does not permit (encourage?) the maximum variance in the use of space. The single sheet of paper that is presented to the examinee, while the stack remains available, is simply to prevent his making impressions on the other sheets, in the course of his drawings, which might be used as guides in making the subsequent drawings.

2. *The stack of cards.* The stack of test cards is kept visible so as to enable the subject to make some anticipatory adjustment in his planning, if he wishes, in deciding where to place his drawings or even to decide how large or small to make them. If the subject asks how many cards there are, the response is, *"Just this stack of cards."*

3. *Placement of the single sheet of paper.* It will be noted that we start the subject off by presenting him with a single sheet with the long axis perpendicular to his body. This is done because it is the usual position when writing or drawing on $8\frac{1}{2} \times 11$ inch paper. However, the subject is *free to change its position,* so that he may decide to shift the paper and have the long axis, for example, parallel to his body. There are a number of issues involved in this matter. For one thing, it is probable that presenting the paper in the "vertical position" while the test card is presented in the "horizontal" position, as we have suggested, maximizes the frequency with which rotations will appear, especially in younger children. (See the related research: Griffith & Taylor, 1960; Hannah, 1958.) We shall consider the possibilities of modifying this and other features of test administration in the section titled "Testing-the-Limits: Experimental–Clinical Methods." (See also Chapter 4).

Another aspect of our suggested "standard" procedure is the meaning behind a subject's decision to rotate the test paper. One *possible* explanation is a tendency toward oppositional behavior. (Such a possibility needs to be checked and explored in various ways, as we shall see.) When the subject changes the position of the paper, a note should be made as part of the record.

4. *Placement of the test card.* The standard placement of the test card provides for a standard perceptual task. Shifting the position of the card may change its Gestalt quality. Hence, if the subject rotates the test card, the examiner should replace it in its standard position, with the added instruction, *"You are supposed to copy it this way."* However, if the subject insists upon having the card in a different position, make a note of this in the record, and then interpret the possible meaning of the reproduction on a different basis. (See the *HABGT Revised Record Form* for further instructions on this point.)

5. *Pencils and eraser.* The use of a medium-soft pencil helps to maximize nuances produced by varying pressures while drawing. Thus, the examiner can later examine the drawings for variations in pressure and consider such possible variations in terms of their meaning as indicators of anxiety, frustration with the task, etc.

The presence of the eraser is suggestive that corrections and erasures may be made, but no explicit directions are given. If the examinee asks whether he may erase or correct, he is told, *"That's up to you."* Some examinees may make more than one attempt at drawing a design. *This is neither encouraged nor discouraged.* Again, if asked about this, the examiner states, *"That's up to you."* When more than one attempt is made in reproducing a design, the examinee's choice as to which he considers best is used as the basis for later scoring. If no choice is made, then the best reproduction is used in later objective scoring (see Chapter 14). However, the several drawings may furnish important clues about the features of the design that are difficult or disturbing to the examinee.

Returning now to the remainder of the administration of the copy phase of the test, when the examinee has completed his reproduction of the design on Card A, the examiner removes this card from sight, with some appropriate comment such as *"That's fine,"* and then places Card 1 directly in front of the examinee with the comment, *"Now copy this drawing as well as you can."* As in the placement of all cards, the base of the card, indicated by the number on the back, is placed toward the examinee. Similarly, when Card 1 has been completed, it is removed and Card 2 is placed in position. This procedure is continued until all test cards have been administered.

The sequence in which the cards are presented is considered important. Although there is no adequate research evidence on this point, clinical experience suggests that variations in sequence influence results. For example, perseveration is more likely to occur on Card 2 when it follows Card 1. The sequence of Cards 4, 5, and 6 seems to maximize difficulties on curved figures, when such a tendency is present. Cards 7 and 8, the most difficult from the viewpoint of perceptual maturity, are given last and might adversely affect the performance of some subjects on later tasks if given earlier in the sequence.

As with any psychological task, the *behavior of the examinee* is sometimes as important as the test response itself. Especially in the early stages of the examiner's experience with this test, copious notes should be taken on all relevant aspects of the examinee's behavior. *His spontaneous comments should be recorded* and examined later for possible significance. Among various aspects of the examinee's methods of work to be recorded the following are the most important: (1) Does he preplan his drawings or does he proceed impulsively or even impetuously? (2) Does he count the number of dots, loops, or sides of figures, or does he proceed haphazardly? (3) Does he make frequent erasures? If so, on what figures and on which parts of these figures does he have difficulty or does he show extra care? (4) Which part of the figure does he tackle first? (5) In what direction does he proceed as he copies the figure? Does he draw from the top down or from the bottom up? Does he draw from the inside out or from the outside in? Does the direction of movement vary from figure to figure? (6) Does he use sketching movements? (7) Does he show unusual blocking on any figures?

The time taken by the examinee in reproducing the designs is not recorded. There is no evidence that this factor correlates significantly with important personality variables.* However, *extreme variation in time* to make the drawings should be noted carefully, and clinical experience will soon indicate to the examiner when such extremes occur. Excessively long time is usually indicative of psychomotor blocking and thus can be an important clinical indicator of a number of types of pathology (e.g., latent catatonic blocking, brain damage, or extreme compulsivity). Unusually rapid performance may also be significant and may indicate one of a number of conditions (e.g., extreme anxiety with a need to "get out of the situation," psychopathic attitude, or strong oppositional tendencies). Hence, future valuable dividends may be gleaned from a manifestation of extreme variations in time.

---

* Marley's study (1982), referred to in Chapter 2, indicates that there is an r of .80 between time taken to complete the copying and recall of the test designs and degree of organic deficit. It must be remembered, however, that many other factors may produce excessive time in copying the designs.

The *HABGT Revised Record Form* contains space and directions for recording these and other features of the test performance.

Other Test Procedures

The *elaboration phase* is the second phase of administration of the test as a projective instrument. Its major purpose is to assist in maximizing those projective reactions to the test which will enable the examiner to offer tentative hypotheses about the particular examinee. This phase of the testing *further reduces the structured quality of the test situation* and thus requires the examinee to impose his own idiosyncratic meaning upon it.

After the copy phase has been completed, the examinee's drawings are *removed from sight*. Again, a stack of paper is provided and placed near the examinee. The examiner instructs something like: *"Well, that was very nice. Now, I'm going to ask you to do something else with these drawings. This time, I'd like you to modify the drawings, or to change them in any way you wish, so as to make them more pleasing to you. Feel free to change them in any way that you like. (They may even remind you of things.) You can change the drawings as little or as much as you like. Just make them more pleasing to yourself. Do you understand what I'd like you to do?"* Any questions are then answered within the framework of these instructions. The wording may be modified to clarify the meaning of the instructions. Thus, for a more sophisticated subject, the examiner might say, *"You might like to make them more esthethic in appearance."* To a young child he might say, *"Say if you can make them better looking."*

The examiner then presents each card in sequence with the instruction: *"Change this one in any way you like so as to make it more pleasing to you."* If the examinee states that he likes the drawing the way it is, he should be told, *"All right, but will you please copy it again the way it is."* This is done for two reasons. (1) Even when the examinee attempts to recopy the drawing, he may reveal aspects of his performance that were not clear the first time, or he may modify it involuntarily. In either case, further evidence becomes available that is useful in later interpretation. (2) The sequence of the drawings, and their placement on the page (pages) needs to be considered, especially if an aberrant placement (deviation in sequence) has occurred.

When time considerations are important, and it is thought to be important to reduce the total time for the testing, certain cards may be omitted from the elaboration phase. Cards A, 2, 4, 6, 7, and 8 will usually furnish a sufficient sample to make all of the necessary deductions. These cards present about all of the important Gestalt qualities found in the entire sample of cards, and can therefore be used for such an abbreviated procedure. Of course, sequence is then modified and may affect some of the possible findings. The saving in time is increased when a few cards are eliminated from this phase, because they are then also eliminated from the next phase, the association phase.

Again, as in the copy phase, notes are taken on the examinee's spontaneous comments and test behavior.

The degree of freedom the examinee exercises in the elaboration phase, the kind of individual creativity he displays, and the definition he imposes upon this ambiguous task all tell us something about the way in which his personality functions. Some subjects are quite anxious when they are asked to work without specific structuring of the task. They become overly defensive and are fearful of revealing unknown aspects about themselves. But these and other subjects often are led to modify the drawings in ways which they do not "consciously intend." Sometimes the very act of drawing the designs, with latent cues derived either from the drawing or their own distortions of the drawing, trigger important deviations in the elaboration phase that were hardly noticeable in the copy phase. Even compulsive individuals, intending only to reproduce the designs faithfully, find themselves modifying them in highly idiosyncratic ways. The relative lack of fantasy and creativity in other subjects is often highlighted. In still others, the need to conform or the excessive and neurotic fear of authority figures becomes evident as they strive only to reproduce the "standard" designs. In some cases, the disintegration or severe regression that occurs that occurs during the elaboration phase is highlighted. They "escape" from any reality controls and engage in "doodling," or present their drawings in a confused jumble, sometimes letting the figures collide or overlap. Occasionally, we see a peculiar fascination with a particular part of a design that intrigues the subject, and it is redrawn with elaborate and excessive care. These and other features sometimes become evident during this phase and provide important clinical leads to understanding the unique features of the individual. Of particular interest is the performance of some brain-damaged patients who struggle impatiently with some aspect of the design that troubles them and that they are unable to reproduce accurately either in the copy phase or in the elaboration phase.

A comparison of the accuracy of nosological predictions based on the copy phase alone as contrasted with a combination of both the copy phase and the elaboration phase (utilizing 130 male adult psychoneurotic subjects, 38 schizophrenics, 119 heterogenous cases with organic brain damage, and 25 hospitalized nonpsychiatric patients) indicated that the latter combination gave improved accuracy of predictions significant at the .05 level of confidence.

The third aspect of procedures to provide projective data about the examinee is termed the *Association Phase*. The chief function of the association phase is to elict the individual's associative content to *both* the original test cards and the elaborations which have been made of them during the elaboration phase. It is assumed that when an individual modifies the design, he is doing so, in part, because of implicit and unconscious cues that his perceptual–motoric behavior stimulated. The *contrast* between the original designs and his elaborations of them is believed—with considerable clinical evidence and some research evidence (Story, 1960)—to increase the likelihood of evoking significant associative material.

The method is quite simple. After the elaboration phase has been completed, the examiner presents stimulus Card A *alongside* the elaboration the examinee has made of it. He then says: *"Now, look at the design on the card and look at the modification you made of it in your drawing. What does each of them remind you of? What could they be? What do they look like or suggest."* The examiner records the association(s) to the card and the association(s) to the elaboration. If the examinee offers an association only to the card, he is then asked, *"And what does the one you made look like or remind you of?"* Conversely, if an association is offered only to the elaboration, the examiner asks, *"And what does the one on the card look like or remind you of?"* The sequence in which the associations are offered is numbered and a notation is made of the stimulus (*O* for original stimulus card, and *E* for the elaboration stimulus) to which the association is given. It is also advisable to ask, *"And what in the drawing made it look like that?"*

A similar procedure is followed with each of the other cards; in each case, the stimulus card is presented alongside the elaboration and the examinee is asked, *"What does each of them remind you of?"*

Of course, as will be illustrated in later chapters, both in the diagnostic process and in the therapeutic process, the clinician may extend this procedure so as to get at conflicts and conflict-situations.

When administration of the HABGT has been completed, the following data are available: (1) drawings made during the copy phase, together with notes and observations concerning the examinee's comments and behavior; (2) drawings made in the elaboration phase, together with comments on the examinee's behavior and verbalizations; and (3) associations given to both the original stimuli and to the elaborations. All of these data, taken together, constitute the material for use in projective interpretation: two samples of perceptual–motoric productions together with the accessory information concerning the sequence in which the drawings are placed on the page(s); two sets of associative comments; verbal behavior; comments on methods of work.

As noted earlier, in order to score on the objective scales that are presented in Chapters 4 and 6, only the material from the copy phase needs to be utilized. In order to develop projective hypotheses, all of the material will need to be considered first separately, and then in combination. In general, projective interpretation follows principles derived from work with all projective instruments. However, there are important additions, as well as some modifications, dependent on the specific stimulus properties of the present test characteristics. These principles for projective interpretation are presented in Chapter 11.

EXPERIMENTAL–CLINICAL METHODS: MICRODIAGNOSIS

In their original volume on the Rorschach, Klopfer and Kelley (1942) discussed some of the values and limitations of varying the testing procedure, after the formal testing had been completed, in order to clarify the meaning of certain ambiguous findings. Shortly thereafter, the present writer proposed a rationale for more regular use of some testing-the-limits procedures (Hutt & Shor, 1946). One of the features of this proposal was to explore the "levels of response." It was assumed that the original responses made to the Rorschach cards represented the level of easily available potentials of the personality. But what were the hidden resources of the personality, and under what conditions could they become available? Thus, in testing-the-limits procedure, it was thought advisable to offer different degrees of suggestions to determine at what point previously unavailable resources could become available.

This, it would seem, would be a major function of any testing-the-limits procedure. Suppose, for example, we have the HABGT record of an individual who has shown tendencies in his test protocol that suggest the possibility of organic brain damage (let us say, trends toward rotation, collision, and regression). The question arises: To what extent are these features fortuitous or accidental, and to what extent are they reliable indicators? As we shall learn in our review of the relevant literature, many types of individuals with brain damage are unable to correct for such deviations, even when they are asked to attempt to do so, whereas emotionally disturbed persons can frequently make appropriate correction when attention is simply called to the deviations with such a comment as, "Is that exactly right?" (Smith & Martin, 1967).

Although the experienced clinician will be able to devise many kinds of ad hoc procedures to test and evaluate questionable responses on the HABGT, I should like to describe some basic methods that may be employed in the clinical–experimental analysis of test behavior. It is usually best to begin the clinical–experimental analysis directly after the copy phase of the test, but it can also be employed after other phases of the test have been completed.

Interview Analysis

If the clinician suspects that some peculiar or abnormal test phenomena have resulted from factors other than those that usually account for their presence, he may proceed by inquiring about the responses in question. Suppose, for instance, that the subject has given an inferior response to one of the cards and this is suspect because he has responded in superior fashion on another, perhaps more difficult test card. The examiner can then present the test card alongside the subject's drawing for that card and ask: "Are these two exactly alike?" If the subject indicates that they are not, the examiner can inquire how they are different. If the answer indicates that the subject perceives accurately how they are different, the examiner can proceed further by asking why the subject made it the way he did. Frequently, the subject will clearly elucidate why he performed the way he did. It may be a matter of carelessness, lack of attention to detail, fear of approaching what seemed to be a difficult task, fatigue, or lack of interest or motivation. The examiner may then ask the subject to try drawing "that one" again, this time taking care "to make your drawing exactly like the one on the card."

The fact that the subject was aware of his error and could clearly perceive what was wrong is important evidence in itself. It may be that the factors noted above were responsible for the "failure." However, it might turn out that the subject is able to perceive accurately but is unable to reproduce the design accurately. Observation may indicate that either gross or fine coordination is poor. The examiner can then proceed to test for coordination by appropriate methods. It might also turn out that the subject had difficulty with some feature of the design, such as making smooth curves, or executing the parts of figures which overlap. In such a case, special procedures, noted below, may be employed to tease out the particular feature which interferes with good performance.

However, it may also happen that the subject is unable to determine how his production differs from the design on the test card. He may be dimly aware that his production is inaccurate, but he may be unable to pinpoint the difficulty, or he may be unaware that his production differs from the design on the test card. These possible characteristics of the interview data may lead the examiner to do some further ad hoc testing with different, possibly simpler, designs to evaluate the nature of the perceptual difficulty. If perceptual problems seem to be associated with the overlapping feature of Card 7, for example, the examiner can present the subject with his own drawings of two overlapping elipses or two overlapping squares to test out the nature of the perceptual problem.

These and similar procedures, based on an interview about the subject's performance, are extremely important in the clinical analysis of test data. Their proper employment may enable the clinician to test out hypotheses about the subject's performance and assist in arriving at an adequate explanation of the nature of the difficulty. They are also very useful in offering a basis for recommendations for remedial or therapeutic assistance. If the subject cannot perceive the nature of his error or cannot correct it even with support and guidance concerning the nature of the error, one may clearly suspect that either perceptual–motoric inadequacy (or slow development), some organic brain damage (if the subject is mature enough for a given design), or mental retardation is present.

Test Performance Analysis

Some of the procedures under this heading overlap with those already discussed in the previous section. Here, however, we are addressing ourselves more explicitly to the question: "What aspects of the test stimuli are causing difficulty for this subject?" The subject may show some evidence of pathological indicators, such as rotation of the figures, severe angulation difficulties, fragmentation, and so on. (See Chapter 4 for definitions of these terms.) If the interview analysis has not offered conclusive evidence of the nature of the problem, the examiner may proceed to test out, through the employment of specific ad hoc procedures, the precise nature of the problem. Such procedures are especially relevant when the test performance is not internally consistent, i.e., when "mistakes" are made inconsistently, or when easy items are difficult for the subject while difficult items are done more adequately.

The types of questions that require clarification are as follows: (1) Are certain features of the test stimuli causing difficulty (i.e., curves, angulation, overlapping, open figures, etc.)? (2) Is the difficulty level of the item causing the problem? (3) Are motivational (and/or fatigue) factors responsible? The task now is to provide the subject with additional test items that will help to clarify the difficulty. If, for instance, the problem seems to relate to curves, the examiner may provide new test stimuli which he now prepares (or has ready), in which the same type of design is offered except that straight lines are substituted for the curves. If angulation seems to be the difficulty, then substitute figures, with different angulation, are presented. If overlapping difficulty is noted, the same figures, but separated, or simpler overlapping figures are now presented. If, on the other hand, motivational factors are suspect, the examination may be repeated on another occasion and better motivation may be encouraged.

If fatigue seems to have been a factor, the test may be repeated with rest periods offered between "sections" of the test.

Some subjects show rotational problems because the test paper is presented in a vertical orientation while the test card is presented in a horizontal orientation (see above). To test out the effect of the discrepant orientations of test card and test paper, the items of the test that are involved may be re-presented, this time with both paper and card in the same orientation. The relation of paper–test card orientation to organic brain damage has been explored by a number of workers (Griffith & Taylor, 1960; Hannah, 1958; Verms, 1974).

Card Sorting

A useful procedure, in some cases, is to ask the subject, after the test proper has been completed, to sort the cards into two piles: one pile containing the designs that he loves or likes most; the other pile containing the designs that he likes least. When this has been done, the examiner may inquire about the first pile: *"What is it about these cards that you like?"* Similarly, he may ask about the other pile: *"What is it about these cards that you don't like?"* The physical characteristics of the sortings may be quite evident. For instance, the subject may place the "easy" items in one pile and the difficult ones in the other. Or he may group the cards on the basis of open versus closed figures, or curves versus straight lines. Inquiry about the choices may prove to be quite revealing, however. Sometimes the cards are grouped on the basis of their symbolic (or unconscious) meaning (Suczek & Klopfer, 1952; Tolor, 1960). If the elaboration and association phases of the test have been completed, the sorting and explanation may be checked against the material obtained in those parts of the test.

Microdiagnosis

All of the above and similar procedures may be subsumed under the rubric *microdiagnosis* (Hutt, 1980). Microdiagnosis, incontrast to the term *macrodiagnosis* (or nomothetic classification), attempts to determine, in *the individual case,* not only which factors contributed to the individual's test performance, but how these factors interacted in producing that particular performance, and *whether or how the performance might be improved.* This is essentially a clinical rather than a psychometric task. It focuses on intraindividual variances rather than on interindividual variances. In sum, the clinician's task is to determine *how* an individual's performance was produced (rather than how it differs from some normative population), what *routes* the individual utilized in that performance (as, for example, whether motivational factors, cognitive factors, perceptual–motoric factors, and the like) contributed to or detracted from the performance, and under what conditions performance might be improved.

Such an approach requires sophistication about the nature of the behavior that is involved as well as ingenuity in *teasing out* the relevant performance factors. The clinician will not rely, solely, on scores or normative data, but rather use them as a *point of departure* for further investigation.

PROCEDURES FOR MALINGERERS AND NONMOTIVATED SUBJECTS

Some patients are very antagonistic to testing even though the examiner has attempted to establish good rapport. Others have characterological problems that interfere with effective effort and may approach the test with a nonchalant or indifferent attitude, making little effort to comply with test directions. These and many other types of individuals who are "unwilling" subjects and those who are willful malingers may produce an HABGT protocol which does not reflect their true capacities. Subjects who are referred by courts or penal agencies present similar problems in testing. The sensitive and ingenious clinician will attempt to deal with such individuals in some appropriate, adaptive manner. Sěpic (1972) found that adults who attempted to malinger on this test have very little success.

The following suggestions may be of some help in such instances. After all testing procedures have been completed, and preferably after a few days have elapsed, the copy phase of the HABGT should be readministered. This may suffice to demonstrate the invalidity of the previous testing since, in some cases, with the passage of time the patient may have forgotten the deliberate distortions he attempted, and make none this time, or quite different ones. Or with the passage of time motivational factors may have changed, if they were simply concurrent with the situation. If, however, significant distortions still occur during retesting, the examinee can be shown the stimulus cards in contrast to his drawings and asked, *"Does your drawing look exactly like mine?"* His response is then taken as the cue for further prodding. For example, *"You say yours is different. Well, tell me how."* And, *"Now try to make one exactly like mine."* The examiner may make use of the discrepancies between the two sets of drawings by the patient to ask him which one is better, and then to say, *"Well, I see you can do much better than you did. Now, try it again, and this time make it exactly like mine."*

Another variation in retesting may prove to be helpful. When read-ministering the test after an interval of time, the test cards may be pre-sented in an inverse position. Most of the figures thereby take on new configurational properties. The malingerer will usually be unable, for ex-ample, to reproduce his "faked" responses in the same way he did origi-nally and evidence of his malingering thus becomes available. The changes in his productions can then be used as a basis for further discus-sion about his attitudes and his "goals" in taking the test.

OTHER METHODS OF ADMINISTRATION

A number of additional methods of administration deserve consider-ation. Some of these have very special purposes, such as the tachistosco-pic method, while others are more generally useful, such as the recall method. In all clinical work, special situations may arise for which there is no clear-cut answer; the creative and experienced practitioner will then devise ad hoc procedures to fit such occasions and make cautious use of the findings. It should be noted that what we have called the copy phase is regarded by most clinicians as the standard procedure, and the findings from this phase are those most frequently presented in research studies.

The Tachistoscopic Method

In a previous volume on the HABGT (Hutt & Briskin, 1960), the tachistoscopic method of administration was suggested "when intracra-nial pathology is suspected." It was thought that this method would im-prove diagnostic differentiation of patients with organic pathology from other nosological entities. This judgment was made, in part, on the basis of clinical experience with adults, and in part on findings by Ross and Schilder (1934) that tachistoscopic presentation results in the production of more primitive forms. Up to the present, only limited research evi-dence has been available to substantiate such claims, but the method still seems highly promising.

The method is essentially similar to that employed in the copy phase, the main difference being in the time of exposure of the stimulus card. The patient is told in substance: *"I'm going to show you some cards, one at a time, that have some designs on them. I shall let you look at the cards for only a few seconds. Then I'll take the card away and ask you to draw the design from memory. Do you understand? Remember, I'll show you the card for only a few seconds. Study it carefully so that you can draw it from memory when I take the card away."*

Card A is then exposed directly in front of the patient for a period of five seconds. It is then removed and the patient is asked to draw the design from memory. The remaining cards are presented in similar fashion, each card being exposed for only five seconds. The patient is free to use as little or as much paper as he wishes, and he is free to erase and correct. If desired, after the patient has completed all nine drawings by tachistoscopic presentation, the regular copy phase of the test may be administered.

The tachistoscopic method may prove to be quite threatening to some organic patients. For this reason, great care should be taken to gain rapport, and ample reassurance should be offered when required. Aside from the reproductions, the patient's behavior during the test is most important. In particular, evidence of feelings of impotence should be closely observed, for such evidence is a compelling hallmark of organic pathology.

A specific test of our hypothesis that the tachistoscopic method would increase diagnostic differentiation of organic pathology has been reported (Snortum, 1965). This study went beyond the testing of this hypothesis in that the effect upon intergroup differences among normals, neurotics, alcoholics, and organics was also explored, but we shall concentrate our discussion on the organic group. A five-second exposure was used, followed by the regular administration of the copy phase. There were 25 subjects in each of the experimental groups: normal, neurotic, alcoholic, and organic. They were matched for age (mean age about 36–37 years) and for education (mean grade about 11th–12th). All were male military personnel. The organic group consisted of 13 cases of encephalopathy due to trauma, 5 cases of encephalopathy due to arteriosclerosis, 4 cases of cerebral thrombosis, and 1 case each of postencephalitic psychomotor epilepsy, cerebral–cortical atrophy, and brain abscess and craniotomy. The neurotic group was a mixed group, as was also the alcoholic group.

A comparison was made of the efficacy of the tachistoscopic versus the copy method in differentiating among the four groups. Scoring of the records was done by the Pascal-Suttell method. On both copy phase and tachistoscopic phase scores, the order, from poorest to best, was organics, alcoholics, neurotics, and normals. Both methods differentiated the organics from normals, the copy phase at the .01 level of significance, and the tachistoscopic phase at the .001 level of significance. The latter method also differentiated the organics from the neurotics ($p = .02$), whereas the copy phase did not. Thus, despite the limitations of this study (small and mixed nosological groups, scores only for the Pascal-Suttell method), the findings serve to indicate the probability that organics are more effectively differentiated by the tachistoscopic than by the copy phase score. Further exploration of this finding seems warranted, using other scores and other populations.

Two other studies offering some indication of the value of the tachistoscopic method may be noted. Lindsay (1954) showed that the method was of value in differentiating among normals, anxieties, and hysterics. Korchin and Basowitz (1954) felt that it was useful as an indicator of ego strength.

It should be emphasized that this method is intended primarily to increase the efficacy of some types of diagnostic differentiation, mainly that of organics. It should not be used alone, but it should be considered a supplementary device that can offer supporting data when needed. At least, for individual diagnostic study, it should be supplemented by the use of the copy phase. Qualitative indicators and configurational scoring, as well as observational data, should all enter the diagnostic picture. Of course, in any well-rounded psychological study, other kinds of psychological test data should also be available. In the author's opinion, in the present stage of our knowledge qualitative and configurational evaluation are more desirable for individual diagnosis than are objective scores. (See Chapters 5 and 9 for discussions of qualitative and configurational evaluation.)

The Recall Method

One of the variants in administering the Bender or the HABGT is the recall method. The usual procedure is to request the examinee to reproduce from memory the designs that he drew during the copy phase. If the copy phase is followed by the recall method, this would possibly affect results that might thereafter be obtained with such other procedures as the elaboration phase and the tachistoscopic method. Hence, a choice has to be made based upon the purpose of the testing, which guides the form of test administration. As we shall see, the recall method has some possible advantages over other methods of administration, mainly in the differentiation of organics from nonorganics. However, neither clinical nor research evidence indicates any overall advantages of this method. Possibly this is one of the principal reasons why only about 20% of psychologists who use the Bender also employ the recall method (Schulberg & Tolor, 1961).

We shall review briefly selected studies that have explored the utility of the recall method. It would be advisable to keep in mind that there is no single method for administration and that methods of scoring and evaluating the results also vary. These factors alone would account for much of the variability in findings. In addition, there are the usual problems of definition of nosological groups, experimental design, and validity criteria that influence all research work in this field.

The earliest experimental study of the efficacy of the Bender recall used sparse and simple criteria (Hanvik & Andersen, 1950). Three groups were compared (on both copy reproductions and recall reproductions): cerebral lesions in the dominant hemisphere; cerebral lesions in the nondominant hemisphere; and controls (consisting of surgical and general medical patients). The only significant differences that were obtained for intergroup comparison on the recall material was that brain-damaged patients showed more rotations than the control groups. The two scores that were used were the average number of designs recalled, and the number of rotations of 30 degrees or more.

In a later study, Tolor (1956) investigated the relative efficacy of the recall of digits and the recall of Bender designs with three groups: organic; convulsive; and psychogenic. The three groups differed significantly in the average number of Bender figures recalled, the means for the three groups being: organics 3.69, convulsive 5.5, and psychogenic 5.53. It was also found that Bender recall differentiated better than digit recall with respect to organicity, but it was not effective in predicting organicity in individual cases. Tolor (1958) did a cross-validational study, this time using groups of schizophrenics, character disorders, and organics. The groups were matched for intelligence and approximately matched for age. Using as his recall score the total number of whole and partly, correctly and incorrectly reproduced designs on recall, the organics did significantly more poorly on recall than the other two groups, and the two functional groups did not differ significantly.

Reznikoff and Olin (1957) also attempted to determine whether organics could be differentiated from schizophrenics on recall. Using three scores for recall, they found that organics did more poorly than schizophrenics on the "Good Recall Score." They also compared the recall scores of the convulsives with the nonconvulsives, and, unlike Tolor, found no significant differences. Another study used geriatric patients (over 60 years of age), and divided the population into three subgroups, matched in age, in terms of organics, doubtfuls, and functionals. It was shown that in both copy and recall phases there were significant differences in scores from the functionals (highest) through the doubtfuls, to the organics (poorest) (Shapiro, et al, 1956). Test materials consisted of six simplified and enlarged Bender-Gestalt designs.

Olin and Reznikoff (1957, 1958) conducted two other studies designed to test the efficacy of the recall method in differentiating diagnostic groups, as well as to explore other factors such as the difficulty of the designs. In these studies they used a modified scoring system adapted from that developed by Pascal and Suttell. In the 1957 study, organics, schizophrenics, and student nurses were compared. An analysis of differences on scores for each design revealed that only on design 4 did the schizophrenic patients do significantly better than the organics. Normals did better than schizophrenics only on design 6, while they did significantly better than organics on designs 2, 5, 6, 7, and 8.

A sophisticated study, utilizing five diagnostic groups (organic, schizophrenic, depressive, neurotic, and character disorder) and scores based on both the Reznikoff and Olin and the author's own revised scoring system obtained highly promising results (Armstrong, 1965). The original number in each group was small (only 20), but the groups were carefully matched, especially in age, the mean age being 33.56 years. The author's revised recall scoring system was better than Reznikoff and Olin's, and it differentiated the organics from the nonorganics remarkably well. There was little overlap in the two groups and " . . . only 21% of nonorganic patients had as high or higher a recall score than the lowest recall score . . . obtained by any organic patient." In addition, it was found that the copy phase score differentiated organics from schizophrenics, from depressives, and from character disorders at the .001 level of significance.

These studies indicate that scores based on the recall reproductions can fairly well differentiate organics from nonorganics, as groups, and there is some evidence that refined scoring may achieve results that are applicable on an individual basis. It is questionable, however, how much better the differentiation is when made on the basis of recall scores alone in comparison with scores based on copy scores alone. Other studies (Stewart, 1957; Stewart & Cunningham, 1958) have proposed other scoring systems based on the recall material by itself. Still others have explored the relation of performance on the recall of designs to intellectual ability and to nonorganic conditions alone (Aaronson, 1957; Gavales & Millon, 1960; Goodstein, Spielberger, Williams, & Dahlstron, 1959; Peek & Olson, 1955).

Studies are needed in which the contribution of memory and of psychomotor versus visual memory are teased out in relation to performance under recall conditions. An especially interesting study along such lines was done by Schwartz and Dennerll (1969). They analyzed recall performance on the Bender of outpatient epileptics. They found that the poorest recall results were obtained with those patients suffering from both grand mal and psychomotor seizures. Results did not appear to be influenced by lateralizable EEG abnormalities, multiple seizure types, or continuing occurrences of grand mal seizures. They concluded that in those patients with grand mal and psychomotor seizures combined, the psychomotor element was crucial and that consequent impairment led to short-term visual memory defects. Another study, by Rogers and Swenson (1975), sought to evaluate the relative contributions of memory and distractibility on Bender-Gestalt recall performance. They used 65 patients who had been referred for evaluation of possible intellectual defects (age range 16 to 78 years), analyzing their performance on the Bender-Gestalt recall and the Wechsler Memory Scale. They were able to conclude that the Bender-Gestalt recall was a good screening measure of memory, whereas the factor of freedom from distractibility did not correlate highly with performance. The correlation of the Bender-Gestalt recall score with the Wechsler Memory Scale score was 0.74.

A recent study by Holland and Wadsworth (1979) investigated the relative efficacy of standard, recall, and BIP administration. It was found that recall and BIP-recall were somewhat superior to copy protocols in differentiating organics from schizophrenics.

Many issues remain to be resolved. In order to evaluate the true significance of the recall method of administering the test, it is imperative to control for exposure time in presenting the test cards before recall is attempted. If subjects are first required to copy the designs before the recall aspects of the test is employed, unknown variations in "experience" with the test designs as well as uncontrolled exposure before recall can contaminate the findings. Well-designed studies in which these factors are evaluated are clearly needed.

Group Methods

The usefulness of the Bender-Gestalt Test or the HABGT as a screening device has been noted previously. This function would seem to be especially important in screening young children in school for further study in connection with severe personality problems, perceptual immaturity, and weak ego development, as well as for possible organic disturbance. Another important function for group administration would be in research, since large numbers of protocols or related information could thus be obtained relatively easily. One study interested in exploring the meanings of the designs to college students obtained the association data to the designs by group administration, without however, requiring that the designs be reproduced (Suczek & Klopfer, 1952). As far back as 1945, this author suggested the possible use of group administration and offered proposals for minimal conditions for such administration (Hutt 1945a).

A number of approaches have been used in the administration of the test as a group procedure. In testing young, immature children, especially, 2–4 children are each given a set of cards arranged in the correct sequence. They are asked to copy the card on the top of the stack and when all have completed this they are then asked to turn to the next card. The remaining cards are copied in a similar fashion. Dinmore (1972), for example, has used this procedure in obtaining developmental scores for young children. This method has the advantage that the examiner can observe unusual behavior during the test and take this into consideration in making individual evaluations. The method is also useful with small groups of psychiatric patients.

More typical group procedures involve testing larger groups—perhaps 15–20 individuals at the same time. A method that has been employed fairly frequently involves the use of enlarged test cards—usually 3–4 times larger than the standard set. Such cards have to be specially prepared, of course, by the examiner or a draftsman. Keogh and Smith used this kind of procedure (1961), placing the test cards in a holder at the front of the room, in clear view of the primary grade children. Tiedeman (1971) utilized this method in a large cross-cultural study in which she examined 7-year-old children in 13 countries. Other investigators have employed special test booklets with the test designs reproduced, one to a page, at the top of the pages. Group testing has also been done by projecting the test designs, with an opaque or slide projector, onto a large screen. Correlations of between .75 and .87 have been obtained between sets of scores derived from individual and group administration with kindergarten children (Becker & Sabatino, 1971; Ruckhaber, 1964). Although this degree of correlation is fairly high, it indicates that considerable variation in results can be obtained in some cases. Keogh and Smith's (1961) study was quite comprehensive. They examined 221 kindergarten children assigned to one of three groups based on a stratified random sampling. One group was given the test individually, another was given the test with special booklets, and the third was shown the enlarged designs on special cards. Using the Pascal-Suttell method of scoring, no significant differences were found among the three methods in relation to average scores. However, no check was made for possible differences that might have been obtained for the same individuals if they had been tested by differing methods. A study done with adults also found no significant *group differences* between individual and group methods of administration (Blum & Nims, 1953).

Such findings suggest that group methods of administration are valuable. One should not conclude, however, that there would not be significant and important differences in individual cases. Of course, group administration loses a great deal of direct observational material that can be highly useful in clinical work. Moreover, we have no evidence, as yet, of the possible effects of group administration on psychiatric or emotionally disturbed individuals. Probably, the most important use of group administration is for screening purposes, especially with primary grade children. These findings can lead to further individual study when appropriate.

Other Experimental Approaches

Isolated attempts have been made to explore still other variations in administration. We have already referred to the study in which multiple-choice selections of test designs were employed (Niehbur & Cohen, 1956). In studying the relative contribution of perceptual and motoric factors in test protocols, a comparison was made of the performance on the standard task and one in which the subjects reproduced the designs by placing pieces of felt on a felt board (McPherson & Pepin, 1955). It was found, incidentally, that performance was influenced primarily by covert perceptual responses.

Other procedures have been employed, principally to increase the test's differential capacity for organicity. One worker employed figures reproduced in relief on plastic plates (Barker, 1949). In this pilot study it was learned that this method appears to be much more sensitive for such differential diagnosis than the conventional method, but no data were presented. Another worker used figures designed with partially raised thumbtacks (Parker, 1954), and also found that brain-injured patients were even more effectively differentiated from nonorganics by this tactual-kinesthetic method than by the standard method.

A simpler and potentially much more useful method, on both practical and theoretical grounds, has been offered by Canter (1966). In this study the results obtained under conventional administration were compared with those in which subjects were asked to reproduce the figures on paper with curved, intersecting lines, called "background interference." As can be expected when figure–ground problems are made more complicated, the organics showed greater decrements under the latter conditions than did a group of nonorganics. In a cross-validational study, almost no overlap was found between organics and nonorganics. In a later study, in which a modified scoring method was employed, Canter (1968) found that the Background Interference Procedure (BIP) did significantly identify brain-damaged patients. Interscorer reliability was high. Song and Song (1969) found that in a study with brain-damaged retardates and other mental retardates, the BIP procedure was effective in differentiating the organics from the nonorganics. Adams and Canter (1969) were able to show that "ability to cope with the BIP effect is fairly well established by age 13." It seemed to have little relationship to intelligence as measured. In a recent study, Pardue (1975) was able to show that the BIP with Pascal-Suttell scoring differentiated male brain-damaged patients from male schizophrenic patients.

Psychologists have been ingenious in their modifications of test administration and test interpretation. It is to be hoped that even more fruitful techniques and theories will gradually emerge from these efforts.

PART II

Test Factors, Test Scales, and Rapid Screening

4
The Psychopathology Scale: Test Factors and Evidence

The 17 factors in the Psychopathology Scale were derived first from extensive clinical experience and then from research studies. Some of these factors are also incorporated in Configurational Scores (see Chapter 5), which provide a simple and rapid basis for *screening purposes*. For more adequate diagnosis, however, the full Scale is advisable, as well as other, supplementary procedures.

Wherever possible the interpretations are founded on experimental evidence derived specifically from the Bender Test or one of its variations. However, it must be noted that there is still a lack of fully adequate, empirical evidence for some of the statements that follow. In such instances we must rely upon extended clinical experience, checked against clinical criteria and behavioral evidence in a wide variety of situations: diagnostic, therapeutic, and consultative. Even when experimental evidence seems to confirm our impressions, we should not regard this as the final word. In some cultural-situational contexts,* and in some individual

---

* I do not believe that any test can be entirely independent of differences in social-cultural influences, although the HABGT is largely independent in such respects. Gilmore, Chandy, and Anderson (1975) found no significant differences between the scores of Mexican American primary grade children and the norms on the Koppitz test, although these children tended to make more errors than "normal" after 7 years of age. No significant differences were found between black and white brain-damaged patients, except in the nonepileptic group, where blacks scored better than whites (Butler, Coursey, & Gatz, 1976).

It should be clearly understood that visual–motor development per se can be affected by developmental experiences in visual–motor behavior. Deprivation of such experiences is particularly likely to retard this development. Marked differences in widely differing cultures can also have their effects on such development. Even such differences in early

(ftnt. cont.)

instances, the end-product proves to have a highly idiosyncratic meaning. It is assumed that the careful clinician will not seize upon any one, or even more than one, bit of evidence to make sweeping generalizations about the individual under study. Rather, each factor, which may have several meanings even for the same patient, should lead to an interpretation that is more in the form of a hypothesis rather than a conclusion. When hypotheses of this kind are used to *explore the possible meaning of the behavior,* and are evaluated against other pieces of evidence, especially against possibly conflicting interpretations, they will have served a useful and creative clinical function. The final clinical summary will then contain *probable* implications of the findings, together with *possible* implications. All clinical statements must be regarded as probabilities rather than as confirmed conclusions.

A number of introductory observations are in order. The interpretations that are offered for each of the test factors were derived, in the main, from clinical and experimental evidence with adults. In most instances, the same or similar interpretations would have comparable validity for children 7 years of age or older. However, two qualifications are needed. First, the level of intelligence, while reflected in perceptual–motoric functioning, is more likely to influence perceptual–motoric functioning in younger children than in adults. Hence, especially with moderately to severely retarded children, the meaning of test behavior may require considerable additional exploration. Second, when children are found to have some significant perceptual lag, their test behavior may be seriously influenced and thus require quite a different interpretation. Of course, in the case of any significant and relevant handicap—such as serious visual defect, gross muscular incoordination, severely limited visual–motoric experience—the results should be evaluated with great caution.

It should also be clear that certain kinds of distortions or deviations in the reproductions may be due to extrinsic factors such as a poor or rough writing surface, errors in the stimulus figures (which we have, unfortunately, observed in some instances), improper pencil for drawing, and hurried conditions of testing. It is assumed that the examiner will duly note such extrinsic factors, *recording them in detail on the Revised Record Form.*

---

experience as living in mountainous regions versus living in a region of plains can affect both perception and motoric phenomena, as has been demonstrated by Segall, Campbell, and Herskovitz (1966). Research evidence indicates, however, that in modern urban societies such differences in visual–motor development have been fairly well equalized by about age 9 or earlier (Greene & Clark, 1973; Sonoda, 1973; Taylor & Thweatt, 1972). Certainly, the kinds of phenomena this chapter deals with are usually attributable to personality rather than developmental differences in visual–motor experience. In any case, the HABGT used as a projective test, depends far more on such personality factors. (See Chapter 4 for other studies.)

Each of the factors discussed below is presumed to be related to specified personality processess or outcomes. The clinician begins by assuming that the factor has the meaning(s) attributed to it. He may suspect other possible meanings. He may also develop alternate or modified hypotheses concerning the significance of a factor as it recurs under different circumstances or is present in a new configuration. (This kind of reinterpretation is especially likely to occur during anlaysis of the elaboration phase material.) Thus, the *process* of interpretation is guided by (but not limited to) the typical meanings of the several factors and is continuously confirmed, modified, or rejected on the basis of new evidence. (In objective scoring, as in our Psychopathology Scale, we assume that the weights represent the typical loadings which the factor represents, and that variances from such loadings tend to cancel themselves out.)

For purposes of scoring for the two objective scales, the examiner need not consider the psychological significance of the 17 test factors. Such psychological interpretations will, however, be needed for projective interpretation of both the *Copy Phase* and the *Elaboration and Association Phases*.

The discussion of test factors is presented under four major groupings: organization, deviations in size, deviations in form, and gross distortion.

FACTORS RELATED TO ORGANIZATION

1. Sequence

DEFINITION

Sequence refers to the relative degree of regularity in the sucessive placement of the drawings on the page(s) used in making the reproductions. The expected order of successive placements is either from *left to right or from top to bottom*. Sequence is scored in terms of the number of shifts that occur as a deviation from the order in succession, *which the examinee has already manifested*. When the examinee places his successive drawings in order from right to left or from bottom to top, this is scored as one shift in sequence. Otherwise, *each time* the sequence is altered it is counted as one shift. Thus, when an examinee has been arranging his drawings from left to right and then places the next figure above or below or to the left, this is counted as a shift in sequence. *The score on Sequence is the total number of shifts.* Charts 1a and 1b illustrate examples and scores for such shifts. If an examinee places each drawing on a separate page, this is considered an *irregular sequence* (see below) and is counted as 2 shifts. (Note: allowance is made and no score for shift

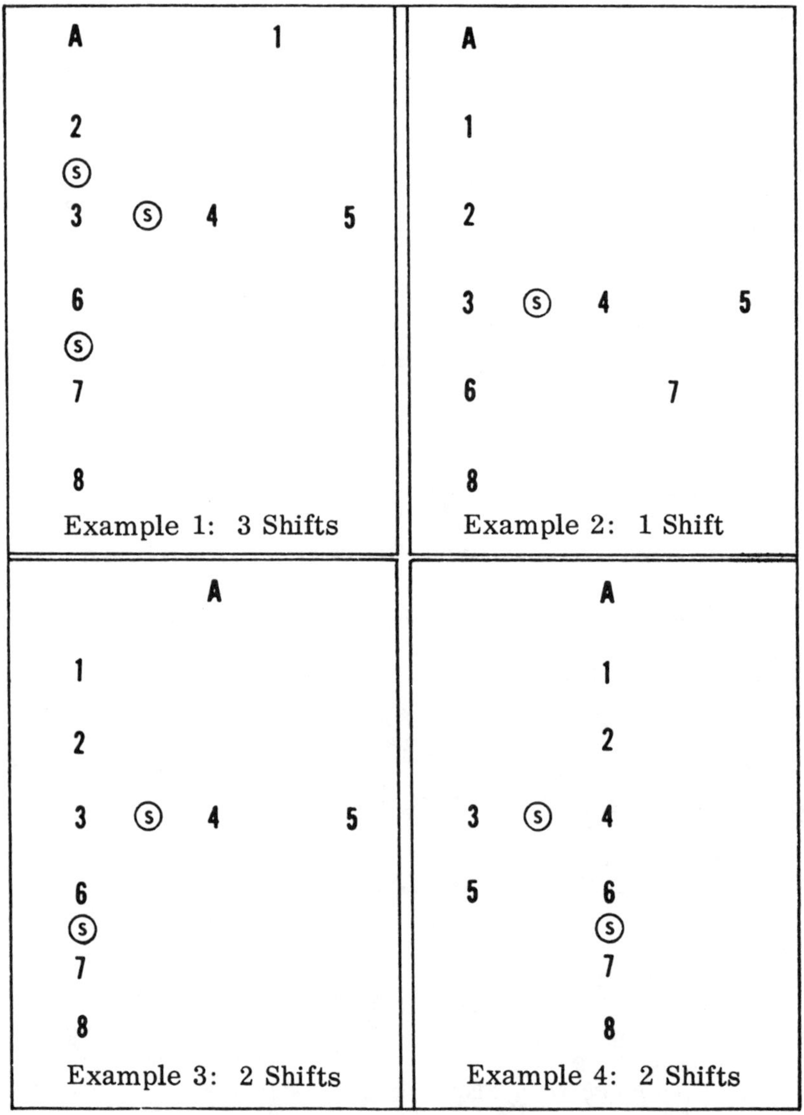

A			**1**		**A**		
2					**1**		
Ⓢ							
3	Ⓢ	**4**		**5**	**2**		
6					**3** Ⓢ **4**		**5**
Ⓢ							
7					**6**	**7**	
8					**8**		
Example 1: 3 Shifts					Example 2: 1 Shift		

A	**A**	
1	**1**	
2	**2**	
3 Ⓢ **4** **5**	**3** Ⓢ **4**	
6	**5** **6**	
Ⓢ	Ⓢ	
7	**7**	
8	**8**	
Example 3: 2 Shifts	Example 4: 2 Shifts	

Chart 1a.   Examples of shifts in sequence. The circled S's indicate the point at which a shift in sequence may be noted. In example 1, the first shift occurs from figures 2 to 3, since previous sequence was from left to right: the same applies to the shift from figures 6 to 7. In example 3, no shift is counted from A to 1, since the general direction of sequence has not yet become manifest, but a shift does occur from figures 3 to 4 since the prior sequence had been from top to bottom.

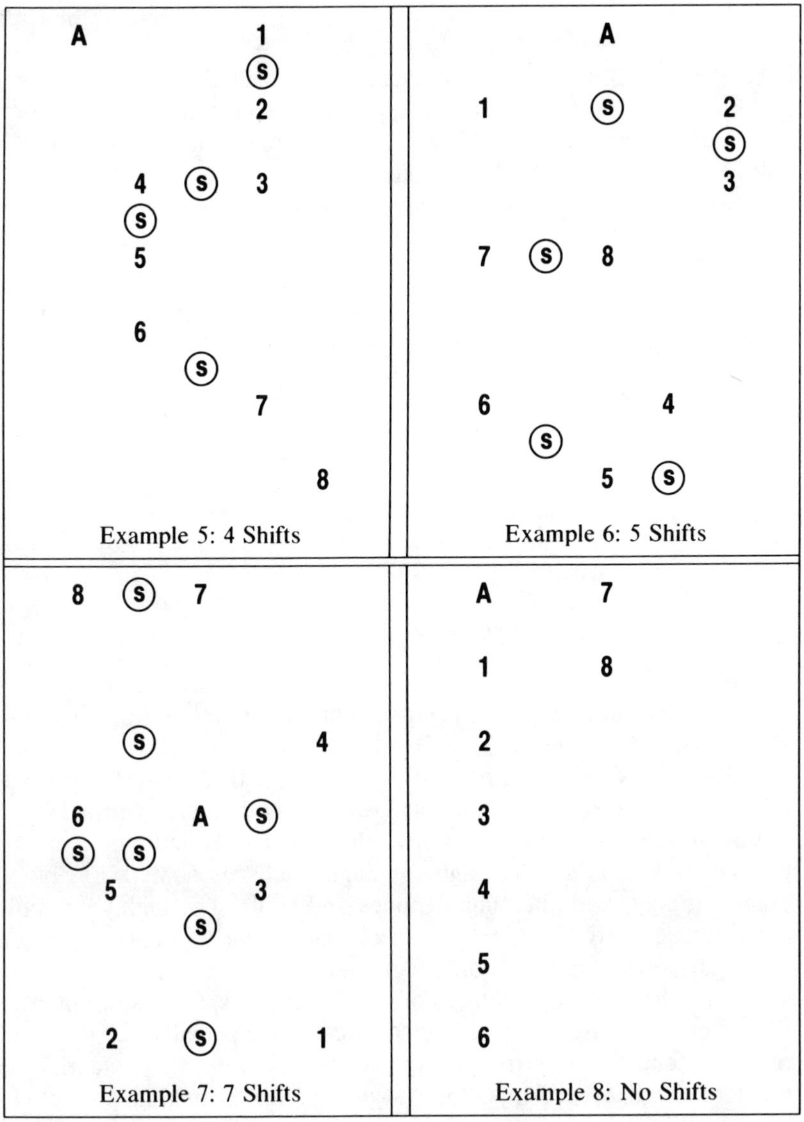

	A	1
		(s)
		2
	4 (s)	3
	(s)	
	5	
	6	
	(s)	
		7
		8

Example 5: 4 Shifts

	A	
1	(s)	2
		(s)
		3
7	(s)	8
6		4
(s)		
	5 (s)	

Example 6: 5 Shifts

8 (s)	7
(s)		4
6	A (s)
(s) (s)	
5		3
(s)	
2 (s)		1

Example 7: 7 Shifts

A	7
1	8
2	
3	
4	
5	
6	

Example 8: No Shifts

Chart 1b.   Examples of unusual Sequence. In Example 5, there are 4 shifts and Sequence is *borderline* confused. In 6, there are 5 shifts and Sequence is irregular. In 7, with 7 shifts, Sequence is *symbolic*. In 8, sequence is *overly-methodical*. (The symbol indicates the point at which a shift occurs.)

71

in sequence is counted, when the examinee reaches the edge of the paper
and places the next figure in the appropriate space below.)

Sequence is characterized as: normal or methodical; overly methodical; irregular; confused or symbolic.

Scores on the Psychopathology Scale (PSV) follow:

Scale Value	Definition
10.0	*Confused or symbolic sequence:* Drawings are placed in a jumble on the page—that is, without any apparent plan—or some symbolic arrangement is evident. Symbolic placements may be a spiral, a figure-8 arangement, or the like.
7.0	*Irregular sequence.* There is *more than one* shift in sequence, but no confusion or jumble can be detected.
4.0	*Overly methodical sequence.* No shift occurs. The drawings are placed in a rigid sequence, without deviation.
1.0	*Normal or methodical sequence.* No shift or only one shift in sequence occurs.

INTERPRETATION

In addition to the research literature on organizational factors in
spontaneous paintings, there is significant but limited research data on the
significance of "sequence" on Bender reproductions (Byrd, 1956; Clawson, 1959; Mosher & Smith, 1965). Only one of these was done on adults
(Mosher & Smith, 1965), and that study was concerned primarily with
brain-damaged patients. We believe that the way an individual organizes
his reproductions on the page (or pages) tells us something about his
organizational and planning attitudes and skills. The highly compulsive
individual is likely to arrange his drawings precisely in correct sequence,
not even permitting the spontaneous adaptations to occur that are suggested by the objective features of the designs or space requirements. On
the other hand, highly anxious neurotics and especially agitated schizophrenics tend to show irregularity to confusion in the sequential placement of the figures. Thus, the "style" of work, in this respect, is an
important indicator of this aspect of personality "style" (Shapiro et al,
1965). It is assumed that the more rigid the personality the more rigid the
cognitive style is likely to be. Thus, normal individuals, unless under
severe stress, tend to use a methodological sequence, whereas neurotics
tend to use either irregular or overly methodological sequences.

Donnelly and Murphy (1974) did a specific study of the relation between sequence and impulse control in psychiatric patients. An analysis
of styles of sequence for 37 bipolar and 30 unipolar depressives revealed
that irregular sequence was indicative of lack of control and was characteristic of bipolar depressives (manic–depressives), while overly methodi-

cal sequence was indicative of (overly) methodical impulse control and was characteristic of unipolar depressives.

The way in which the ego controls behavior, making it overly rigid or spontaneous in functioning, is important in the total evaluation of the personality. For this reason, in *inferential analyses* of records (see Chapter 9), *sequence* is considered early in the development of hypotheses about the individual. A confused sequence is very likely to be indicative of a highly disturbed individual, and is frequently found in the records of anxious schizophrenics and patients with delirium, dissociative and toxic psychoses, and manic or hypomanic conditions.

Our own count of the frequency of three types of sequences in the records of 80 "normal" college students, matched individually for age and sex (40 males and 40 females) with 80 outpatient neurotics (mainly anxiety and mixed reactions), shows the following:

Sequence	Normal	Overly Methodical	Irregular
Normals	62	13	5
Neurotics	9	41	30

Monheit (1983) found that 85.4% of her severely disturbed adolescents and 80.0% of her delinquent adolescents while only 40.0% of her normals received scores above 1.0 on this factor. Thus, as a single indicator of some form of emotional disturbance, this test factor is important.

Another consideration in interpreting sequence is the point in the record at which a shift occurs. Possible hypotheses concerning causative factors in producing the shift may yield a harvest of important hypotheses about the individual. Was it the particular design that caused some upset? The data in the elaboration and association phases may be quite revealing. Was it the point on the page that had been reached? An example of shifts in sequence that occur on this basis is that of the individual who follows a regular sequence, lines up his drawings on one side of the page, then follows the same pattern on the other edge of the page, but suddenly finds himself out of room on the page and then crowds the remaining figures either at the bottom of the page, or indiscriminately in blank spaces left on the page. The lack of anticipatory planning and the borderline ego control that are thus made manifest may uncover an aspect of this individual's functioning that was not manifest in other areas of his social behavior, in other test situations, or in interview. The examiner will observe the individual's behavior closely when shifts of this nature occur, in the search for evidence of anxiety, disorganization, or even regression. Psychological characteristics that may be related to such functioning include: low frustration tolerance, high latent anxiety, indecisiveness, excessive rigidity, covert feelings of inadequacy, and compulsive doubting.

Sequential progression in the placement of the figures from right to left may indicate negativistic or rebellious tendencies in the personality. The examiner should also check the possibility that cultural factors may have contributed to such functioning.

Placement of each figure on a separate page (usually in or near the center) is likely to indicate egocentricity, as well as oppositional characteristics. In our sample of 80 neurotics referred to above, 6 of the 8 patients who were judged to be narcissistic showed this characteristic.

In general, patients use either a single sheet of paper or two sheets, using only about half of the second sheet. The use of more than two sheets should be regarded as unusual and occurs most typically among psychopaths, egocentric individuals, manics, and schizophrenics with ideas of grandiosity.

2. Position of the First Drawing

DEFINITION

This factor refers to the placement of figure A on the page, whether the examinee uses a single page for all the drawings or uses more than one page.

Values on the Psychopathology Scale are:

Scale Value	Definition
10.0	*Abnormal placement, severe:* Any portion of Figure A is *within one inch of any edge of the paper.*
5.0	*Egocentric placement:* Any portion of Figure A is within a 3-inch square centered on the page.
1.0	*Normal placement:* All of Figure A lies *within* the upper third of the page, and *no portion* is less than one inch from any edge of the page.

INTERPRETATION

It has been our belief, based primarily on clinical experience, that the placement of the first figure on the page is reflective of the individual's orientation with respect to his world-space. Our own research experience with the Adience-Abience Scale (see, later), indicates that those who place Figure A in some atypical position on the page tend to be "abient" (that is, avoidant of perceptual contact with the real world). Placement near the center of the page, especially if the figure is enlarged, tends to be associated with such personality attributes as narcissism, egocentrism, and passive oppositionalism. Bender (1938) and Pascal and Suttell (1951) suggested that such placement for adults is indicative of severe psychopathology, although other factors may also account for such placement. The work of Brown (1965) and Tripp (1957) supported the conclusion that central placement of the individual's orientation toward the world suggests egocentrism. In one of the few experimental studies of this phenomenon, Gordon (1982) found that a group of 58 clinic children, ages 6–12 years, with diagnoses of behavior, personality, or neurotic disorders, compared with a control group of healthy, nonpsychiatric children showed a significantly higher percentage of central placements in the former group (p = .028).

These considerations and published findings led us to review our own data. We were able to compare the records of 140 carefully selected normal adults with those of roughly matched groups (both sexes) of 150 out-patient neurotics and 155 chronic schizophrenics. We found that only 13 normals showed any abnormal placements while 56 neurotics and 74 schizophrenics showed such placements. These intergroup differences are statistically significant (.01 level or better). Moreover, an analysis of egocentric placement (center of the page) revealed the following figures: 4 normals, 12 neurotics, and 17 schizophrenics.

These findings led us to revise the scale values for this factor.

We should emphasize that abnormal performance on *any test factor* may be due, in unusual circumstances, to factors other than pathology. Hence, as we have emphasized repeatedly, the clinician should not rely on scores, alone, for final interpretation of a test record, but should *always consider special circumstances* in each, individual case.

3. Use of Space

DEFINITION

This refers exclusively to the spacing between *successive or adjacent drawings*. The criterion is *always* the preceding or adjacent figure, and space is judged in terms of the *relevant axis* of that figure. Thus, when space is judged in relation to two figures in the same horizontal plane, the *horizontal* axis of the drawing at the *left* is considered. When space is judged in relation to two figures in the same *vertical* plane, the vertical axis of the drawing *above* is considered. When the drawing is placed between two figures (either to the left or above), the relevant axis of the *nearer* figure is considered.

This factor can be either normal or abnormal. It is *abnormal* if the space between two successive drawings is either *more than half the size* of the relevant axis of the preceding or adjacent figure, or is *less than one-fourth the size* of that axis.

Scores on the Psychopathology Scale follow:

Scale Value   Definition

10.0   *Abnormal use of space:* Space is scored as *abnormal* if it is
            either excessively constricted or excessively expansive, as
            defined above. Abnormal use of space must occur in *two or
            more instances* to be scored as *abnormal.*

1.0   *Normal use of space:* Excessive use of space is noted in *less
            than two instances.*

INTERPRETATION

This factor seems to be related to basic modes of personality adaptation as manifested in perceptual–motoric performance. There is considerable evidence concerning this relationship derived from studies of drawing and painting, especially in children, but also in disturbed adults. More directly pertinent to our use of these factors is the work on perception conducted by many investigators. Piaget (1950) had proposed that the tendency toward "centralization" is very pronounced in young children. This type of diffusion in perception causes size overstimulation. As children develop they decentralize attention and can "scan" more, so that this tendency decreases with age and by the adult level individuals do not make consistent estimation errors and veridical size perception appears. Another study compared size estimation in emotionally disturbed children with that in schizophrenic adults (Davis, Cromwell, & Held, 1967). Using the Harris materials (Harris, 1957), which consist of pictures of a square, a dominance scene, an acceptance scene, a rejection scene, an overprotective scene, and a neutral scene, they were able to show: (1) children (mean age 11 years) tended to overestimate size; (2) there were differences in size estimation of withdrawn as compared with acting out and disturbed children; (3) paranoid and good premorbid schizophrenics underestimated size whereas nonparanoid and poor premorbids overestimated size. Such findings indicate that both perceptual maturity and emotional adjustment influence size estimation.

In our test factor we are dealing with the *relative* estimation–reproduction of successive figures. Thus we believe we are maximizing our measure of perceptual–motoric behavior in terms of adaptive factors more than in terms of perceptual maturation factors. Strong supportive evidence for this definition of our factor as a personality measure can be found in the studies by Byrd (1956) and by Clawson (1959). The specific interpretations we have previously suggested are "confirmed" in these researches. Moreover, our own data in connection with the Psychopathology Scale (differences between normal and neurotic and between neurotic and schizophrenic groups are significant at the .01 level) and with the Adience–Abience Scale (in which successive cross-validations supported

the use of this factor) offer further support for the following interpretations. Additional support has been found in studies by Culbertson and
Gunn (1966) and by Molodnosky (1972).

An excessive amount of space between successive drawings tends to
correlate with behavior that is characterized as hostile, "acting out," and
assertive. Constricted use of space is related to passivity, withdrawn
behavior, and schizoid tendencies. The possibility of repressed hostility
and of masochistic trends may also be associated with constriction. In
general, abnormal use of space is indicative of some form of emotional
maladjustment, the precise nature of which may be more fully inferred
from further analysis of this and other factors on the HABGT.

A recent study on adolescents (Brannigan & Benowitz, 1975) found
that excessive use of space was associated with emotional maladjustment
and could be used as an index in this regard.

We believe that we can generalize to the assertion that use of space is
one important indication of the individual's attitudinal orientation of himself in relation to the world. More specifically, whether hostile feelings are
openly and appropriately expressed or whether they are suppressed and
distorted can often be inferred from this stylistic feature of the reproductions. Actively paranoidal adults tend to use excessive space and tend to
reproduce the figures as much smaller than the stimuli. Frequently they
compress all of the drawings into less than half of a page, make them very
small, and leave much space between figures.

4. Collision

DEFINITION

Collision refers to the actual running together or overlapping of one
figure by another. The perimeter of one figure must either *touch* or *overlap* the perimeter of another figure. If the line of dots or circles of one
figure intrudes into the open space of an adjacent figure, but there is no
actual touching or overlapping of the perimeter, this is *not* counted as
collision; rather it is considered a collision tendency, and is so scored and
interpreted. (See chart 2 for sample scorings.)

There are seven subcategories of collision and collision tendency:

Scale Value	Definition
10.0	*Collision, extreme:* Collision occurs more than twice.
8.5	*Collision, moderate:* Collision occurs 2 times.
7.0	*Collision, present:* Collision occurs once only.
5.5	*Collision tendency, extreme:* Occurs more than twice.
4.0	*Collision tendency, moderate:* Occurs twice.
2.5	*Collision tendency, present:* Occurs once only.
1.0	*No collision or collision tendency.*

When the phenomena of both *collision* and *collision tendency* are present in the same record, the scores for both are summated, but in no case can the total score for this factor be more than 10.0

INTERPRETATION

The author's major hypothesis with respect to this phenomenon, as stated in a previous publication (Hutt & Briskin, 1960), was that it was indicative of "a marked disturbance in ego function." Two qualifications must be added. (1) Collision and, especially, collision tendency are related to general developmental factors which govern motor control and perceptual acuity, so that one would expect such phenomena to appear relatively more frequently, even in normal cases, in very young children, say below 7 years of age. (2) These phenomena may also occur as a result of peripheral neurological impairment and muscular disturbances that affect motor control. We believe that when brain damage is accompanied by loss in ego control, collision or collision tendency may occur on the HABGT. However, they may also occur without brain damage when there is a significant psychological disturbance in this area. Reflected in the phenomena are poor anticipatory planning, difficulty with figure–ground relationships (which shows up even more clearly on overlapping figures like design 7), and extreme degrees of impulsivity.

The phenomena do not occur with great frequency in any unselected population so that statistical tests of significance in comparisons of clinical subgroups are not readily obtainable. When the factor is present it is likely to have important, clinical significance.

In addition to our own data, we should like to refer to some studies that evaluated this factor, but not necessarily our criteria for scoring it. The study by Byrd (1956) utilized our former definition of this factor. He compared the frequency of the occurrence of the collision phenomenon in 4 age groups of 50 children in need of psychotherapy with 50 children who were judged to be well adjusted. In the 8–9-year-old group the frequencies were 11 and 7, respectively; in the 10–11-year-old group they were 11 and 5, respectively; in the 12–13-year-old group they were 5 and 6, respectively; and in the 14–15-year-old group they were 7 and 0, respectively. At the upper age level the difference was significant at the .02 level. When the age groups are combined, we find 37 instances of collision in the group needing psychotherapy and 18 instances in the well-adjusted group—a statistically significant difference (beyond the .01 level). Obviously, developmental factors may account for the greater frequency in the younger groups. More significant is the fact that the comparison of the oldest groups, in which we may assume considerable heterogeneity in severity of maladjustment and in adequacy of good adjustment, reveals *no cases of collision* in the "normal" group and 7 (out of 50) cases in the other group.

Clawson (1959) included this factor in an aggregate score called "use of white space." Her comparisons involved a "clinic" group (heterogeneous), and a "normal" group. Analysis of her data lend some indirect support to the validity of our hypothesis of the relationship between collision and ego control, especially in terms of congruent Rorschach data.

In terms of the capacity of this factor to assist in differentiating brain-damaged groups from other psychiatric and normal groups, two studies may be noted. In one, using a measure of "overlap designs," Hain (1964) found this factor to have a high, discriminating weight in terms of a total, successful differentiating score. The "test sign" was given a weight of 3, and only 3 other test signs (with weights of 4) out of 15 significant "test signs" had a higher weight. In a study by Mosher and Smith (1965) in which comparisons were made between 142 brain-damaged cases and 28 neurological cases (without brain damage) and 92 schizophrenics, collision was found to discriminate at the .05 level. We would expect that, at the adult level, collision would be found infrequently in a schizophrenic group such as was used in this study (acute schizophrenics who had been returned to active military duty), so that the finding of some significant difference is all the more impressive.

The author's data in which 80 normal college students were compared with 95 cases of confirmed brain damage (miscellaneous, adult group), yielded the following figures. Among the college group there was only one case of a collision tendency and one of actual collision (respective scores of 2.5 and 7.0). Among the brain-damaged group there were: 4 cases of collision, score 10.0; 5 cases of collision, score 8.5; 5 cases of collision, score 7.0; and 3 cases of collision, score 2.5. In terms of total groups, the difference in psychopathology scores on this factor is significant at the .001 level.

Two other studies that have previously been cited (Lacks, 1984; Marley, 1982) found this test factor highly significant in differentiating between organics and other psychiatric patient groups. The phenomenon of collision was also studied by Monheit (1984) in her research on adolescents. It contributed significantly (ranking 8th among the 17 psychopathology test factors borrowed from Hutt) in discriminating normals from severely disturbed and delinquent adolescents.

In the broadest terms, then collision and collision tendency are indicative of loss of control, primarily due to cortical dysfunction but also a result of severe difficulty in impulse control. In relatively infrequent instances, peripheral nerve or muscle damage may produce collisions, but the investigator can easily test out such possibilities.

We do not have developmental data, particularly for ages below 9 years, which might affect the interpretation of this test factor at those age levels.

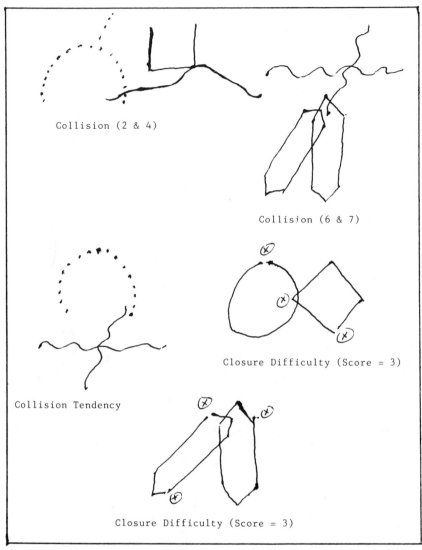

Collision (2 & 4)

Collision (6 & 7)

Collision Tendency

Closure Difficulty (Score = 3)

Closure Difficulty (Score = 3)

Chart 2.   Scoring examples of Collision, Collision Tendency, and Closure Difficulties.

5. Shift in the Position of the Paper

DEFINITION

This factor refers to the actual rotation of the test paper from the vertical position, in which it is presented, to the horizontal position (or a shift approximating 90 degrees). (This factor should not be confused with *rotation* or *perceptual rotation,* as defined in Factor 10 below.) Three degrees of paper rotation are considered.

Scale Value	Definition
10.0	*Rotation of paper on all designs.*
7.0	*Rotation of paper on 3 to 8 designs.*
5.5	*Rotation of paper on 1 or 2 designs.*
1.0	*No rotation of paper.*

INTERPRETATION

It will be recalled that, with our procedure, the test paper is presented so that its vertical axis, the longer axis, is at a right angle to the subject's body, while the test card is presented so that the longer axis is paralleled to the subject's body. This procedure is followed so as *to maximize the incongruence between the two axes,* thus increasing the perceptual dissonance of the test situation. The resulting tension experienced causes some subjects to attempt to shift either the paper or the test cards. (It should be remembered that the subject is told to copy the designs in the designated procedure.) It was assumed that healthy individuals (making allowance for developmental factors that might influence results) *would inhibit rearranging either paper or test card,* and adapt comfortably to the test situation.

Our clinical experience indicated that when, *under the standard test administration,* the subject shifts the position of the paper, such shifts are indicative of latent or passive oppositional tendencies. This finding is of major clinical significance in that it is indicative of repressed aggression or is part of a characterological pattern of oppositionalism. We have observed rotation of the paper in clinical cases of paranoid schizophrenia, severe personality disturbance, and sociopathy.

When the subject rotates the test paper, and especially when the subject continues to do so even when reminded that this is not the way it is supposed to be, the careful clinician will inquire about this *after* the test has been completed. Infrequently, cultural conditions or some misunderstanding of test directions will be a *contributing factor.* Typically, rotation of the paper reflects a personality dimension that might otherwise escape the clinician's attention.

Occasionally, rotation of the paper is the result of the OBS patient's attempt to deal with, what is for him, a difficult perceptual figure-ground problem.

There is research evidence (Griffith & Taylor, 1961; Hannah, 1958) that shows that fewer perceptual rotations are produced when the test card and the test paper are aligned so that the comparable axes are congruent. Studies by Hasazi, Allen, and Wohlford (1971) and Allen (1968) showed that mentally retarded subjects produced more errors (such as rotations and fragmentations) when the standard presentation was made in comparison with modified presentations (i.e., congruent axes). *This is to be expected* precisely because the standard presentation is *intended* to maximize perceptual discrepancies. Allen and Frank (1963) argue that standard presentation introduces significant size inaccuracies (as compared with modified procedures), implying that the modified procedures are, therefore, better. (Subjects were children with an average age of 8 years 5 months!) Of course, developmental limitations will produce more errors under standard conditions, and developmental status should be taken into account. But if the objective of our test procedure is to maximize perceptual discrepancies (and tension) in order to uncover psychopathological phenomena, we contend that the standard presentation will be clinically more rewarding.

FACTORS RELATED TO CHANGES IN THE GESTALT

The factors discussed in this section have to do with some degree of change in the quality of the Gestalt. The Gestalt is not destroyed or severely distorted, as may result from the operation of factors described in the next section, but it is altered in some qualitative way. Such changes are thought to represent psychological derivatives of a more specific nature than those discussed in the preceding section.

6. Closure Difficulty

DEFINITION

This factor refers to difficulty in "joining" parts within a figure or two adjacent figures that touch each other. The figures on which closure difficulty may occur are *A, 2, 4, 7, and 8.* Problems in "joining" may occur in connection with completing the circle or the diamond in figure A, in completing the circles in figure 2, in joining the sides of figure 4 or the junction of the curve and the open square in the same figure, and in joining the sides or connecting the adjacent parts in figures 7 and 8. The difficulty may be manifested in a number of ways: gaps at the point of joining; "overshooting the joining" (overlap at this point); erasures or corrections at the point of joining; and, noticeably, increased line pressure or redrawing at such points (see Chart 2).

The *raw score* on this factor is the total number of closure difficulties that occur, but there are two special provisions: (1) no more than 2 closure difficulties may be counted on any one figure; and (2) on figure 2, count 2 closure difficulties as a raw score of 1, and 3 or more closure difficulties as a raw score of 2.

There are five subcategories of this factor: very severe, severe, moderate, mild, and absent.

Scale Value	Definition
10.0	*Very severe:* Raw score is 9 or above.
7.75	*Severe:* Raw score is 6 to 8.
5.5	*Moderate:* Raw score is 3 to 5.
3.25	*Mild:* Raw score is 1 to 2.
1.0	*Absent:* No closure difficulties.

INTERPRETATION

Our major hypothesis to closure difficulty is that this phenomenon represents, at the visual–motor level, difficulty in maintaining adequate interpersonal relationships. Subhypotheses include the association between closure difficulty and fearfulness in interpersonal relationships, and the association between this phenomenon and emotional disturbance in general, in which there usually tends to be a problem in sustaining adequate and consistent cathexes and external objects. Of course, as with most phenomena, one should not expect anything like a near-perfect linear relationship with the complex end-product—some specific personality characteristic. Rather, it should be considered as *one part of a possible configuration* that expresses this linkage. Hence, our hypothesis would be supported if general trends in the predicted direction proved to be significant.

Apart from our own extensive clinical experience that supports these hypotheses, there are some research data that also lend some support. Byrd's (1956) study found that there were consistent and significant differences (at the .01 level) between well-adjusted children and children in need of psychotherapy in this test factor at age levels 8–15. If his age level data are combined, the significance of the difference is greater than .001. We would assume that this finding, while not a direct test of our major hypothesis, is consistent with the hypothesis. It should be noted that Byrd's analysis was performed with a measure of closure difficulty that is far cruder than our present measure. Clawson (1959) found that the symptom of interpersonal problems was significantly predicted by a rough measure of closure difficulty, and similarly a measure on the Rorschach was also predictable. Another indirect test was provided in Guertin's (1954b) research, in which factor analysis of Bender records of 100 adult psychiatric patients disclosed a statistical factor called "unstable cloture" (with a measure derived from Billingslea's scoring criteria). This factor, with a high loading among catatonics, was thought to be indicative of "emotional imbalance." Additional support for a similar factor may be found in Hain's (1964) study. A much more specific test of the hypothesis was provided in Story's (1960) study of alcoholics. Using a comparison of alcoholics with a control group of nonalcoholics, he found that each of two derived measures of closure difficulty separated these groups at the .01 level of significance. In our own comparison of a neurotic group with a comparable college group, we found mean closure scores of 5.7 and 3.1, respectively, and the difference significant at the .01 level.

One of the studies that attempted a validation of Hutt's Bender signs as well as a developmental analysis of these signs (Flint, 1965), compared the presence of these signs in 10-year-olds with adults (average age of 19.9 years). Her criterion measure was a paper-and-pencil test, the Institute for Personality and Abilities Testing 16 Personality Factor Questionnaire. Unfortunately, *especially as pertains to the HABGT factor of closure,* she employed the 4 × 6 inch cards published by the American Orthopsychiatric Association. (The amplitude of the curves and the configurations on test designs involving curvature are very different from the HABGT designs.) Questions have also been raised concerning the validity of the IPAT scales with respect to comparability of children's and adults' phenomena. Nevertheless, Flint found that the factor of "curvature" was valid (i.e., correlated with comparable test factors on the IPAT) and consistent over the age-interval studied.

Thus, in a general way, we can say that closure difficulty seems to be an important indication of some form(s) of emotional maladjustment associated with severity of psychopathology, and, more specifically, there is some support for the hypothesis relating to interpersonal problems.

7. Crossing Difficulty

DEFINITION

This factor refers to difficulty in executing the crossing(s) that occur on figures 6 and 7. It is manifested by redrawings, sketching, erasing, or markedly increasing the line pressure at the point where lines cross.

When figure 6 is drawn as two tangential curves, this is *not counted* as crossing difficulty, but two noncrossing curves *do count* as crossing difficulty. The raw score is the total number of times this difficulty occurs.

Scale Value	Definition
10.0	*Severe:* Raw score = 3.
7.0	*Moderate:* Raw score = 2.
4.0	*Moderate:* Raw score = 1.
1.0	*Absent:* Raw score = 0.

INTERPRETATION

It is believed that this manifestation is an indication of psychological blocking and is correlated with such behavior as indecisiveness, compulsive doubting, and phobias. It is also likely to be represented in behavior at the level of difficulty in interpersonal relations, although perhaps not as specifically as in Factor 6.

In the author's clinical experience this factor is almost invariably present when some significant form of blocking is present, although the opposite is not necessarily true. The factor has also withstood the more general tests of significance in the item validation of both the Psychopathology Scale and the Adience–Abience Scale.

There have been two studies in which measures based on some aspect of crossing difficulty have been tested. In both studies (Calwson, 1959; Story, 1960), the results have shown some support for the contention that the factor is significant, but its more precise meaning awaits further research.

8. Curvature Difficulty

DEFINITION

This difficulty refers to *any obvious change* in the nature of the curves in figures 4, 5, and 6. Such changes occur when: there is an increase or decrease in the amplitude of the curve; the curve is replaced by straight or spiked lines; the curve is flattened; the curve is made very unevenly or irregularly; the number of loops on figures 4 and 6 is either increased or decreased. The raw score is the total number of figures on which such changes occur.

For scoring purposes, slight irregularities in curvature *are not counted. It should be emphasized* that the changed curvature must be *obvious,* as indicated above.

Scale Value   Definition
10.0   *Severe:* Raw score = 3.
7.0   *Moderate:* Raw score = 2.
4.0   *Mild:* Raw score = 1.
1.0   *Absent:* Raw score = 0.

INTERPRETATION

Our own findings, both clinical and statistical, indicate that this factor is a highly sensitive indicator of emotional disturbance. Increases in curvature are thought to be indicative of increases in, or overly active responses in, emotionality, whereas decreases have a polar opposite meaning. Emotionally labile patients tend to produce increased curvature and depressive patients tend to produce decreased curvature. Irregularity in curve production is associated with irregularity in emotional behavior, and often, especially if associated with increase in curvature, with hostile acting out. On this factor, like all others, one should not expect there to be a simple linear relationship between curvature change and behavioral change, although such a relationship is probably more likely on this factor than on most other factors. It seems to be a rather direct expression of the pattern of internal emotional feeling.

Psychologists have long been interested in bodily and behavioral manifestations of emotional experience. Line movement, especially as represented in the drawing of curves, has been found to relate fairly well to this aspect of personality (Allport, 1937; Wolff, 1943). With respect to Bender reproductions, changes in curvature seem to reflect, rather clearly, shifting changes in emotional expression. In two separate studies involving factor analytic methods with psychiatric patients, it was found that propensity toward what is called curvilinear movements was related to "poor emotional control" (Guertin, 1952), and that curvilinear distortion was related to impulsiveness (Guertin, 1954). Byrd (1956) found curvature difficulty to differentiate well-adjusted from "poorly" adjusted children at all levels from 8 to 15 years. Clawson (1959) found, similarly, that "clinic children drew the curved line of figures out of proportion," and that "the deviation was in the direction of increased curvature." The frequency of occurrence, in her sample, did not permit an adequate test of the significance of the direction of shift in relation to specific personality manifestations. Story (1960) discovered that the nature of the change in curvature sensitively reflected such personality manifestations in alcoholics. Finally, in a subgroup of the author's experimental neurotic population ($N = 12$), increased curvature was significantly related to increased emotionality, while in another subgroup ($N = 15$), decreased curvature was significantly related to decreased emotionality. In both subgroups, independent clinical judgments were available concerning the criterion of emotionality, and changes in curvature were scored by means of the scale values on the Psychopathology Scale. Corroborative research supporting the usefulness of this factors may be found in the studies by Kai (1972) and by Brannigan and Benowitz (1975) for children and adolescents, respectively.

9. Change in Angulation

DEFINITION

This change refers to an increase or decrease, by *15 degrees or more,* of the angulation *within* stimulus figures 2, 3, 4, 5, 6, and 7. In figure 2, a change of 15 degrees or more in the angle the columns make with the horizontal rows is the criterion. In figure 3 it is a change in the angle made by the columns of dots. In figure 4 it is the angle of the curve in relation to the open square. In figure 5 it is the angle of the external dots in relation to a presumed horizontal line. In figure 6 it is the angle at which the two curves cross. In figure 7 it is the angle of intersection of the two figures. The score is the number of figures on which the defined degree of change is present.

Scoring can be greatly facilitated by use of the *Scoring Template,* furnished by Grune & Stratton.

Scale Value	Definition
10.0	*Changed angulation on 5 figures.*
8.0	*Changed angulation on 4 figures.*
6.0	*Changed angulation on 3 figures.*
4.0	*Changed angulation on 2 figures.*
2.0	*Changed angulation on 1 figure.*
1.0	*No changes in angulation.*

INTERPRETATION

Our major hypothesis is that significant changes in degree of angulation reflect difficulty in dealing with affective stimuli, and in turn are related to problems in affective control and control of impulses. *Increased angulation,* by which we mean a change in the direction of rectangularity, is related to *decreased affectivity,* while *decreased angulation,* by which we mean a change in the direction of greater acuteness of the angle, is related to *increased affectivity.* We have also suggested that inaccuracy in reproducing angles is often associated with organic brain damage, and may be related to mental retardation, as well. The latter hypothesis is clearly related to the correlation between developmental and intellectual factors and accuracy in reproducing angles. The presence of angle difficulty in organics seems, however, to be attributable much more to difficulties with figure–ground problems and to primary disturbances in perception than to intellectual factors, per se.

There is substantial evidence that this factor assists in differentiating well-adjusted from poorly adjusted individuals. These findings could have been anticipated since the latter group is thought to have far greater problems in impulse control and in handling affectivity. A specific test of the hypothesis that alcoholics, who tend to suppress affect and have problems in handling affect, would perform adversely on this factor in comparison with nonalcoholics was made (Story, 1960). One measure of change in angulation was a shift in the angulation of the columns of circles in figure 2 toward the vertical position or even by a reversal of the "slant" of the columns. The other measure consisted of rotation of the upright hexagon in figure 7. On the first measure the level of statistical difference was .01, while it was .05 on the latter, both findings being consistent with the above hypothesis. Byrd (1956) found that, except for the 8–9-year-old group, children in need of psychotherapy did significantly more poorly than well-adjusted children. It is interesting to note that Byrd's data indicate that from age 10 through age 15, the relative frequencies of changes in angulation remain about constant, suggesting that age is not a significant factor above 9 years. Clawson (1959) found an even greater degree of significance in the difference between school and clinic children, the level of significance being .001. The fact that in both of these studies some children in the "good" groups showed difficulty in angulation may be indicative that some of these children also had emotional problems or that the measure, by itself, is insufficiently differentiating for such groups. In the authors' experimental groups of neurotics and college students ($N = 80$ in each group), the significance of the difference in angulation score (as defined) was above .001. A separate test was made of 14 individuals in the neurotic group who were clinically judged to be overly affective or bland in affect. Their combined angulation score was 6.7, while that of the college group was 1.9, the difference being significant at the .001 level. No test was made of differences between increased and decreased angulation.

Three other studies supply data on the efficacy of this factor in differentiating organics from nonorganics. In Mosher and Smith's (1965) study, angulation and change in slope, both rated by the criterion suggested by Peek and Quast (1951), were found to differentiate organics from nonorganics at the .01 level. Hain (1964) developed a score to identify brain damage in which 15 Bender-Gestalt signs were retained after item analysis. In the final measure for brain damage, difficulty with acute angles was retained and given a weight of 3, only three other signs having the greater weight of 4. The total score differentiated between organics, psychiatric patients, and controls. Wiener (1966) found that angulation difficulty significantly discriminated minimal neurological deficit in 8–10-year-olds.

Finally, as Lacks (1984) has reported, in a comparison of cases with organic dysfunction (N = 85) with those suffering from personality disorder (N = 123) and psychoses (N = 141), all adults, it was found that 41% of the organics while only 15% of the personality disorder cases and only 17% of the psychotics had angulation difficulty (as scored only for figures 2 and 3). This statistically significant finding highlights the discriminatory power when *severe difficulty in angulation* is the criterion. It does not, however, answer the question of how less severe angulation difficulties are reflected in normals as compared with psychiatric cases.

FACTORS RELATED TO DISTORTION OF THE GESTALT

The following seven factors are considered to be indicative of severe psychopathology. The eighth factor will be considered separately. Although their occurrence may, on occasion, be attributable to factors other than psychopathology, their presence in a test record should raise the question of a severe disturbance. We would expect their occurrence to be only occasional in neurotic groups and significantly more frequent in psychotic and organic groups. They may also occur, however, as a consequence of transient and severe trauma, but would not be expected in such cases after recovery from the immediate effects of such trauma. Distortions typically represent loss of some aspect of ego control and are therefore to be regarded as serious.

10. Perceptual Rotation

DEFINITION

This factor refers to the reproduction of the *entire* test figure with a rotation of its major axis *while the stimulus card and the test paper are in their normal, standard positions*. This factor is called "perceptual" rotation to distinguish it from factor 7, Shift in the Position of the Paper. This factor is *not* scored if only a segment of the figure is rotated (as when there is a shift in the position of the external line in figure 5). Similarly, change in only some of the columns of figure 2 is *not* scored as rotation. *The score is the highest score obtained.*

The Scoring Template will be found helpful for this factor.

Scale Value	Definition
10.0	*Severe rotation:* Rotation of 80–180 degrees on *any one figure.* (Pathognomic.)
7.0	*Moderate rotation:* Rotation of 15–79 degrees on *any one figure.* (Indicative of personality disturbance.)
4.0	*Mild rotation:* Rotation of 5–14 degrees on any one figure. (Possible personality problem, relatively minor.)
1.0	*No rotation:* No rotation more than 4 degrees.

INTERPRETATION

In evaluating the possible meaning of perceptual rotations, consideration needs to be given to both the degree of rotation and the frequency with which it appears. Although we do not score for frequency of rotation in our Psychopathology Scale (for empirical reasons in connection with that scale), clinical interpretation will be more meaningful when this factor is also considered. It should also be noted that rotation is an end product in behavior and that many factors may contribute to it: e.g., age, intelligence, nature of the stimulus, degree of congruence between axes of test figure and test paper, and type of pathology. What this really means is that such factors should properly be taken into account in evaluating the possible significance of rotation as indicative of psychopathology. But, of course, such considerations are important in all individual psychological evaluations.

Severe perceptual rotation is usually indicative of profound disturbance in some aspect of ego functioning, unless accounted for by some other clearly defined factor. In an earlier publication (Hutt & Briskin, 1960) we stated:" . . . it is most frequently found in the records of individuals who are psychotic, have intracranial pathology, or are mentally defective." Commenting on this allegation, Tolor and Schulberg (1963) say " . . . the multiplicity of diagnostic interpretations assigned to some of the test factors clearly diminish their value for making specific diagnostic judgments and . . . some type of ego impairment represents the only common denominator. . . . " Such despair is not warranted; human behavior and tests of human behavior turn out to be complex things, and to seek an overly simplified view of such phenomena is to demonstrate a relatively naive view of the science of psychology.

The fact is that diverse groups show relatively high frequencies in rotations, but there appears to be a commonality underlying this—a disturbance or inadequacy in some aspect of ego functions. For example, Fuller and Chagnon (1962) found that, as they measured them, there were significant differences in frequencies of rotations from normal children

(1.90), through emotionally disturbed children (15.00), to schizophrenics (24.62). Griffith and Taylor (1960) found significantly more rotations among organic patients than among nonorganic patients, and they also found the following percentage frequencies for rotations (defined as angular displacement of 45 degrees or more): mental defectives, 55.9%; organics, 40.8%; and, schizophrenic, neurotic, organic, "other," and character disorder, 22.8%. In a later study (Griffith & Taylor, 1961), they also reported that intelligence was correlated with frequency of rotations. Such findings as these seem to indicate that frequency of rotations is complexly related to type and severity of psychopathology; and that low level of intelligence may contribute an inordinate share of rotations. But if one is analyzing an individual record in which intelligence level is at least average and both severity and frequency of rotational difficulty are noted, psychopathology becomes highly suspect and other test (as well as clinical) indicators can be utilized to elucidate the specific meaning of the phenomena.

A considerable amount of research work has been devoted to the problem of rotations, some of which has been summarized in Chapter 2. In an analysis of the significance of rotations in connection with abnormal EEG's of children, Chorost, Spivack, and Levine (1959) shrewdly conclude that, despite problems of base rates in such populations, children who produce rotations are more likely to have abnormal EEG's than children who do not make such rotations. Hanvik and Andersen (1950) had found that, compared with a control group, organics produced more frequent rotations. Moreover, Mark and Morrow (1955) found that organics had significantly more rotations than a nonorganic, psychiatric comparison group. Hain's (1964) scoring scheme gives the highest weighting to rotations as an element in his score for identifying brain damage.

It should be emphasized that the position in which the test paper is presented, viz-a-viz the test cards, is important in relation to the phenomenon of rotation. As indicated, we prefer that the test paper be presented in a vertical orientation (with the long axis in a vertical position). The discrepancy between the axis of the paper and that of the test cards (which have the long axis in a horizontal position) maximizes the frequency and degree of rotations. Developmental studies indicate that rotations, particularly on designs A, 3, 4, and 7, tend to occur more frequently among very young children, but by age 9 years normal children rarely show rotational difficulties (Black, 1973; Weiss, 1971a). These findings obtain with the test paper in the "normal" orientation. Frequency of rotations occurs more often with the paper presented in a vertical orientation. Verms (1974) found that among psychiatric patients without organic brain damage, presentation of the test paper in the vertical position produced significantly more frequent rotations than when the test paper was presented in a horizontal position. However, this study, which involved a large number of patients ($N = 349$), showed that the position of the paper was not significant with brain-damaged patients; presumably, the neurological deficit was, by itself, sufficient to induce the rotation phenomenon.

A comparison of heroin users with nonopiate psychiatric patients indicated that the users of heroin tended to rotate the designs more frequently than the nonusers (Korim, 1974).

It has been found that gifted children like to rotate the position of the paper to a horizontal position and rarely show the phenomenon of rotation of the drawings (Bravo, 1972). The reasons for the preference in having the paper in a horizontal orientation is unknown, but one can speculate that gifted children tend to be more creative, individualistic, and oppositional.

There is little doubt that ability to reproduce the designs without rotations is, in part, a function of the development of cognitive capacities. Rock (1974) has demonstrated that accurate perception of form involves, to some extent, the recognition of the concepts of "top," "bottom," and "sides." When cognitive functions are immature or when they have been disrupted, rotational phenomena tend to occur.

In work with children, we should like to cite again the studies by Byrd (1956) and Clawson (1959). The former found that the factor of rotation significantly differentiated the well adjusted children from those in need of psychotherapy at all age levels, 8–15. The incidence of rotations among the oldest group (14–15 year olds) was only 1 in a population of 50 well-adjusted children. The latter study found that when rotation was counted whenever the degree of rotation was equal to 15 degrees or more, this differentiated the school from the clinic population at the .001 level of significance. Surprisingly, "School and clinic children made about the same amount of rotation (90° to 180°)." A possible explanation for this finding is that large rotations in children often are more indicative of oppositional trends than of severity of pathology. Our own data with adults does not support the hypothesis that larger degrees of rotation are less significant diagnostically. Using our revised scale for measuring rotation we found the following: a mean score of 7.9 among 95 heterogeneous organic cases; a mean score of 7.2 among 100 heterogeneous cases of schizophrenia; a mean score of 4.3 among 80 neurotic cases; and a mean score of 1.5 among the 80 college students. Chi square tests for intergroup differences indicated that the only intergroup differences which did not reach the probability level of .01 was that between organics and schizophrenics.

The recent studies of Marley (1982) and Lacks (1984) confirmed the diagnostic validity of this factor. In Lack's study, *severe rotation* was found in 28% of the records of organics, in 13% of the records of psychotics, and in only 9% of the records of personality disorders. It should be noted that both Marley and Lacks used the Orthopsychiatric cards that probably produce fewer rotations than the HABGT cards.

The author's clinical experience suggests that mild degrees of rotation in the clockwise direction are often associated with depressive reactions. Counterclockwise rotations, especially but not necessarily mild in degree, are indicative of oppositional tendencies. Story (1960), testing the hypothesis that mild degrees of counterclockwise rotation were indicative of oppositional tendencies, and using only rotations on figure 7 in which the degree of rotation was in the range 5–20 degrees, found that this measure differentiated alcoholics from nonalcoholics at the .05 level of significance.

An important characteristic of the phenomenon of rotation concerns the degree of awareness of the patient of his rotational error. In general, there is clinical and experimental evidence to suggest that awareness of the patient of his rotation is indicative of transitional difficulties in the perceptual area. Regressed schizophrenics and organics are usually unaware that their reproductions show rotation. Thus, when rotation occurs, it is advisable to check the protocol on the elaboration phase for similar rotations and to test for degree of awareness during the testing-the-limits phase of the procedure.

Another important "limits" testing in connection with rotations, suggested in a previous publication (Hutt, 1960), is the capacity to correct rotations when they are pointed out by the examiner. When the individual is unable or not easily able to make a correct, nonrotated reproduction, even when asked to "correct the drawing so that it looks just like the one on the card," there is confirmatory evidence of the probability of either an organic condition, or a severely regressed psychotic condition. A test of this hypothesis was made by Smith and Martin (1967). They compared a group of 25 neurologically impaired patients with a group of 25 non-neurologically impaired patients. The impaired group made a significantly greater number of rotations and required a significantly greater number of cues to correct rotations. These workers felt that the ability to correct rotations is a more discriminating index of neurological impairment than frequency of rotations.

In clinical work, the clinician will wish to make use of all the factors we have discussed in evaluating the significance of rotations: degree of rotation; frequency of rotation; awareness of occurrence of rotation; and ability to correct rotation. In addition, related data from the test will assist greatly in reaching a more precise formulation of the meaning of the rotation in terms of the context in which it occurs. Of course, developmental level and intellectual level will influence the interpretation of the meaning of the rotation.

11. Retrogression

DEFINITION

Retrogression refers to the substitution of a more primitive Gestalt form for the more mature Gestalt of the stimulus figure. The most common forms of retrogression are as follows: substitution of impulsive loops for reasonably well-formed circles (as in figure 2); substitution of dashes for dots (as in figures 1, 3, and 5); and substitution of dots for circles (as in figure 2). The criterion for counting such phenomena as retrogression is its occurrence *at least twice on any given figure*. The psychopathology scale value then depends upon the number of times this criterion of retrogression is met.

Scale Value	Definition
10.0	*Severe:* Criterion met in *more* than 2 figures.
7.0	*Moderate:* Criterion met in 2 figures.
4.0	*Mild:* Criterion met in 1 figure.
1.0	No regression as defined.

INTERPRETATION

Strictly speaking, retrogression should be differentiated from developmental immaturity in the perceptual–motoric sphere, for by this term we are implying *some form of reversion to an older mode of behavior* rather than simply a present inadequacy. In clinical evaluation of retrogression on this test we should consider whether there is evidence of higher levels of functioning, and only when such discrepancies occur should we consider the phenomena under question to be an instance of retrogression.

Our general hypothesis is that retrogression occurs under conditions of relatively severe and chronic defense against trauma and is indicative of some degree of failure in ego integration and functioning. We expect that *some types of schizophrenic adults* would manifest this phenomenon. Such types would be characterized by disorganization of the personality and inadequate compensation for chronic conflict. However, neurotics with intense anxiety and ineffectual defenses should also be expected to display it. The problem of evaluating retrogression in children is much more complicated because developmental factors intrude much more significantly in performance, especially below the age level of approximately 9 years. It should also be noted that the points in the testing at which retrogression appears may be of considerable significance: whether in the copy phase or the elaboration phase; whether on difficult figures or on easy figures; whether in "open" designs or in "closed" designs. The possible significance of these associations requires clinical analysis, as we have indicated in previous chapters, and as we shall illustrate with case material in Part III of this book.

Various investigators have studied retrogression (or regression) on the Bender records. It is difficult to integrate the meaning of their findings because quite different definitions of retrogression have been utilized and quite variable criteria of suspected regression in behavior have been chosen. However, our analysis of these findings suggests that, generally, they consider retrogression to be indicative of some major disruption in functioning. There is not any consensus as to whether this is the result of regression in the usual sense or whether it is some form of malfunctioning. Thus, for instance, Suttell and Pascal (1952) compared the functioning of schizophrenics with both neurotics and normal children, using items from their own scoring scheme (based, in part, on previous suggestions by Hutt). They concluded that disruption of learned, regulatory responses sometimes accounts for the "regressive" phenomenon, and at other times maturation is the important factor. In this study schizophrenics and neurotics could not clearly be differentiated. One suspects that their criteria of regression accounted for these ambiguous results. On the other hand, studies by Guertin (1954c, 1955) indicate that, at least in the case of what is termed "disorganized hebephrenics," retrogressive phenomena occur significantly more frequently than other "forms" of schizophrenia. Clawson (1959), using five criteria of Bender regression similar to our own, found that 23 of 80 school children and 57 of 80 clinic children, varying in age from 7 to 12 years, showed this phenomenon. The difference in frequencies was significant at the .001 level. She believes: "The so-called regressive signs . . . are evidence of lag in maturation rather than reversion to earlier modes of behavior," although it is difficult to learn on what basis she reaches this conclusion. However, it is interesting to note that, in agreement with this author, she believes that " . . . judgment of regression is warranted only if there is evidence of more mature forms . . . in the record."

Ames (1974), in a study of 92 older subjects between the ages of 57 and 92, separated these individuals on the basis of Rorschach data into normal adult, intact presenile, medium presenile, and deteriorated adults. The Bender records provided differentiation among these groups at a highly significant level ($p < .001$). Retrogressive features of the Bender records contributed to this differentiation. The regressive substitution of dashes for circles, especially, and for dots, has been found to be associated with emotional problems in children, particularly with agressive behavior (Brown, 1965; Kai, 1972). Of course, regression in children is far less significant than the same phenomenon in adults.

The discriminatory power of this test factor was demonstrated in

Monheit's study (1983) in which 75.3% of the severely disturbed adolescents revealed this phenomenon whereas only 8.4% of her normal adolescents showed any evidence of retrogression. The severe disruptive effects on perceptual-motoric functioning is clearly evidenced in Lack's (1984) findings in which it was found that 42% of her organic group revealed retrogression and that 21% of patients with personality disorders and 18% of psychotics also revealed retrogression. She points out that this *single test factor* did not discriminate statistically between the two psychiatric groups but it did discriminate between these groups and the organic group.

Our own clinical experience indicates that the presence of this test factor is *always* indicative of severe psychopathology in adult records, and our own statistical findings strongly support the discriminatory power of retrogression, especially as part of the total Psychopathology Scale.

12. Simplification

DEFINITION

Simplification refers to the reproduction of the stimulus as a *simpler figure* or one that is *much simpler to draw*. The following are examples of simplification: drawing the two parts of figure A as noncontiguous; reducing the number of elements in figures 1, 2, 3, and 5, by *at least 3 less* than in the stimulus; reducing the number of curves in figure 6; and reproducing the parts of figures 7 and 8 as rectangles or crude elipses. Simplification is *not scored* when either fragmentation or retrogression is involved; i.e., only one phenomenon is scored per drawing.

Scale Value	Definition
10.0	*Severe:* Present on *more* than 2 figures.
7.0	*Moderate:* Present on 2 figures.
4.0	*Mild:* Present on 1 figure.
1.0	None.

INTERPRETATION

At the psychological level, Simplification seems to represent a decrease in cathexes to external objects or tasks, or, in more behavioral terms, it represents an attempt to reduce the expenditure of energy required in completing a task or dealing with a situation. Although it sometimes occurs as a result of deliberate decrease in effort on the part of the examinee, primarily related to oppositional tendencies or a need to malinger, it usually seems to be related to difficulties in impulse control and the executive functions of the ego. Simplification does not, necessarily, re-

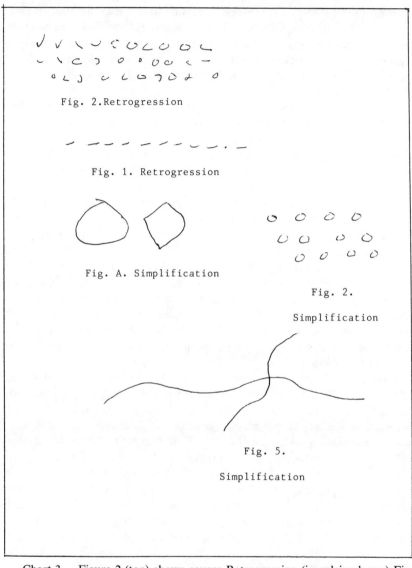

Fig. 2.Retrogression

Fig. 1. Retrogression

Fig. A. Simplification

Fig. 2.

Simplification

Fig. 5.

Simplification

Chart 3.   Figure 2 (top) shows severe Retrogression (impulsive loops) Figure 1 (near top), shows impulsive dashes, instead of dots. Figure A (middle) shows gross separation of the parts, hence Simplification. Figures 2 and 5, (near bottom) show gross reduction in the number of elements—hence, Simplification.

flect a profound distrubance in ego functions, but it may be present as a derivative of such disturbance. Hence, one expects to find it in organic cases and it is often associated with feelings of impotence in such cases. When other test indications of profound ego disturbance occur, the presence of Simplification can then be regarded as confirmatory evidence of such disturbance.

Surprisingly little specific research evidence has been directed to this test factor, whether because of lack of confidence that this seemingly simple phenomenon is important, or because of lack of clarity about its meaning and definition. Our own hypotheses concerning it were derived, in the first place, from clinical observations of the relationship of this factor to other personality manifestations. Later, some statistical evidence was gathered. For example, this factor withstood the tests of item validation in the construction of the Psychopathology Scale and the Adience-Abience Scale. More specifically, we found the following frequencies of occurrence of some degree of simplification in our experimental populations: 1 of 80 college students; 6 of 80 neurotics; 8 of 100 schizophrenics; and 13 of 95 organics. Thus, there is a significant difference between the occurrence of this phenomenon in both organics and schizophrenics and that in "normals." However, Simplification does not occur with high frequency in any subgroup, so that while it may add to the meaning of a total score in psychopathology, it does not by itself constitute a reliable differentiator.

Further evidence of the significance of this test factor may be found in Lack's publication (1984), in which it is found that 49% of patients with organic brain dysfunction show Simplification. It is also found with some degree of frequency in psychotic records (20%) and in the records of patients with personality disorders (17%). Monheit (1983) found that 79.8% of her emotionally disturbed (severe) adolescents showed simplification, but she also found that 27.4% of her normals also showed some degree of this phenomenon. I would suspect that her scorers scored for Simplification "too leniently" and perhaps scored for this factor when *our criterion* (as above) was not strictly met. Our scoring samples (Chart 3) illustrate examples of Simplification as well as of Retrogression.

13. Fragmentation

DEFINITION

Fragmentation refers to the essential destruction of the Gestalt. It can be manifested in a number of ways. The most common are as follows: the reproduction is obviously unfinished or incomplete; or the Gestalt is drawn as if composed of separate parts, i.e., the parts are grossly separated so that the Gestalt is lost.

Scale Value	Definition
10.0	*Severe:* Present on more than 2 figures.
7.0	*Moderate:* Present on 2 figures.
4.0	*Mild:* Present on only 1 figure.
1.0	*None.*

INTERPRETATION

Fragmentation represents a severe disturbance in perceptual–motoric functioning and seems to be associated with decrement in the capacities for abstracting and synthesizing. It should therefore be expected to occur in diverse types of pathology in which the individual suffers damage in these functions. Although its absolute frequency of occurrence is not very great in the total clinical population, as has been demonstrated in many studies of neurotic, psychotic, and brain-damaged individuals, its appearance in a given record is highly significant of profound impairment. Various workers have defined and measured this type of distortion in diverse ways, so that results are not directly comparable. However, what Peek and Quast (1951) call "major distortion," what Pascal and Suttell (1951) call "distortion" and "part of design missing," and what Hain (1964) calls "distortion" are all closely related to our factor. Almost invariably in these and other studies this factor is shown to have high differentiating power between psychotics and normals and between organics and nonorganics, and is therefore given considerable weight in scores presumably measuring severity of psychopathology. Our own analysis of this factor also led to its inclusion in the Psychopathology Scale. One example of its efficacy may suffice: a comparison of mean scores on Fragmentation of the neurotic group with the heterogeneous psychotic group yielded a score of 1.1 for the former and 7.2 for the latter, the difference being significant at the .001 level.

The data furnished by Lacks (1984) clearly indicate that Fragmentation occurs only infrequently in patients with personality disorders (6%), but occurs somewhat more frequently among psychotics (10%) and with a reasonable degree of frequency among OBS patients (27%). Again, we may conclude that when this phenomenon occurs it is highly pathognomic.

Fragmentation, as measured, rarely occurs in the records of young children. For example, in one study of 400 cases ranging in age from 8 to 15, only 8 instances of fragmentation were noted (Byrd, 1956). Below age level 10 one would suspect that is has quite different meaning than above this age level and might be more closely related to developmental factors than to psychopathology. However, qualitative analysis of this factor may be rewarding, even in young cases.

14. Overlapping Difficulty

DEFINITION

This factor refers to the specified types of difficulty with overlapping (figure 7) and contiguous figures (figures A and 4). This type of difficulty involves: gross overlapping where none exists in the stimulus figures (A and 4); failure to reproduce a portion of the overlapping (in 7); simplification or distortion of portions of either figure at the point of overlap (in 7).

Scale Value	Definition
10.0	*Severe*: Overlapping on more than 1 figure.
5.5	*Moderate*: Overlapping on 1 figure.
1.0	*None*.

INTERPRETATION

Our present definition of this factor deviates considerably from previous definitions that we have offered and distinguishes it more clearly from Closure Difficulty, on the one hand, and Simplification and Fragmentation, on the other. Our experience had suggested that this difficulty was most closely associated with some types of diffuse brain damage, and that this factor was extremely sensitive to such damage. The work reported by Hain (1964) and by Mosher and Smith (1965) seem to support this contention. We do not yet have adequate tests of the hypothesis, and probably adequate tests would have to involve a greater sampling than the material the HABGT offers. However, we do have convincing evidence of the power of this factor to distinguish the organic group, in general, from the nonorganic (with $N = 95$ and $N = 180$, respectively) in our experimental population. The former group attained a mean score of 5.6, whereas the latter group attained a mean score of 1.3, the difference in means being significant at the .01 level. With such heterogeneous groups, which would tend to attenuate the significance of the difference, such results are promising.

Lacks' study (1984) offers confirmatory evidence. Organics committed this error 45% of the time, a statistically significant difference from the percentage of errors committed by either personality disorders (26%) or psychotics (26%).

15. Elaboration or Doodling

DEFINITION

This factor refers to doodling or elaboration on the reproduction in which the form is markedly changed. The elaboration can include the addition of loops or curlicues, or the addition of lines or curves that change the Gestalt. This factor should be differentiated from Factor 22, Perseveration.

Scale Value	Definition
10.0	*Severe*: Present on *more* than 2 figures.
7.0	*Moderate*: Present on 2 figures.
4.0	*Mild*: Present on 1 figure only.
1.0	*None*.

INTERPRETATION

Anyone who has had occasion to examine the HABGT records of agitated patients will have noticed the presence of this phenomenon. It appears to be associated with problems in impulse control and intense, overt anxiety. However, we must also note that we have observed its presence in the records of some mentally retarded individuals as well as some organics. Hence, we suspect that the phenomenon is the complex and indirect end product of a number of intervening processes. The author has never observed this phenomenon in well-adjusted adults or in the records of compulsive neurotics. We should, however, be careful to distinguish doodling and elaboration, as defined, from minor or occasional embellishments of the figure, *which do not essentially distort the Gestalt*. When the phenomenon does involve distortion of the Gestalt it is very likely to be indicative of some severe disturbance in ego control. It appears to be a significant contributor to measures or judgments of psychopathology, but not all types of psychopathology necessarily manifest it. Item validation in connection with both the Psychopathology and Adience–Abience Scales confirmed its contributory role in these measures. Qualitive analyses of clinical records have also demonstrated its clinical usefulness.

The Pascal-Suttell scoring method (Pascal & Suttell, 1951) contains a number of examples of scores which involve phenomena very similar to this Elaboration factor. The scoring method developed by Hain (1964) also contains a "sign," called "added embellishment," which is given a medium weighting in this scheme. In Byrd's (1956) study of children's records, the phenomenon appeared infrequently, but it *never* appeared in

200 records of well-adjusted school children, only in those children needing psychotherapy. The contrast in frequency of occurrence in adult schizophrenic records is marked: it occurred in 12 of the 100 records of our chronic schizophrenic population.

In her recent work Koppitz (1975a) has added "spontaneous elaborations or additions to design" as another "emotional indicator." Her experience shows that this phenomenon is "rare and occur(s) almost exclusively on Bender Test records of children who are overwhelmed by fears and anxieties. . . . " The occurrence of the same phenomenon in adults is more likely, however, to be even more serious, and is indicative of some loss of control over reality factors or retreat into fantasy.

16. Perseveration

DEFINITION

Perseveration refers to either of *two types* of perseverative phenomena: (a) perseveration in which elements of a previous design are utilized in a *succeeding design* when they are not present in the stimulus figure; and (b) perseveration of the elements present in a given figure *beyond the limits* called for in the stimulus. An example of perseveration of type (a) is the use of dots in figure 2 (instead of circles) perseverated from the dots used in figure 1. An example of perseveration of type (b) is the presence in figure 1 of 14 or more dots instead of the 12 dots present in the stimulus design. Another example is the presence of 12 or more columns of circles in figure 2 instead of the 10 columns present in the stimulus design. The criterion for scoring the presence of perseveration is the *occurrence of 2 or more* of the perseverated elements in the case of type (a), or the *addition of 2 or more elements* (perseverated) within the same figure in the case of type (b).

Scale Value	Definition
10.0	*Severe*: Present in *more* than 2 figures.
7.0	*Moderate*: Present in 2 figures.
4.0	*Mild*: Present in one figure *only*.
1.0	*None*.

INTERPRETATION

Perseveration, as defined, seems to represent either an inability to shift "set," or a rigidity in the maintenance of an established "set." In either case it represents a markedly decreased degree of spontaneous and adaptive ego control. It is probably reinforced by a decrease in reality test functions. We had originally suspected that perseveration of type (b) was more significant than type (a) in persons with organic insult, but additional findings suggest that both types are about equally significant in organic damage. A mild degree of perseveration, however, such as the infrequent addition of a single element (like adding a single dot in figure 1) probably has quite a different kind of significance. It may, for example, represent some degree of carelessness in execution or some degree of inaccuracy in counting in the case of children. *Severe perseveration*, as defined, is almost always pathognomic in adult records and is most frequently associated with the records of organics and deteriorated schizophrenics. It should also be noted that severe mental retardates of almost all types frequently manifest this phenomenon, as the author's study of such cases (see Chapter 6) indicated.

The apparently opposite phenomenon, namely the *reduction* in the number of elements from the number in the stimulus designs, seems to represent an entirely different kind of phenomenon, and we have therefore included it in the Simplification factor. Pascal and Suttell (1951) combine these two phenomena in a single score and call it "number of dots (or circles)." They find that this score adds some weight to their general measure of psychopathology.

Perseveration is found most frequently in connection with figures 1,2, and 5. It may be found less frequently on figure 3, and still less frequently on figure 6. Perseveration, type (a), is found most frequently on figure 2, perhaps because this figure is immediately preceded by figure 1, and in both figures the examinee is required to repeat the element a large number of times.

The author's research data yielded the following mean scores: college students, 1.04; neurotics, 1.90; schizophrenics, 4.70; organics, 5.97. Tests of the significance of these differences show that both organics and schizophrenics, as groups, are differentiable from the "normal" and neurotic groups (.01 level), but there is no significant difference between "normals" and neurotics, although there is a trend indicating neurotics to be inferior. Clinical observation suggests that highly anxious neurotics tend to perform differently from other types of neurotics.

Mosher and Smith (1965) found that perseveration of type (a) differentiated organics from controls at the .01 level of significance. The factor of perseveration, as measured by Hain (1964), was given the highest possible weight in the score that was used to discriminate organics from both controls and other psychiatric cases. In 300 cases, ranging in age from 10 to 15 years, Byrd (1956) found seven cases showing perseveration (as measured) in the psychotherapy group, and only one case in the well-adjusted group. Obviously, frequency of occurrence is not sufficiently great to make this measure useful in a score for such groups. He also reported that in the 8–9-year-old group more cases with perseveration (6) occurred in the well-adjusted than in the psychotherapy group (1). Although the usefulness of this factor is especially limited with children below 10 years of age, *severe perseveration* still warrants serious consideration as a pathognomic indicator, in our judgment, and should be evaluated clinically when it occurs.

Other data pointing to the usefulness of this factor may be found in Wursts's (1974) study, which extracted perseveration as one of the basic factors in visual perception, and that of Korim (1974), in which heroin users were found to manifest this phenomenon significantly more often than nonopiate subjects.

That perseveration occurs particularly frequently in organic records is confirmed in Lacks' research (1984). She found that this phenomenon occurred in 56% of such records, the frequency being statistically significantly greater than that found in the records of patients with significantly greater than that found in the records of patients with personality disorders (31%) or those of psychotics (32%). Although this test factor adds to the total configuration which is diagnostic of organics, it must be emphasized that nonorganic factors may produce perseverative behavior. Hence, in individual diagnosis, as we shall emphasize in later discussions, experimental–clinical–testing, first to determine whether the subject is aware of his perseverative behavior, and second whether the subject can, with motivation, voluntarily decrease or eliminate such behavior.

17. Redrawing of the Total Figure

DEFINITION

Redrawing refers to a second attempt to reproduce a figure when the first attempt (which may not necessarily include reproduction of the total figure) is left without complete erasure or is simply crossed out. On rare occasions more than two attempts may be made to reproduce a figure.

Scale Value	Definition
10.0	*Very severe*: Present 4 times or more.
7.75	*Severe*: Present 3 times.
5.5	*Moderate*: Present 2 times.
3.25	*Mild*: Present 1 time.
1.0	*None*.

INTERPRETATION

Scattered references may be found in Bender research literature, but surprisingly little systematic research effort has been devoted to this factor. We believe that one of two conditions generally produces Redrawing.

Table 4.1
Data for Various Groups on Redrawing

Category	N	Mean Score	SD
Normals	150	1.05	1.04
Outpatient neurotics	150	1.78	1.96
Chronic schizophrenics	155	3.12	2.10
Organics	147	4.01	2.19

One is the absence of adequate anticipatory planning and the other is an overly self-critical attitude, usually combined with the former condition. When this phenomenon is marked (i.e., occurs more than once) it is probably significant. A single occurrence, while scored, may only indicate a high degree of current anxiety.

Some scoring schemes that have been published for Bender-Gestalt protocols include this item. Pascal and Suttell (1951) give it considerable weight in their scoring scheme. Koppitz (1975a) includes it as one of the factors in her list of "emotional indicators." The phenomenon probably occurs more frequently in the records of young children than in older subjects. We have reanalyzed our own data, using the scoring indicated above, and have obtained the findings indicated in Table 4.1. Significant differences in mean score are found between groups of organics and schizophrenics on the one hand ($p < .01$), and neurotics and "normals" on the other.

When redrawing, as defined, occurs in the records of organic patients, it is usually indicative of their feeling of impotence in perceiving and reproducing the designs, particularly those designs in which there are figure–ground problems (such as figures 3 and 7). In such instances parieto–temporal brain damage may have occurred and experimental–clinical–testing is highly advisable.

THE PSYCHOPATHOLOGY SCALE—3rd EDITION

Despite our caveats and reservations about objective measurements, we have also noted that they possess important attributes. They are replicable, they can be utilized for comparative purposes, and they can be the foundations for normative analyses. If objective measures are utilized with full awareness of their inherent limitations, they can contribute significantly to clinical application. It is largely when they are taken literally at face value, without recognition that they are based on assumptions which do not necessarily hold in the individual case, and particularly in the individual clinical case, that their use may be inaccurate if not hazardous.

In this chapter we shall present the Psychopathology Scale, which can be utilized in the clinical study of individuals. It can also be utilized for many other purposes, including group comparisons and many research functions. The scale rests on the general assumption that global measures based on the projective characteristics of test behavior are of value. Human behavior is quite complex and can best be understood, in the author's view, if the total, complex response is not broken down into atomistic, meaningless units. The complex response contains a unique quality; the single elements into which this response may logically be reduced no longer define this quality, nor can they be reconstructed by logical means into the end product by some arithmetical construction. The complex response may, on the other hand, be evaluated in terms of its necessary antecedents and consequences; the separate, atomistic elements do not necessarily, and usually do not, manifest the same relationships.

The Psychopathology Scale attempts to provide a global measure of the degree of psychopathology manifested on the HABGT. Psychopathology is considered to vary from a very small amount, which may characterize the so-called "normal" individual, to a very great amount, which may characterize the very disturbed individual. The degree of psychopathology varies on a continuum and is assumed to possess a linear quality, so that a higher score on psychopathology represents a higher degree of psychopathology.

The Psychopathology Scale is derived from the copy phase of the HABGT. Work on this scale was begun in 1958–1959, and a preliminary form of the scale was published in 1960 (Hutt & Briskin). It was called The 19-Factor Scale, since it was then based on the scoring of 19 factors, each of which contributed to the total score. Based on an analysis of comparisons of well-adjusted controls and two groups of patients, it was found that the scale differentiated the controls ($N = 50$) from psychiatric patients ($N = 20$) and from hospitalized deaf, mentally retarded patients ($N = 169$) ($p < .001$). These crude analyses seemed promising and led to further refinement and study of the scale.

The present Psychopathology Scale represents the culmination of a great number of research studies. It consists of 17 factors, each of which is defined in objective terms. The factors are scored on a scale from 1 to 10. Scores may range from a minimum of 17.0 to a maximum of 170.00, the total range being 150 points. In the following discussion we shall present the scale, then offer our present normative findings and summaries of research studies, and finally discuss some uses to which the scale may be put.

As noted earlier, the Psychopathology Scale is based on scores derived from the subject's productions in the *Copy Phase,* only. Each factor

Table 4.2

The Psychopathology Scale—3rd Edition

Factor	Raw Score	Scale Value
1. *Sequence*		
Confused or symbolic		10.0
Irregular		7.0
Overly methodical		4.0
Normal		1.0
2. *Position, 1st Drawing*		
Abnormal, severe	(See criteria)	10.0
Egocentric placement	(See criteria)	5.0
Normal	(See criteria)	1.0
3. *Use of Space*		
Abnormal	(See criteria)	10.0
Normal	(See criteria)	1.0
4. *Collision*	(See directions)	
Extreme	Occurs more than 2 times	10.0
Moderate	Occurs 2 times	8.5
Present	Occurs 1 time	7.0
Tendency, extreme	Occurs more than 2 times	5.5
Tendency, moderate	Occurs 2 times	4.0
Tendency, present	Occurs 1 time	2.5
No collision		1.0
5. *Shift of Paper*		
On all figures		10.0
For 3–8 figures		7.0
For 1–2 figures		5.5
No rotation		1.0
6. *Closure Difficulty*	(See criteria)	
Very severe	9	10.0
Severe	6–8	7.75
Moderate	3–5	5.5
Mild	1–2	3.25
Absent	0	1.0
7. *Crossing Difficulty*		
Severe	3 or more	10.0
Moderate	2	7.0
Mild	1	4.0
Absent	0	1.0
8. *Curvature Difficulty*		
Severe	3	10.0
Moderate	2	7.0
Mild	1	4.0
Absent	0	1.0
9. *Change in Angulation*		
On 5 figures	(See criteria)	10.0
On 4 figures	(See criteria)	8.0
On 3 figures	(See criteria)	6.0

Table 4.2 (continued)

Factor	Raw Score	Scale Value
On 2 figures	(See criteria)	4.0
On 1 figure	(See criteria)	2.0
None present		1.0
10. *Perceptual Rotation*		
Severe	80–180 degrees	10.0
Moderate	15–79 degrees	7.0
Mild	5–14 degrees	4.0
None	Less than 5 degrees	1.0
11. *Retrogression*	(See criteria)	
Severe	On more than 2 figures	10.0
Moderate	On 2 figures	7.0
Mild	On 1 figure	4.0
None		1.0
12. *Simplification*	(See criteria)	
Severe	On more than 2 figures	10.0
Moderate	On 2 figures	7.0
Mild	On 1 figure	4.0
None		1.0
13. *Fragmentation*		
Severe	On more than 2 figures	10.0
Moderate	On 2 figures	7.0
Mild	On 1 figure	4.0
None		1.0
14. *Overlapping Difficulty*		
Severe	On more than 1 figure	10.0
Moderate	On 1 figure	5.5
None		1.0
15. *Elaboration*		
Severe	On more than 2 figures	10.0
Moderate	On 2 figures	7.0
Mild	On 1 figure	4.0
None		1.0
16. *Perseveration*	(See criteria)	
Severe	On more than 2 figures	10.0
Moderate	On 2 figures	7.0
Mild	On 1 figure	4.0
None		1.0
17. *Redrawing, Total Figure*		
Very severe	4 or more times	10.0
Severe	3 times	7.75
Moderate	2 times	5.5
Mild	1 time	3.25
None		1.0

is given, first a raw score, and then this score is translated into a Scaled Score, based on the definitions given previously in this chapter. It should be emphasized that *these scores are based on reproduction of the Hutt Adaptation of the Bender–Gestalt designs, as discussed in the earlier portion of this work*. The use of *any other cards, such as those published by the American Orthopsychiatric Association, may and probably will, result in differing test phenomena*. Therefore, our scorings and normative findings may not be applicable when other designs are used.

The Psychopathology Scale (Table 4.2) Score is the sum of the scaled scores on all 17 test factors.

Additional directions for scoring and a Scoring Template to facilitate scoring are provided on the Record Form for the Hutt Adaptation of the Bender–Gestalt Test, published by Grune & Stratton.

Normative Findings

We have accumulated norms for several well-defined groups of adults. Experience has indicated that, above age 10 years, age is not a significant factor in the Psychopathology Scale score (see later discussion). Table 4.3 presents these normative data for adults.

A few comments may be in order concerning the nature of these normative groups. Both sexes were grouped in our analysis. The outpatient neurotics were selected from both the author's own practice and that of other clinical psychologists. It is not assumed that they are typical of a random selection of neurotics. The inpatient neurotics were hospitalized for a variety of neurotic syndromes, mostly severe anxiety or depression. Similarly, the unipolar depressives were hospitalized for a very severe depressive condition. The outpatient schizophrenics were being treated by clinical psychologists and psychiatrists (43 and 17, respectively). The chronic schizophrenic population was drawn from state mental hospitals and probably represents a larger proportion of indigent psychotics than may be found in psychiatric hospitals in general. All of the organic brain-damage cases were selected on the basis of clinically verified neurological examination and represent cases with chronic disease processes or traumatic brain injury.

An analysis of the differences among means reveals the following. Differences between means are significant at the .001 level or better, except in two instances. The difference between inpatient neurotics and unipolar depressives reaches the level of only .01. The difference between chronic schizophrenics and the organic brain-damaged group reaches the probability level of .05. Thus it may be said, on the basis of these findings, that the Psychopathology Scale scores provide significant differentiation between most groups of patients. The questionable difference between

Table 4.3
Revised Normative Data for the
Psychopathology Scale

Group	N	Mean	SD
Normals*	140	32.8	4.9
Outpatient neurotics	150	53.0	9.5
Inpatient neurotics	55	61.7	8.7
Unipolar depressives	68	66.2	6.4
Outpatient schizophrenics	60	78.3	11.8
Chronic schizophrenics	155	97.1	12.1
Organic brain damage	147	101.1	14.5

* This group consisted of 80 individuals who were
"screened" for evidence of disturbance and 60 "unselected" college students.

the depressives and the inpatient neurotics may be due to the fact that
there was much overlapping in clinical pathology between these two
groups. The organic group is a very heterogeneous group and is not
claimed to be representative of typical organic cases. Moreover, it is
likely that some of the patients in the chronic schizophrenic group suffered from some form of brain dysfunction.

It should be emphasized that although these data indicate the value of
the scale *in differentiating groups,* they do not indicate that individual
cases can be "defined" in terms of the scale score alone. We have emphasized the hazards of utilizing any clinical score, no matter how high its
putative value, in making clinical diagnoses; much more information is
necessary in the individual case.

Now let us examine the findings for children. Table 4.4 presents these
tentative normative data.

The "normals" reported in Table 4.4 are unselected cases, the only
restriction in their sampling being that they had not been referred for

Table 4.4
Normative Data for the Psychopathology
Scale: Children

CA (years)	Type of Group	N	Mean	SD
10	Normals	28	43.8	6.2
	Disturbed	40	59.7	10.0
11	Normals	35	41.2	7.3
	Disturbed	43	58.4	10.2
12	Normals	39	42.3	7.6
	Disturbed	36	57.1	9.8

special study by the school psychologist or clinic. All of the "disturbed" cases are individuals who had been reported by their teachers as showing problems in their personal or social adjustment. It will be noted that the means for the disturbed children at these ages are very similar although slightly higher than the norms reported in Table 4.3 for outpatient neurotic adults. We have reason, therefore, to assume that children who are disturbed in these age ranges to not perform very differently from outpatient neurotics on this scale. The means for the normal children are, however, significantly higher than the means for the normal adult population ($p < .001$). Apparently our scale is somewhat affected by the maturation factor although these differences are not striking.* In the main, our data indicate that very high scores on the Psychopathology Scale, for these age groups, can differentiate disturbed from normal children ($p < .001$) and can be interpreted in much the same manner as is done for adults. Again, we caution that in the individual case more than a high Psychopathology Scale score is needed before reaching the conclusion that an individual child is disturbed. The Psychopathology Scale score, rather, should be taken as suggestive, only. It is also interesting to note that, both for "normal" and "disturbed" children, there is no discernable trend, between the ages of 10 and 12 years, of any significant change in mean scores. Thus, although there is a slight difference between the means for children and adults, the maturation factor does not appear to operate significantly within the 10–12-year-old groups. We assume that this is also the case above 12 years of age.

We do not yet have adequate data for children below 10 years of age, although our extensive clinical experience with this procedure for such children indicates that the scale is "roughly" applicable for nonretarded children down to about 8 years of age.

As to the question of objectivity in scoring, or *interjudge reliability*. As reported in our earlier edition of this work (Hutt, 1969a), the correlation between the total scores on the Psychopathology Scale for two "experienced" scorers for 100 schizophrenic cases was .96, indicating adequate objectivity. The reliabilities for the 17 factors of the scale ranged from a low of .76 for the factor of Simplification to a high of 1.00 for Shift of Paper. Only 3 of the 17 factors yielded a reliability coefficient of less than .81 (Perceptual Rotation, Simplification, and Overlapping). A series of subsequent studies (Miller & Hutt, 1975) showed that only slightly lower interscorer reliabilities were obtained when one scorer was relatively inexperienced and the other experienced. The rho obtained was .895 for a population of schizophrenic patients. Moreover, in the latter

---

* Monheit (1983) found some age differences beyond age 13, but it is not clear whether age, alone, or personality dysfunction contributed to such differences.

publication it was shown that the three major components of the scale (Organizational Factors, Changes in Gestalt, and Distortions of the Gestalt) were also separately reliable.

Interscorer reliability for the Psychopathology Scale was studied in a research project with male delinquents (Hutt & Dates, 1977). Three scorers were employed; they scored the records independently. The Kendall Coefficient of Concordance for these scorers for pretreatment conditions was .91. The records were rescored independently after a period of 40 weeks of therapy. The Coefficient obtained was then .95. The reliability of this Scale was also found to be high over the same 40–week period, the r's being .85 and .89 for two treatment groups and .92 for a control group.

Taken together, these findings indicate high test–retest and interscorer reliabilities for the Psychopathology Scale for both adults and children.

A study of *test–retest reliability* with 40 hospitalized patients over a two-week period yielded rho's of .87 for the males and .83 for the females (Miller & Hutt, 1975). Further analysis indicated that both patients who obtained high Psychopathology Scale scores and those who obtained low scores obtained high test–retest reliability.

Data concerning the possible *relationships between Psychopathology Scale scores and chronological age, sex, and intelligence* have also been obtained. All of our data indicate that, at least above 15 years of age, Psychopathology score and age are not significantly correlated (Research Report #43, 1964; Hutt & Miller, 1976). Data presented in Table 4.3 also suggest that the relationship is not important, at least down to age 10 years for children who are not retarded. Neither does there appear to be a significant relationship between sex and Psychopathology score, as revealed by study of the data in the same publications. The question of the relationship between intelligence and Psychopathology score is a more complicated matter. It would appear that at lower age levels (below 10 years of age) and for mentally retarded individuals at even higher age levels, there is a small but significant relationship between the two variables. In our study of deaf–retarded individuals, the r reached the level of .55, which would indicate about 30% of commonality between the two variables. This conclusion is very tentative, however, since the measure of intelligence used in that study (Research Report #43, 1964) was quite unreliable and since the population studied was quite exceptional. Our evidence suggests, however, that at the adult level, intelligence and Psychopathology score are *not* significantly correlated. Using highest school grade reached as a rough estimate of intelligence, for a population of 100 outpatient individuals, an r of .004 was obtained between "intelligence" and Psychopathology score (Hutt & Miller, 1976).

Uses of the Psychopathology Scale

There appear to be many possible uses for the Psychopathology Scale. In the research area there are many interesting issues that can be investigated. Aside from replication and extended study of some of the issues we have already discussed, the scale can be used in studying various clinical populations and in analyzing the contribution of degree of psychopathology to clinical and therapeutic improvement. VandenBos (1973), for instance, utilized the scale in research on the problem of "focusing" in relation to therapeutic improvement. The scale should be useful in comparisons among various cultural and social groups as well as in cross-cultural studies. Of course, the interrelationships between the Psychopathology Scale score and other criteria of psychopathology would be a fascinating area of exploration. These are but a few of the possibilities.

There are many ways in which the Scale can be used in clinical practice. (1) *Initial screening.* Scores can be obtained by trained nonprofessionals as well as by psychologists, and subjects with high scores can then be selected for further study. (2) *Analysis of psychopathology.* The record can be studied to evaluate the nature of the psychological or organic dysfunction. Our clinical and research findings with respect to the several factors, as well as general research on such functions, can lead to fruitful areas of investigation in the individual case. (3) The Scale is particularly useful in work with subjects who have *linguistic and/or cultural handicaps* since it is based on performance that is largely independent of such factors. (4) *Well–defended subjects.* Many of our personality tests are based on *verbal* responses to test stimuli. This can sometimes prove to be a serious limitation in cases in which verbal defense of facade can conceal, rather than reveal, pathology.

It should be remembered, however, that this one measure of psychopathology, like any other single, objective measure of the phenomenon, is limited in validity. A high Psychopathology Scale score should be taken as the *starting point* for the evaluation of probable psychopathology, not as the conclusion. *High scores are more likely to be significant than low scores, however.* The clinician will also wish to consider both the normative scores for a particular population against whom the patient is being compared, and the standard deviations in scores for those populations. For instance, let us say that a patient's Psychopathology Scale score is 75. In judging whether the patient is more likely to be properly categorized as a neurotic or a schizophrenic, one would consider that while this score places him slightly below the mean of outpatient schizophrenics (78.3), and thus is presumptive evidence that he may belong in that category, his score is still within 2 sigmas above the mean of inpatient neurotics (61.7). Thus, from a statistical viewpoint one could say that, judged on the basis of this criterion alone, he has a much higher probability of falling within the psychotic population than the inpatient neurotic population. The probability of "correct" categorization would be increased by the utilization of a configurational analysis (see Chapter 5). Clinical assessment would be greatly enhanced, of course, through inferential analysis (see Chapter 9).

5

Rapid Screening with HABGT Factors: The Configurational Approach

There is an apparent need for rapid psychological screening procedures, as many recent publications, particularly in the BGT area, attest (Lacks, 1984; Marley, 1982; Monheit, 1983; Tolor & Brannigan, 1980). This evidence indicates that rapid screening with this test is not only efficient, but is significantly accurate, especially in differentiating patients with OBS from other psychiatric patients and from normals. In the case of screening for organicity, the HABGT test factors not only reach a positive identification of this condition of approximately 80% or better, but testing and scoring are also rapid and highly reliable. The case for positive identification of other psychiatric conditions has not been researched adequately, but recent findings indicate that Configurational Analysis is highly promising.

It should be emphasized that *screening* is not *diagnosis,* nor is it *psychodiagnosis.* As we have stressed, the latter two procedures require the evaluation of much more data than any one test can supply: developmental history; medical and drug record; cultural conditions, if unusual; and the subject's motivation in taking psychological tests. Screening should, therefore, be regarded as a *preliminary* findings, on the basis of which further psychological and medical investigation are warranted.

We shall now discuss our approach utilizing configurational analysis. As we have noted previously, we should not expect to find perfect agreement between any configuration of test signs and a particular nosological category. The presentation of certain configurational patterns that are frequently associated with certain psychiatric categories is intended, rather, to indicate *commonly occurring, associated conditions.* The utilization of such configurations should *not,* therefore, lead to automatic diagnostic designations of individuals. They can be highly useful for group comparisons and for further analysis of individuals who are suspected of having a particular psychiatric condition. In the case of individuals, configurational analysis leads, rather, to an inference that this individual, who shows test behavior commonly associated with a particular psychiatric category, *may* also belong to that category. However, since each nosological category is, itself, quite heterogeneous, and since even configurations of test phenomena may result from varying causes, the clinician will wish to explore the basis for the particular configurational finding. The essential test of the validity of any configurational pattern in discriminating between nosological categories is not whether all individuals who show that configuration fall within a given psychiatric group, but whether groups of individuals classified within a given psychiatric category are significantly distinguishable from other psychiatric groups in terms of that configuration. There have been many studies attesting to the great diversity within the category of so-called schizophrenia. There is considerable evidence that individuals with the same or similar organic brain damage differ in their behavior responses. Neuroses and character disorders are even more heterogeneous in terms of underlying pathologies. Nevertheless, if nosological categories have any merit, it is because they manifest, in each instance, some common attributes. The configuration on test phenomena assumes that, *as a group,* people are distinguishable from other people who show another configuration on the test. The configurations that we shall present serve this function. They have met the tests of clinical experience and research validation.

The following sets of configurations constitute a third revision based on reported findings in the literature and further validation against the author's own research data. The normative groups, matched for age and sex, consisted of the following: outpatient neurotics (N = 150); chronic schizophrenics (N = 155); unipolar depressives (N = 68); organic brain-damaged patients (N = 150) and normals (N = 140). The mean age for the total population was 30 years and 3 months. The groups varied somewhat in highest mean educational grade level, the lowest being the schizophrenic population (with a mean grade of 7.8) and the highest being the outpatient population (with a mean grade of 10.7). Our research findings indicate that grade level in adults is not significantly correlated with psychopathology score (Hutt & Miller, 1976).

It will be noted that each factor in the configuration is given a weight of either 1 or 2. These weights were assigned empirically on the basis of the discriminatory capacity of the component. The score for a given configuration is simply the total of the scores obtained on the relevant components. We also indicate the *marginal and critical* scores for each configuration. If an individual's score for a given configuration falls within the marginal range, his assignment to that nosological category should be regarded as questionable even though further clinical study may, indeed, indicate that he belongs to that category. If, on the other hand, his score falls within the range of critical scores for that configuration, his *statistical* placement in that category is quite probable. Even so, as we have indicated, the clinician will wish to test the significance of the findings by means of what we have called Testing-the-Limits. This procedure is especially relevant with subjects whose configuration scores suggest that they have organic brain damage. Not only will such procedures help to validate the diagnostic categorization, but they will assist in defining the nature of the organic defect; i.e., difficulties in spatial perceptions are related to defects of the parietal area of the brain; difficulties in motor coordination are related to defects in the motor or frontal area.

Previous studies that have attempted to evaluate the effectiveness of configurational analysis and of the relative merits of clinical versus actuarial analysis of Bender-Gestalt records have been inconsistent in their findings. An older study (Goldberg, 1959) showed that clinicians were better able to differentiate organic from nonorganic Bender records than chance expectancy, but that the Pacal-Suttell scores gave better differentiation. There were two interesting aspects to this study. One was that more experienced raters were less confident in their judgments than less experienced raters, but obtained better (more correct) results. The other was that the most experienced rater (the present writer), who was the least confident, but who took the most time in examining and evaluating the records, obtained better results than any of the other judges or the Pascal-Suttell scores, obtaining a "diagnostic hit rate" of 83%! The probable reason for this finding is that the "expert" was not only more experienced, but took into careful consideration both the "signs" of organicity and the inconsistencies in the records, thus tending to eliminate false positives of "doubtful" organics were classified as organics when the configuration showed some strong, but insufficient organic characteristics. In other words, configurational analysis can be improved in effectiveness when it is buttressed by careful, painstaking evaluation of the nature of the findings. The author feels quite sure that success in differentiating organics from nonorganics could be significantly improved if Testing-the-Limits were included in the total procedure.

Another study, by Bruhn and Reed (1975), posed the problem of differentiating 20 nonorganic college students who attempted to simulate brain damage in their Bender records from 33 organic patients. In this study the Pascal-Suttell score did not differentiate the two groups, but a certified clinical psychologist was able to do so with 89% accuracy. In a cross-validation study by the same authors, they found that clinicians, utilizing the findings from the pilot study, were able to identify all of the malingerers correctly.

In contrast, there is the study by Lyle and Quast (1976). Their subjects were in the age range 15–20 years. Using recall scores, they investigated their efficacy in separting three groups: those subjects who were showing symptoms of Huntington's disease ($N = 21$); those subjects who developed Huntington's disease after the Bender-Gestalt Test had been administered ($N = 22$); and those subjects whose parents had had Huntington's disease but who were themselves free of such symptoms ($N = 46$). Clinicians were also asked to separate the records into the three groups. In general, successful placements by the two methods were about the same, both methods achieving only about 67%–68% accuracy of placement. It should be noted, however, that the rationale for separating the three groups is quite questionable. Moreover, clinicians were not told to look for signs of Huntington's disease, but were asked to evaluate for organicity. The study leaves many unanswered questions, such as how much experience did the clinicians have with organic Bender records, how much did they know about Huntington's disease, and how different were the three groups, in actual fact, with respect to organicity? Finally, recall scores, as derived and used in a global fashion (i.e., simply the number of correctly recalled designs) are not necessarily related to organicity, much less to finely differentiated nuances between subjects who would later develop Huntington's disease, but had not as yet manifested the disease, and those who were already showing overt symptoms of the disease.

The fact that configurational scoring can be quite effective in differentiating *some groups* was demonstrated in two studies. Bilu and Weiss (1974), using a configuration involving seven components, were able to differentiate 81 inpatient psychotics from 81 outpatient nonpsychotics with reasonable accuracy and effectiveness. Johnson (1973), using configurational indicators of depression, was able to find significant results with this method. Even a single specific indicator can sometimes be used to highlight a particular psychiatric condition, as Donnelly and Murphy (1974) did in finding that irregular sequence was associated with lack of impulse control in bipolar depressives, while overly methodical sequence was associated with overly methodical impulse (or constriction) in unipolar depressives.

Both Lacks (1984) and Marley (1982) report that Hutt's "old" configurations, using 12 test factors in Lacks' studies and less than 12 (plus other factors and "recall") in Marley's publication, were highly effective in differentiating patients with organic brain damage from other patient groups. Lack utilized the Orthopsychiatric cards, while Marley used her own modification (not completely specified) of these cards. Our "configurations" and weights are based *on the HABGT cards,* which may produce more errors by patients than were found in these other studies.

Our own data, utilizing the revised Configurations that follow, produced the following findings: critical scores differentiated normals and neurotics from schizophrenics and organics at the .001 level or better; all differences of depressives, schizophrenics and organics from each other were at the .01 level or better. Thus, for psychiatric, nosological placement, the critical scores for each nosological category, with the exception or the "mentally retarded," can be used for screening purposes with reasonable accuracy. We shall comment, later, on the mentally retarded category.

In scoring for Configurational Analysis, utilize the definitions and scores from the Psychopathology Scale. *Only the Copy Phase of the test is used in configurational scoring.* To test for the subject's inclusion in a particular configuration *only those factors in the configuration* need to be scored. Thus, for Organic Brain Damage, only 8 factors need be scored. Line incoordination, as defined in Chapter 8 need not be scored, but can be evaluated in terms of the definition that is described.

Organic Brain Damage

In utilizing the following configurational phenomena, it should be emphasized that such factors as age at the time of the injury or disease, severity of brain damage, degree of localization, and laterality of the damage, as well as the personality of the individual, will affect the findings. The relevant factors and their weights are listed in Table 5.1.

There are other test indicators of possible organic brain damage. One of the most important behavioral manifestations is the subject's manifestation of impotence or great difficulty in perceiving or executing the design. He may also show evidence of this characteristic by redrawing part or all of the figure one or more times. Other subjects will begin to doodle or produce elaborations. Still others will "concretize" the drawings by making them into a real object rather than a design. However, none of these indicators showed adequate power to differentiate this group from other groups on a statistical basis.

Both Marley (1982) and Lacks (1984) found that the time taken by a subject, if especially long, was indicative of possible OBS. Although this observation is accurate, our data do not justify its inclusion in our configurational schemata. Some organic brain damaged patients do take an inordinate amount of time to complete their reproductions. This is typically an indication of their perceptual-figure ground difficulties and is an indication of their feeling of *impotence* in completing the task. Such patients may

Table 5.1
Organic Brain Damage

PS #	Test Factor & Score	Weight	Frequency %
4	Collion, moderate (8.5)	2	61
9	Angulation, 4 figures (8.0)	2	45
10	Rotation, severe (10.0)	2	29
12	Simplification, severe (10.0)	2	48
13	Fragmentation, severe (10.0)	2	21
14	Overlapping, severe (10.0)	2	38
16	Perseveration, moderate (7.0)	2	58
6	Closure difficulty, severe (7.0)	1	70
*	Line incoordination	1	61

Critical scores: 10 and above
Marginal scores: 7–9

* See discussion in Chapter 8.
Some of the phenomena, as scored in table 5.1, such as rotation, fragmentation, and overlapping, occur relatively infrequently, but when they do occur they are likely to be highly pathognomic.

take more than 20 minutes to complete the Copy Phase of the test. When this is observed by the examiner it should certainly be taken into account in evaluation of the patient. However, it should be noted that many obsessive-compulsive patients also take an inordinate amount of time with the task, reflecting in such cases their "perfectionism" or blocking. The clinician will easily be able to determine whether the subject is showing such personality characteristics or, as in the case of OBS conditions, is showing feelings of impotence.

The Schizophrenias

Our criterion population, on which this configuration is based, consisted of 155 chronic (process) schizophrenics. The vast majority of these *hospitalized* patients were categorized as either paranoids or as mixed types of schizophrenias (79%). There were 92 males and 63 females in the group.

Of course, as is well known, schizophrenics are an extremely heterogeneous population, and vary considerably in the severity of their psychopathology. Hence, careful clinical study as well as "screening" are usually indicated.

Sometimes an individual indicator in Table 5.2 is highly pathognomic of schizophrenia, as when extreme elaboration (indicative of delusional thinking), or when extreme crowding of the 9 figures into a small section of one page, or when placement of the first figure is highly unusual (such as placement in the lower right corner of the page) is manifest. In such

Table 5.2
The Schizophrenias

PS #	Test Factor & Score	Weight	Frequency %
1	Confused/Symbolic sequence (10.0)	2	21
2	Abn. placement, 1st figure (10.0)	2	23
3	Space: abnormal (10.0)	1	18
6	Closure, severe (7.75)	1	61
8	Curvature, severe (10.0)	1	45
10	Rotation, moderate (7.0)	1	18
11	Retrogression, moderate (7.0)	2	32
12	Simplification, moderate (7.0)	1	27
13	Fragmentation, moderate (7.0)	1	15
15	Elaboration, moderate (7.0)	2	18

Critical scores: 7 and above
Marginal scores: 4–6

instances, even when the total configuration score is relatively low, the clinician will suspect some severe psychopathology.

Unipolar Depression

This particular configuration was derived from a population of 68 hospitalized patients diagnosed as having unipolar depression. The configuration for bipolar depressives is not presented at this time since our sample of such patients is limited. Moreover, many bipolar depressives subsequently develop some form of schizophrenia, and in our experience are not clearly distinguishable from that category. There were 32 females and 36 males in our sample (Table 5.3).

Table 5.3
Unipolar Depression

PS #	Test Factor and Score	Weight	Frequency %
1	Overly methodical sequence (4.0)	2	32
*	Severe compression of space, 4/more figures	2	22
7	Severe crossing difficulty (10.0)	1	17
8	Curvature, severe (Flat) (10.0)	2	38
9	Angulation, severe (increased) (10.0)	1	17

Critical scores: 6 and above
Marginal scores: 4–5

* See chapter 8 for definition.

It should be noted that critical scores discriminated 73% of unipolar depressives accurately.

Table 5.4
Essential Psychoneuroses

PS #	Test Factor & Scores	Weight	Frequency %
1	Irregular/methodical sequence (4.0)	2	20
7	Crossing difficulty, mod. (7.0)	2	19
8	Curvature diff., moderate (7.0)	1	36
9	Angulation diff., mild (6.0)	2	27
*	Isolated changes, size, moderate	2	37
*	Inconsistent/uneven lines	1	22
*	Constriction in size, severe	2	24
*	Excessive use of margin	2	33
*	Inconsistent direction of movement, marked	1	12

Critical scores: 8 or above
Marginal scores: 4–7

* See Chapter 8.
Critical scores correctly identified 73% of our neurotic group.

Essential Psychoneuroses

Neuroses differ markedly in severity and type. Our sample of 150 patients is based on nonhospitalized or outpatient neurotics of whom 81 were females and 69 were males. Patients with clearly diagnosable character disturbances were excluded. The test protocols of these patients only very infrequently showed gross test disturbances such as destruction of the Gestalt or elaborations. Rather, they presented an accumulation of relatively minor changes in some aspects of the designs or their placement (Table 5.4).

Mental Retardation, Moderate and Severe

Mental retardation at these levels may be the consequence of many interrelated factors, including genetic and constitutional factors, severe social–cultural deprivation, and severe emotional maladjustment. Unlike cases with profound mental retardation, organic brain damage is less likely to be evident (Hutt & Gibby, 1976).

It might be added that moderately and severely mentally retarded *adults* rarely execute figures 7 and 8 successfully. Adequate completion of these designs should make the clinician wary of concluding that the individual is, in fact, mentally retarded. A special problem that the clinician will wish to take into account in evaluating HABGT records is the quality of motivation. Sometimes subjects will do less well than they could because of low aspiration level (Table 5.5).

Table 5.5
Moderate and Severe Mental Retardation

PS #	Test Factor and Scores	Weight	Frequency %
1	Irregular sequence (7.0)	2	67
4	Collision tendency (4.0)	1	36
6	Closure difficulty, severe (10.0)	2	59
10	Perceptual reversal (180) (10.0)	2	30
13	Fragmentation, figs. 7,8 (10.0)	2	49
14	Overlapping difficulty, moderate (5.5)	2	36
*	Very irreg, spacing of figures	2	38
*	Increasing diff., figs 5, 6, 7, & 8.	2	73

Critical scores: 8 and above
Marginal scores: 5–7

* See Chapter 8 for definitions.
When an adult subject can reproduce the simpler figures but shows great difficulty with the more difficult figures, the most likely inference is that lack of mental maturity is causing the difficulty.

Emotional Disturbance in Adolescence

Through the kind cooperation of Sylvia Monheit, a random sample of her "normal" and "severely emotionally disturbed" male adolescents was obtained (1983). These populations, ranging in age from 12 years 9 months to 16 years 3 months were fairly evenly distributed among the several age groups. Blacks and white pupils were approximately equal in numbers, and a small sampling of Hispanics (12%) as well as scattered samples of other ethnic minorities were included. All children were American born and lived in San Francisco. The Copy Phase of the HABGT (Orthopsychiatric cards) was scored on the Configurational Schema presented in Table 5.6.

Table 5.6
Emotional Disturbance in Adolescents

PS #	Test Factor and Score	Weight
1	Sequence (4.0)	2
2	Position 1st Figure, Abnormal (10.0)	1
*	Position 1st Figure, Central Placement	1
3	Use of Space (10.0)	2
6	Closure Difficulty (7.75)	2
9	Angulation (6.0)	2
11	Retrogression (7.0)	2
14	Overlapping (5/5)	2

* See Chapter 8 for definitions.

It should be noted that "normals were defined by teacher judgments and excluded those with acting-out behavior or unverified absence from school. These children had passing grades in school and met the criteria of a check-list (Byrd, 1956). Those with records of organic or neurological problems were excluded. The emotionally disturbed children were selected on the basis of professional evaluations (psychiatrist or psychologist), and among other criteria, had manifested (for at least six months) at least two of the following characteristics: pervasive inability to learn, unsatisfactory interpersonal relationships, bizarre affect or behavior, pervasive depression or lability, persistent psychosomatic symptoms, or severe disturbance in thought processes. Thus, this groups was presumably *severely disturbed.*

A preliminary analysis of the Configurational Scores of 40 "normals" and 40 "disturbed" pupils revealed the following. Mean scores and SDs were: 3.95 ± 2.40 for "normals"; and, 11.225 ± 2.44 "disturbed." The SD of the difference in means is 3.42, significant beyond the .001 level! Moreover, only 7.5% of the "normals" obtained scores above 6 while 95.0% of the "disturbed" had scores above 6.

We have, therefore, tentatively established the following criteria Configurational scoring:

Marginal Scores   = 7–8
Critical Score   = 9 and above

The Critical Score on this configuration yields no false positives for "normals" and correctly identifies 82.5% of the "emotionally disturbed" group.*

Although these findings are highly significant, they need further confirmation. Moreover, it should be remembered that the "disturbed" group presumably included the most severely disturbed youngsters, including cases of psychosis, depression, and borderline personality. Hence, the diagnostic efficiency of this configuration would be expected to be somewhat lower for less "disturbed" pupils. Nevertheless, as a *screening procedure,* the Configuration seems to have considerable promise.

It is, of course, worth noting that when the test protocol of an adolescent manifests *any of the test indicators of destruction of the Gestalt* (such as simplification, fragmentation, retrogression, and perseveration), one should be alert to the presence of severe psychopathology and check the record further. Indeed, Monheit, in a personal note to the writer, commented that 23 of the 40 severely disturbed subjects showed "fragmentation" (57.7%), but *none* of the "normals" showed this phenome-

---

* For an extended discussion of the full findings of this study, see Hutt, M. L. & Manheit, S., 1985. *Psychological Reports,* in press.

non. Typically, however, one does not find such a high percentage of records with fragmentation (a highly pathological indicator) in an unselected group of either adult psychiatric patients or adolescent psychiatric patients. Further study is needed to determine what kinds of adolescent disturbances manifest such severe distortions in HABGT records. Finally, it should be noted, also, that the findings presented in this section are *not* based on the HABGT test cards.

6

The Adience-Abience Scale and Psychopathology

The Adience–Abience Scale represents an attempt to measure a basic characteristic of the individual's perceptual orientation toward the world. The concept of adience–abience, and its preliminary measuring device, were first introduced by the writer in 1960 (Hutt & Briskin, 1960). The concept was further elaborated in a research study some years later (Hutt & Feuerefile, 1963) and in the earlier edition of this book (Hutt, 1969a).

Perceptual adience–abience is conceived as a primary defensive operation of the personality. People differ markedly in their perceptual "openness" or "closedness" (perceptual approach–avoidance) to the world. It is believed that as a consequence of favorable perceptual contact with the world, on the one hand, or of unfavorable or traumatic experience, on the other, the young infant, and later the child, tends to develop either an approach-oriented position or an avoidance-oriented position, respectively, in his perceptual interactions with the external and his internal world. This aspect of perceptual style is thought to be the primary mode of a mediating experience and serves as a foundation for the later development of other defensive and coping operations of the personality. It is assumed that once such a style has begun to develop, it tends to become self-reinforcing. Therefore, it persists unless dramatic circumstances cause it to change. It is inferred that adient individuals are more likely to be open to new varieties of learning experience and can profit from them more than others, whereas abient individuals tend to block out new experiences and profit less from such exposures. This perceptual, personality style is *not* assumed to be coordinate with other aspects of approach–avoidance behaviors, such as extroversive tendencies or aggressiveness in overt behavior.

Although we expect that other aspects of defensive behavior may be correlated with abient tendencies, we also see significant differences. Perceptual vigilance (Postman, 1953), for example, is conceived to be a defense by the person, which enables him to alter his behavior *after* he has perceived a "danger," whereas perceptual abience blocks the person's awareness from receiving perceptual input. Field dependence (Witkin, Dyke, Faterson, Goodenough, & Karp, 1967) may also be related to perceptual abience, but it defines a defensive style of being overly reliant on the visual field, whereas abience, again, is a blocking of that visual field. Other defensive, perceptual concepts have been proposed by Sullivan (1953) (selective attention), Jung (1939) (introversion), Guilford (1959) (experimentally derived measures of introversion), Schachtel (1959) (autocentrism), Gardner and Long (1960) (leveling–sharpening), and Petrie (1967) (augmentation–reduction). All of these have in common some defensive operation manifested in the perceptual response after the stimulus has been perceived. In contrast, the concept of adience–abience relates to a *failure of the organism to process the visual input,* i.e., unawareness (more or less) that a visual stimulus is present (VonBékésy, 1967). Based on our view of present knowledge concerning the other types of defenses, we believe that these are secondary phenomena, i.e., reactive. In contrast, our conception of perceptual adience–abience is perhaps closest to the concept of Schneirla (1959) who in an intensive review of the development of what he terms underlying "biphasic" processes of approach-withdrawal in behavior stated: "Much evidence shows that in *all* animals the species-typical pattern of behavior is based upon biphasic, functionally opposed mechanisms insuring approach or withdrawal reactions according to whether stimuli of low or high intensity, respectively, are in effect."

We have sketched the probable significance of adience–abience phenomena in relation to child development (Hutt, 1976a) and mental retardation (Hutt, 1976b), and in our review of the research evidence, below, we shall comment about this.

The derivation of the items of the Adience–Abience Scale came from extensive experience with the HABGT with a great variety of clinical patients. It was observed that certain types of test behavior were related to certain types of personality constellations. The first scale developed for the purpose of measuring adience–abience rested on these observations and on test factors that were being employed in the Psychopathology Scale. However, the definitions and measuring units of the Adience–

Abience Scale were *differentiated from and weighted differently than* similar items of the other scale. Based upon further clinical experience, tested through various research studies, the scale has been revised so that we now have the Scale for Perceptual Adience–Abience, 2nd revision. We shall now present this scale and then discuss normative findings, research evaluations, and implications for use.

Scale for Perceptual Adience–Abience
2nd Revision*

General Directions

1. Use the Copy Phase text protocol based on the HABGT test cards, and score the drawings for each of the following factors by circling the weight that is appropriate for that factor.† When none of the definitions apply, the weight of that factor is 0.
2. When scorable, each factor is assigned a weight from +2(high adience) to −2 (high abience).
3. The uncorrected score is the algebraic sum of the circled scores.
4. The *Corrected Adience–Abience Score* is obtained by adding +25 to the uncorrected score. The range in Corrected Scores is from +1 to +38; high scores reflect high degrees of adience while low scores reflect high degrees of abience.
5. For Factors 1 and 2, use either the Scoring Template or Table 1 in this volume.

Factors Relating to Space and Size

1. *Height and Width*
   a. There are *no* instances in which *either* height or width is *less* than   +1
       the limits indicated.
   b. There are *1 or 2* instances in which *either* height or width is *less*   0
       than the limits indicated.
   c. There are *3 or more* instances in which *either* height or width is   −2
       less than the limits indicated.
2. *Height, Only*
   a. There are *no* instances in which height is *less* than the limits   +1
       indicated.
   b. There is *only 1* instance in which height is *less* than the limits   −1
       indicated.
   c. There is *more than 1 instance* in which the height is *less* than the   −2
       limits indicated.

---

* This Scale is reproduced in the *HABGT Revised Record Form,*
3rd edition, published by Grune & Stratton, Inc.
   † These definitions differ in some important respects from those applicable to the Psychopathology Scale. Use these definitions, only, for this scale.

Scale for Perceptual Adience–Abience
2nd Revision*

---

3. *Use of Page* (Calculated by imagining a line drawn around all of the drawings and estimating the amount of space utilized in the drawings.)
    a. Uses *more* than three-fourths of the page, and *no more* than 3 +2
        figures are within 1 inch of the left margin of the page.
    b. Uses *more* than three-fourths of the page, but *more* than 3 figures +1
        are within 1 inch of the left margin of the page.
    c. Uses *less* than three-fourths of the page, but *no more* than 3 fig- −1
        ures are within 1 inch of the left margin of the page.
    d. Uses *less* than three-fourths of the page, and *more* than 3 figures −2
        are within 1 inch of the left margin of the page.

Factors Relating to Organization

4. *Sequence* (Defined as a shift in the direction of successive placements of the figures; i.e., when successive placements have been from left to right, a shift occurs when the next figure is placed above, below, or to the left of the preceding figure, etc. When the edge of the paper has been reached the next placement would normally be at the opposite side of the page—as if the page were a sphere.)
    a. Methodical sequence: less than 3 shifts. +1
    b. Irregular or confused sequence: it is *irregular* when 3 or more −2
        shifts occur; it is *confused* when there is an obvious jumble in
        placement and no apparent plan is evident.
5. *Placement of First Figure*
    a. Normal placement: at least 1 inch from the top and left edges of +2
        the page, and not otherwise an abnormal placement.
    b. Normal placement: between ¾ and 1 inch from the top of the page, +1
        and at least 1 inch from the left edge of the page, but not otherwise
        an abnormal placement.
    c. Abnormal placement: less than ¾ inch from the top edge, or less −1
        than 1 inch from the left edge, but not below the upper half of the
        page.
    d. Abnormal placement: center of figure is within 1 inch of the center −2
        of the page, or below the upper half of the page.

Factors Related to Change in Form of Gestalt

6. *Closure Difficulty* (Defined as an obvious failure in accurate closure within a figure or at the joining of contiguous figures. In the case of circles, for example, there is a gap in the closing of the circle, or an overshooting of the closing; in the case of straight-line figures, the joining at an apex is unclosed or overshot; in contiguous figures, there is a gap or overshooting at the junction of the figures. *Score only for figures A, 2, 4, 7, and 8.* Note: *no more than 2 closure difficulties* are counted for a single figure, and on figure 2,

Scale for Perceptual Adience–Abience
2nd Revision*

count 2 closure difficulties as a score of 1, and more than 2 difficulties as a score of 2.)

   a. Normal closure difficulty: 5 or less closure difficulties.   +1

   b. Moderate closure difficulty: between 6 and 8 closure difficulties. −1

   c. Severe closure difficulty: 9 or more closure difficulties.   −2

7. *Crossing Difficulty* (Defined as any obvious difficulty in the crossing on figures 6 and 7, manifested by redrawing, sketching, erasing, or increased line pressure where the lines cross. On figure 6, when the two curves do not cross cleanly—as when there is a merging of the two lines—this is counted as a crossing difficulty, but when the two curves are drawn as tangential, this is *not* counted as crossing difficulty. Note: there may be two instances of crossing difficulty on figure 7.)

   a. No crossing difficulty.   +1

   b. Moderate crossing difficulty: only 1 instance.   −1

   c. Marked crossing difficulty: two or more instances.   −2

8. *Change in Angulation* (Defined as a shift of *15 degrees or more* of the angulation *within* the figure, e.g., when the columns of figure 2 are shifted toward the upright or toward the horizontal. *Score only on figures 2, 3, 5, 6, and 7.* Use the Scoring Template, using the central axis of each figure as the referent. *Increased* angulation means that the angle within the figure has been made more *acute; decreased* angulation means that the angle within the figure has been made more *rectangular,* e.g., when the secant on figure 5 has been shifted toward the upright position, or when the left-hand figure in design 7 has been shifted toward the horizon.)

   a. No instance of either increased or decreased angulation.   +2

   b. Increased angulation: present on only 1 figure, and there is no +1 instance of decreased angulation.

   c. Excessive increased angulation: present on more than 1 figure, but 0 there is no instance of decreased angulation.

   d. Decreased angulation: present on only 1 figure, and there is no −1 instance of increased angulation.

   e. Excessive decreased angulation: present on more than 1 figure, −2 and there is no instance of increased angulation.

Factors Related to Distortion

9. *Rotation* (Defined as a shift in the axis of *the total figure*—not the paper—from the standard orientation of the card).

   a. Absent or mild: no rotation of more than 14 degrees.   +1

   b. Moderate: any rotation of 15-79 degrees.   −1

   c. Severe: any rotation of 80 degrees or more.   −2

Scale for Perceptual Adience–Abience
2nd Revision*

10. *Fragmentation* (Defined as the breaking of the Gestalt into component parts or the *gross separation* of the 2 parts of the figure as in figures A, 4, and 7).
   a. No fragmentation present.   +1
   b. Fragmentation on only 1 figure.   −1
   c. Marked fragmentation: present on 2 or more figures   −2
11. *Simplification* (Defined as the use of a "substitute figure" which is simpler to draw—e.g., the substitution of a rectangle for a hexagon in figure 7—other than by fragmentation or by making symmetrical figures out of asymmetrical ones.)
   a. No simplification present.   0
   b. Moderate simplification: present on only 1 figure.   −1
   c. Marked simplification: present on 2 or more figures.   −2
12. *Elaboration* (Defined an any obvious elaboration or doodling).
   a. No elaboration present.   0
   b. Elaboration present on 1 or more figures.   −2

Normative Findings

At present we have fairly well-established norms on adience–abience for adults, based on slightly more than 500 cases, and these are presented in Table 6.1. Our norms for older children are based on a much more restricted sample and are presented in Table 6.2 as tentative norms for these groups.

It will be noted that there is a steady decrease in the mean Adience–Abience Scale scores as one proceeds down the table from "normals" to organic brain-damaged cases, while the standard deviations increase through the same progression. The differences between each of the pairs of means reaches a *p* value of .001 or better. Thus the adience–abience score is able to differentiate quite satisfactorily among these groups. Tests

Table 6.1
Normative Data for the
Adience–Abience Scale, 2nd Revision

Group	N	Mean	SD
Normals	140	25.8	3.5
Outpatient neurotics	125	23.8	3.6
Inpatient neurotics	55	21.0	3.8
Chronic schizophrenics	155	18.3	5.1
Organic brain damage	98	15.1	6.2

Table 6.2
Tentative Normative Data for the
Adience–Abience Scale: Children

Group	CA Range (years)	N	Mean	SD
Normals*	10–12	102	21.3	3.9
Disturbed*	10–12	109	18.2	4.1
Boys' Club**	10–16	120	17.7	2.6

* These populations are described in connection with Table 4.3.
** These cases were drawn from Project Gamit, a research project in connection with the Boys' Club of Royal Oak, Mich., which is, as yet, unpublished.

were run to determine the relevance of chronological age and sex in relation to these scores. For all of the subpopulations both age and sex were insignificantly related ($p < .01$). The only group for whom we had data on education was a population of outpatients being treated at the Psychology Clinic of the University of Detroit. Utilizing highest grade achieved as a rough indication of "intelligence," it was found that the correlation of Adience–Abience score with educational grade was .052 ($p < .001$; $N = 100$). Thus, we can suggest that for this group, at least, intelligence, as estimated, is unrelated to the Adience–Abience score.

We have lumped the age groups since we have no reason to believe that age, within this range, significantly affects Adience–Abience score. (See later discussion.) The large majority of the Boys/Girls Club children were in the 11–13 age categories; most of these children had been referred to the Club in connection with delinquent acts against persons or property.

The norm for Adience–Abience for "normals" is comparable to that of inpatient neurotic adults reported in Table 6.1; it is 4.5 points lower than the norm for "normal" adults. Hence different norms are justifiable for children. The differences between the "normal" children and each of the problem populations of children are significant at the .001 level. The difference between the norms for the "disturbed" and "Boys/Girls Club" groups is statistically insignificant ($p < .05$), if we demand a higher order of probability.

Clinical experience has suggested that the higher the Adience–Abience score the more likely, other things being equal, that the child will be able to profit from a large variety of "learning" or "therapeutic" experiences. If the score is above 21 on the revised scale, the chances are good that significant improvement may be expected. The meaning of scores for children below 10 years of age remains to be explored, and great care should be taken in attempting to extrapolate from these findings to younger groups.

Research Findings

Let us consider aspects of the reliability of the Adience–Abience Scale. In one study, a rho of .912 was obtained for scores obtained with two judges, one experienced in scoring and the other relatively inexperienced, for a sample of schizophrenic patients (Hutt & Miller, 1975). Other studies, in progress, reveal comparable results, the lowest interjudge correlation obtained being .90 and the highest .94. We can conclude that objectivity in scoring is fairly high. With regard to test–retest reliability there are more extensive data. In the same study noted above, test–retest correlations, over an interval of two weeks, for each of two different groups were found to be .84. Moreover, the four major components of the scale also proved to be quite reliable, the highest reliability being found for the component of "Organization" and the lowest for "Form of Gestalt." In the Gamit project (Hutt & Dates, 1977), with 120 cases, test–retest results over a 40-week period of time yielded an r of .968 ($N = 120$) for children in the age range 10–16 years. Only four cases showed what would be judged to be a significant shift in adience–abience position on a clinical basis.

The problem of validity is, of course, a much more complicated one and demands difficult criteria for meaningful evaluation. We shall present summaries of a number of studies on this score, treating them in a historical perspective.

Our first study, part of the development of the original scale, was done on a population of deaf–retardates. In this study (Hutt & Feuerefile, 1963), a preliminary analysis and a cross-validation analysis were performed. In the preliminary study, 30 cases were selected randomly from the total population of approximately 200 patients. The copy phase of the HABGT records of these individuals were then scored in terms of the preliminary form of the Adience–Abience Scale, and these records were then dichotomized into two groups: 15 cases relatively high in adience and 15 cases relatively high in abience. In order to test the construct validity of the adience–abience measure, these two groups were compared on six criteria, presumably related to the general hypothesis that more adient individuals would show more effective intellectual and interpersonal functioning than those who were higher on the abient end of the scale. It must be remembered that we were dealing with a highly selected population at the lower end of the intelligence scale, and that this fact would tend to attenuate possible positive findings. Despite such limitations, all but one

Table 6.3
A Comparison of Individuals Who Differ in Adience–Abience,
Based on Six Criterion Variables*

Criterion Variable	High Adient Group (N = 15)	High Abient Group (N = 15)	t	p (one-tail)
HABGT score on Psychopathology	70.1	130.4	13.33	<.01
Rating on Psychopathology	2.0	3.2	3.33	<.01
Goodenough I.Q.	70.6	44.9	4.33	<.01
Rating of intellectual impairment	3.1	4.1	2.86	<.01
Age at admission to hospital (months)	175.9	120.6	2.24	<.02
Length of hospitalization	112.1	147.8	1.20	>.05

* For all personality variables, higher scores indicate greater degree of psychopathology.

of the tests turned out to be quite significant, as the data in Table 6.3 indicate.

All of the differences are in the expected direction, but one (length of hospitalization) does not reach a frequently accepted level of statistical significance. The data indicate that our measure of adience–abience does discriminate, for this highly restricted group, along the lines of our *a priori* conceptualization. Adience is apparently related to more effective adjustment and one can infer that it is related to capacity for making more effective use of one's experience.

In the cross-validation study, the remainder of the experimental population was utilized. Four of the criterion variables used in the phase of the study were retained, and three were added, but our analysis will be limited to two of these three additional criteria (since one is not directly pertinent to our present discussion). Moreover, separate analyses are presented for males and females, since (1) other data from this research project indicated that females tended to show more psychopathology than males, and (2) there were differences in adience–abience scores between females and males for this population. A revised form of the adience–abience scale was used. An additional test was made for the possible relationship between age and adience–abience score. A correlation of .09 was obtained between these variables, which is not statistically signifi-

Table 6.4

Adience–Abience Means and Differences for Extreme
Groups on Six Criterion Variables

Variable	Sex	Mean, High Group	Mean, Low Group	t	p (one-tail)
Rating on	M	14.6 (16)*	17.3 (16)	2.39	<.02
Psychopathology	F	12.3 (10)	15.9 (10)	2.04	<.05
Goodenough I.Q.	M	21.5 (16)	11.4 (16)	4.41	<.01
	F	16.4 (12)	8.6 (12)	3.63	<.01
Rating, on	M	14.7 (18)	14.8 (18)	.14	>.25
intellectual	F	9.9 (10)	14.4 (10)	3.21	<.01
impairment					
Age at admission	M	16.4 (23)	12.5 (23)	2.68	<.01
to hospital	F	17.3 (13)	8.5 (13)	4.90	<.01
Wechsler	M	20.4 (15)	11.2 (15)	4.47	<.01
performance I. Q.	F	16.6 (11)	9.0 (11)	3.76	<.01
Rating on overt	M	22.6 (23)	15.0 (23)	3.45	<.01
hostility	F	13.9 (13)	12.0 (13)	.95	>.05

* Numbers in parentheses represent the N in each group.

cant. In the present analysis we compare the means in corrected adience–
abience scores of the groups of males and females who lie within the
upper 25% of the distribution on each of the criterion variables, since
some of these variables are either noncontinuous or are not normally
distributed. Table 6.4 presents our findings.

As predicted, individuals who are high in ratings on psychopathology
tend to be more abient than those who are low in such ratings, the differences being considered significant in view of the limited validity of the
psychopathology ratings. As predicted, adience is associated with better
intellectual performance, on both the Goodenough and the Wechsler
scales, the findings being highly significant. We did not obtain a significant
difference for males on the rating of intellectual impairment, but did for
females. This discrepancy is consistent with the impressions of the clinical staff of the deaf–retarded project that the male population was far less
impaired in intellectual functioning than the female population, and ratings of males had lower reliability. It is apparent that age of admission is
highly significant in relation to adience–abience in the expected direction:
those who were institutionalized earlier were more abient. Our findings on
ratings of hostility are difficult to interpret, not only because they are
inconsistent, but also because this criterion variable turned out to have
very limited validity, as judged by other data obtained in the research
project.

There is apparently some degree of commonality between our measure of adience–abience, on the one hand, and psychopathology and intelligence on the other. A correlation of .69 was obtained for 114 cases between our HABGT score on the psychopathology Scale and on the Adience–Abience Scale. This is not inconsistent with our conceptualization that abient individuals would tend to be more maladjusted. However, there is still sufficient noncommonality to make these measures separately meaningful. Various correlations between measures of intelligence, ranging from .28 to .73, were obtained for different samplings of this population. Again, we would expect that individuals who were higher in adience would tend to rate and function as more intelligent, or be less impaired intellectually, other things being equal. There is sufficient noncommonality between such measures, however, to indicate that somewhat different functions are being tapped.

All in all, the findings from both phases of the deaf-retarded study suggest that the Adience–Abience Scale enables us to make at least roughly accurate predictions in terms of our major hypothesis, and that therefore this scale has significant possibilities.

Other tests of the scale's predictive potential were made and will be reported briefly, as suggestive rather than conclusive. The interested reader will wish to examine the data in research publications that are being prepared.

The first of these concerned the prediction of "movement" in psychotherapy. It was hypothesized that those who were higher in adience, as measured, would tend to make greater improvement from dynamically oriented, uncovering therapy, than those who were higher in abience. From our own population of psychotherapy cases, we selected those individuals, ranging in age from 18 to 35 years at the beginning of therapy, on whom we had ratings of degree of therapeutic change. There were 42 such cases in all. All of these had been given the HABGT during the early stages of the therapeutic program. The rating scale involved global judgments concerning: symptomatic improvement, ego functioning, degree of maturity, and absence of pathological anxiety. Each of these was rated on a 7-point scale and the scores were then averaged. The Adience–Abience Scale scores were obtained independently of any knowledge of these ratings so as to avoid possible contamination. Our test of the efficacy of the adience–abience measure was its capacity to discriminate between the upper third and the lower third ($N = 14$ in each group) in overall psychotherapeutic change, as rated. The findings are presented in Table 6.5.

This significant finding is limited by many considerations. No attempt was made to control for other factors than those already noted, such as initial degree of psychopathology, motivation for therapeutic change, age,

Table 6.5
Means and p Values for
Adience–Abience
Scores of Two Extreme Groups
Differing in Therapeutic Change

Group (N = 14 each)	Mean Score
High in change	29.7
Low in change	23.9
p (one-tail) for mean difference = .01	

etc. The distribution by sex in the two groups was roughly equal, with 8 females in the high group and 7 females in the low group. What appears to indicate promise for the measure of adience–abience is that it discriminated effectively between these two "extreme" groups. This tends to support the notion that adient persons can better profit from at least this type of learning experience.

Our next presentation of findings deals with adience–abience differences between two groups of hospitalized schizophrenic patients. From a population of 100 such patients, we selected the HABGT records of those who had been hospitalized for less than 6 months and those who had been hospitalized for more than 5 years. We wished to test the Adience–Abience Scale's power in differentiating between these two groups, on the assumption that those who had been hospitalized for a long period of time were more likely to be unable to profit from experience (and change) than those who had been hospitalized for less than 6 months and then discharged. Obviously, the two groups must have differed in severity of psychopathology, among other things. Nevertheless, if differences were found between the two groups in the expected direction (that the discharge group would be higher in adience), we would have reason to believe the measure to have some possible value in line with our general theory.

We were able to find 22 cases with hospitalization above 5 years (13 males and 9 females), and selected 20 of these cases, leaving out 2 males. We also found 12 cases with less than 6 months of hospitalization, including 7 males and 5 females. Again, no attempt was made to control for other possibly significant factors, such as intelligence and socioeconomic status, that might influence results. However, at this stage we were still only interested in the general tendency for the Adience–Abience Scale to predict along the lines of our theoretical view. We found that the high hospitalization group had a mean Adience–Abience score of 18.1, while the low hospitalization group had a mean score of 22.6. The difference between the means turns out to be significant at the .01 level (one-tail test), and in the expected direction.

Two other studies deserve special note. In a rigorous study of the predictive power of the Adience–Abience Scale score, we attempted to determine whether schizophrenics who scored higher on the scale had better "inner resources" than those who scored lower (Hutt, 1969b). Two groups of 40 cases each were matched on the basis of age, sex, and length of hospitalization. The groups differed significantly on Adience–Abience scores. They were compared on two tests of creativity: accuracy in reproduction of the figures, and number and quality of associations on the association phase of the procedure. It was found that the two groups were statistically and significantly different on both measures, strongly suggesting the power of the scores on the Adience–Abience measure to tap differences in patients with comparable clinical diagnoses.

A critical study was performed by Credidio (1975). In an attempt to evaluate the construct validity of our measure of adience–abience, he compared two groups of college students who differed in scores on adience–abience with respect to their performance on the Gottschaldt Figures Test. This test yielded an independent measure of perception of novel stimuli and the accurate reproduction of such stimuli. As predicted, those who were high in adience performed significantly better than those who were low in adience or high in abience.

These studies support the predictive and construct validity aspects of the Adience–Abience Scale. Other studies have attempted to evaluate the relationship of this scale to other aspects of the personality. Two studies (Kachorek, 1969; McConville, 1970) explored the relationship of adience–abience to measures of field dependence–independence. As expected, there was a slight tendency for these measures to be related, but the degree of relationship was not statistically significant. Thus, we have some evidence that different functions are being tapped. Similarly, Meyer (1973) has shown that there may be a very small positive relationship between altruistic behavior, as measured by a special test, and adience–abience. In general we find that, as expected, our measure of adience–abience is essentially independent of these other aspects of the personality.

The interrelationship of our Psychopathology Scale and our Adience–Abience Scale has also been investigated with a population of individuals in outpatient therapy (Hutt & Miller, 1976). It was found that the two measures had some degree of commonality (about 15%–18%) in this population, but were essentially independent. However, in the same study, the two measures showed a much higher degree of commonality (40%-60%) in a population of hospitalized schizophrenics. It appears that these measures have much more in common at the extreme in pschopathology.

This last finding is supported in a study by Hutt and Dates (1977). In this study, in which groups of delinquent children were given either individual or group psychotherapy (N = 40 for each group), the intercorrelations between Psychopathology Scale scores and Adience–Abience scores were −.622 and −.636 respectively *before* treatment, but were −.476 and −.401, respectively, *after* treatment. By contrast, in a control population (N = 40), over the same period, the r's were −.657 and −.666. Taken together with changes in mean score in psychopathology over the same time-period, presumably as the result of treatment, the findings suggest that "as adience increases (or abience decreases), less commonality obtains between the Adience–Abience and the Psychopathology Scales." These findings increase the likelihood of our contention that as psychopathology increases, the two scales have less in common.

Implications for Use of the Adience–Abience Scale

We have already dealt with some of the research uses and problems in connection with this scale. The problem of its validity is, of course, by no means settled despite some important evidence of its construct and predictive validities. One of the most important research areas is that of determining under what kinds of conditions adience–abience can be permanently or temporarily modified, if need be. Cross-cultural and experiential effects need to be understood in relation to the phenomenon. The nature of the relationship of adience–abience to other aspects of the personality needs to be much more fully understood. These are but a few of the research areas requiring investigation. We believe that present evidence concerning this scale justifies the effort required in such studies.

At the clinical level there are many possible areas of application. The scale might be used for screening and selection of candidates who are most likely to be ready for some form of ameliorative or therapeutic management. It is useful in any consideration of the nature of the individual's pathology and ego resources. Comparison of findings on this scale with other aspects of the individual's functioning can make the clinical picture much clearer.

If, as we believe, an adient perceptual style is conducive to effective cognitive functioning and healthy personality development, the scale can have important applications in mental health programs. We have detailed some of these possibilities in a chapter of a book about mental health in children (Hutt, 1976a). The scale may be particularly useful in dealing with problems of mental retardation, both in clarifying the exact nature of the retardation and in coping more effectively with it (Hutt, 1976b).

7

Case Illustration: Psychopathology and Configurational Scoring

We shall now present the HABGT record of a very disturbed, male adult in order to illustrate the problems of scoring with the Psychopathology Scale and Configurational analysis. We have selected this record (Copy Phase only) because it demonstrates many of the psychopathological distortions in such records. The major clinical issue in this instance is whether the subject is simply severely neurotic or whether he is psychotic. For this purpose only Configurational scoring might be needed to determine what additional clinical procedures might be helpful. However, even in such cases, scoring on the Psychopathology Scale will offer some evidence concerning the severity of the pathology.

We shall first, therefore, illustrate scoring on the Psychopathology Scale and then complete the rapid Configurational analysis that seems indicated. Following this, we shall comment briefly on some clinical aspects of the case. Bill, as we shall call him, was a white, 38-year-old male, hospitalized for serious social problems.

In scoring the *Copy Phase* of the test, we shall follow the order of the test factors presented in Chapter 4 (and in the Revised Record Form, 3rd edition), commenting on the particular phenomena for each test factor, then providing the raw score (or position in terms of severity of distortion on the test factor), and then indicating the Scale Value on the test factor.

1. *Sequence:* The subject shifts his order in reproducing the test figures, first from 3 (the arrowhead) to 4, and then again from 7 to 8. Thus, there are 2 shifts (irregular sequence). *Scale Value = 7.0.*

2. *Position, 1st Figure:* The subject starts figure A near the center of the page, then completes it (meanwhile redrawing the circle) slightly

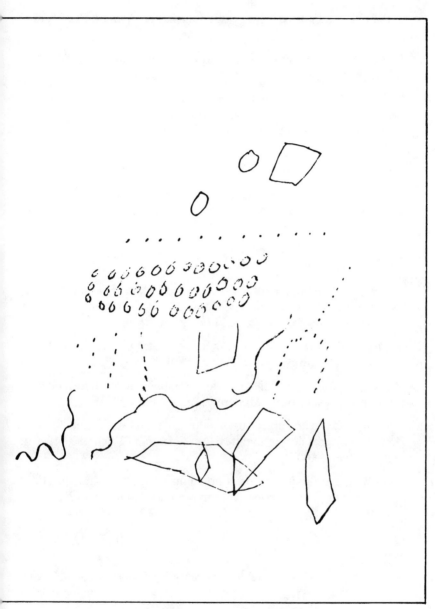

Plate 2.   Bill: Copy Phase. A "Disturbed" Personality

to the right and above. This is an *egocentic placement. Scale Value* = 5.0.

3. *Use of Space:* In terms of the criteria, this record is *excessively constricted. Scale Value* = 10.0

4. *Collision:* Note the actual collision between figures 3 and 6, and between 7 and 8. (There is a questionable *collision tendency* between figures 4 and 6; not counted) (*Collision, moderate*). *Scale Value* = 8.5.

5. *Rotation of Paper:* Not present. *Scale Value* = 1.0.

6. *Closure Difficulty:* There are 2 instances of this phenomenon on figure A and 2 (more than 2 instances on figure 2), 1 on 7 and 2 on 8. Raw score is 7 (Severe). *Scale Value* = 7.75.

7. *Crossing Difficulty:* Present on figures 6 and 7. Raw score is 2 (Moderate). *Scale Value* = 7.0.

8. *Curvature Difficulty:* Flattens curve on 4. There is a questionable change on 5. On 6 the curve is flattened and is irregular. The raw score is 2 or possibly 3. *Scale Value* = 7.0–10.0.

9. *Angulation.* The criterion of changed angulation is met on figures 2, 3, 6, and 7 (4 figures). *Scale Value* = 8.0.

10. *Perceptual Rotation:* Mild rotation is noted on 5 while moderate rotation is present on 8 (Moderate). *Scale Value* = 7.0.

11. *Retrogression:* The subject uses loops on 2, and dashes on 3 and 5. Hence, retrogression is manifest on more than 2 figures (Severe). *Scale Value* = 10.0.

12. *Simplification:* Simplification is noted on A, 3, and 7. It is questionable on 8. Simplification is severe (more than 2 figures). *Scale Value* = 10.0.

13. *Fragmentation:* Present on A, 4, 6, and 7. More than 2 figures (Severe). *Scale Value* = 10.0.

14. *Overlapping Difficulty:* Present on figure 7 (Moderate). *Scale Value* = 5.5.

15. *Elaboration:* Not Present. *Scale Value* = 1.0.

16. *Perseveration:* Type b is noted on figure 2 (2 extra columns) (Mild). *Scale Value:* 4.0.

17. *Redrawing.* Figure A (Mild). *Scale Value* = 3.25.

When these Scaled Scores are summed, the total is 112.0 to 115.0. Now, turning to table 4.2, we find that the subject's score is more than 1 standard deviation *above* the mean for schizophrenics (97.1). It is also higher than the mean for OBS patients. There is little question then that this is the test record of an individual with very severe psychopathology. The Psychopathology Score does *not* indicate what type of psychopathology may be present, although the very high score suggests it is more severe, by far, than that demonstrated on this test by groups of in-patient neurotics. The quality of the distortions suggests the possibility of schizophrenic indicators (in terms of poor ego control, poor anticipatory planning, impulsive behavior on the test, and *some* loss of reality testing), but no strong evidence is noted of typical organic signs. Testing-of-the-limits procedures might be used at this point to differentiate organic from nonorganic phenomena. For didactic purposes, however, we shall proceed to analyze the test protocol for the schizophrenic configuration.

CONFIGURATIONAL ANALYSIS

Table 5.2 enables us to complete a *rapid screening* of this record, utilizing the scale values for the schizophrenic configuration, in order to determine whether Bill's performance falls into that category. (We might, of course, also check the record against other configurations, but as indicated we shall not do so at this time.)

Table 7.1 presents the findings on the configuration for schizophrenia.

Table 7.1
Configurational Analysis

Factor No.	Factor Name	Weight
1	Confused Sequence	0
2	Abnormal Placement	2
3	Abnormal Spacing	1
6	Closure (severe)	1
8	Curvature (severe)	0–1
10	Rotation (moderate)	1
11	Retrogression (severe)	2
12	Simplification (severe)	1
13	Fragmentation (severe)	1
15	Elaboration (absent)	0

Configuration Score = 9–10

Critical Score = 7 or above

Bill's Configuration clearly falls within the category of schizophrenics. This finding lends additional weight to the conclusion that he suffers not only from a severe form of psychopathology, but that this form is *probably* in the schizophrenic category.

Clinical study, which need not be detailed at this point, revealed that Bill had been psychologically disturbed from about the age of 28 years, and that his behavior had become progressively worse over the intervening years. At the time of hospitalization, he could no longer maintain himself in his interpersonal relations and had begun to show periods of violent acting-out behavior. The final diagnosis was: chronic, undifferentiated schizophrenia.

It would be interesting to analyze this record through inferential analysis, but we shall defer such analysis until later chapters.

PART III

Intensive Diagnosis and Therapeutic Applications

8
A Summary of Other Test Factors

Before we proceed with presentations and discussion of more intensive clinical evaluations (psychodiagnosis) and with methods of testing the significance of certain test responses as well as of making therapeutic use of such responses, we shall present some other test factors that have not been included in our objective scales. Some of these factors may have considerable clinical value in exploring or "explaining" the subject's test and extra-test behavior. They have not, however, been included in our objective scales because, thus far, they have not met the statistical criteria we have employed. It may be, however, that further study of these "other" test factors may result in their later inclusion in our scales or in other scales. It may also be that some of these factors require redefinition or more suitable criteria for evaluation.

We have selected these additional test factors based both on our own clinical experience and the research published by others as well as ourselves. The examiner should familiarize himself with the relevant data so that improved, in-depth clinical analysis may be the outcome.

The factors are grouped in the same manner as was done in Chapter 4.

FACTORS RELATED TO ORGANIZATION

Use of Space (Compression Versus Expansion)

DEFINITION

This factor refers to the size of reproductions in relation to the test stimuli upon which they were based. Table 8.1 indicates the "normal" limits for each figure in terms of height and width. A reproduction is considered to be *compressed* if either of its dimensions is less than the limits in Table 8.1. It is considered *expanded* if either of its dimensions exceeds these limits. This factor is no longer included in the Psychopathology Scale but a variation of it is included in the Adience–Abience Scale.

INTERPRETATION

We have already referred to research evidence concerning this factor. Constricted or compressed use of space tends to be related to withdrawn, fearful, and covertly hostile modes of behavior. Expansive use of space is related to overly assertive, rebellious, and egocentric modes of behavior. Sometimes all figures are either constricted or expanded. In such instances the probability that the hypotheses we have advanced are relevant is very great. When only a few of the figures are constricted or expanded the probability should be regarded as less likely. When both constriction and expansion are present in the same record, it is likely that the personality is characterized by ambivalent modes of approach–avoidance behavior. We do not have precise figures to corroborate it, but the author's distinct clinical impression is that patients whom he has seen in

Table 8.1
Normal Height and Width Limits for
Factor 4 (in inches)*

Figure No.	Height Limits	Width Limits
A	0.67 to 1.00	1.18 to 1.97
1		3.11 to 5.20
2	0.27 to 0.40	2.94 to 4.96
3	0.67 to 1.10	1.14 to 1.89
4	1.10 to 1.81	1.00 to 1.67
5	0.79 to 1.34	0.79 to 1.34
6	1.02 to 1.76	1.97 to 3.31
7	0.97 to 1.53	1.10 to 1.81
8	0.35 to 0.59	1.85 to 3.07

* The package of Revised Record Forms contains
a scoring template for these limits.

the course of psychotherapy who have shown wide mood fluctuations have shown this ambivalent characteristic in their HABGT records.

Use of the Margin

DEFINITION

This factor refers to the placement of any portion of a figure within one-half inch of any of the edges of the test paper. Abnormal use of the margin consists in the occurrence of this phenomenon on seven or more of the figures. Although we continue to favor the use of this factor in developing projective hypotheses; we do not include it in either the Psychopathology Scale or the Adience–Abience Scale.

INTERPRETATION

Excessive use of the margin is often indicative of covert anxiety and may represent an attempt to maintain control through the use of external support. In extreme cases of severe anxiety, and in some paranoidal conditions, all of the figures "hug" the margin very closely. It is sometimes found in the records of patients with organic brain damage and can possibly be interpreted in such instances as a compensatory attempt to maintain control and to reduce feelings of impotence. The author's clinical experience supports these hypotheses, but it must be noted that due to the relative infrequency of occurrence (in adults) and the absence of adequate criterion data there has not been a sufficient empirical foundation for inclusion of this factor in the Psychopathology or Adience–Abience Scales. However, we can furnish the following data. Among the "normal" college population ($N = 80$) only one case occurred that could be rated as abnormal use of the margin. Among the comparative neurotic group ($N = 80$) there were 4 such cases among 42 anxiety neurotics and 3 such cases among the remaining neurotics with miscellaneous syndromes. However, in a group of 50 comparable paranoid schizophrenics (active, process), there were 9 instances of this phenomenon. In the clinical work in which the author has had opportunity to observe psychoneurotic individuals in the course of long-term therapy, this phenomenon has occurred frequently whenever there was severe, covert anxiety.

Byrd (1956) found only one instance of excessive use of the margin among the 200 cases of children he studied, but it should be noted that his criterion was different from the one suggested here. On the other hand, Clawson (1959), using a composite of three criteria of "page cohesion" based on what she termed "edge tendency," "top tendency," and "bottom tendency," found 21 instances among the school population but 34 instances among the clinic population. Separately, none of these three elements in her composite reached statistical significance in tests comparing the two groups. Combining the three elements, the test of significance reached the .05 level. This finding lends support to the possible interpretation of the use of "edging" even in the case of children, but the power of the hypothesis must be considered weaker than in adults. Nevertheless, extreme instances of the use of the margin should be given careful consideration in terms of our hypothesis.

Shift in the Position of the Stimulus Card

DEFINITION

This factor refers to changing the position of the stimulus card from its "standard" position with the long axis parallel to the examinee's body to one approximately 90 degrees from this position, i.e., with the short axis parallel to the body.

Some of the same conditions as those that cause the examinee to shift the position of the paper apply to this factor. There are no research data, other than those obtained by the author, to support this interpretation. A check of the two groups of individuals who were employed in testing other factors, 80 college students and 80 outpatients neurotics, showed the following: there were 7 instances in the college group in which the card was shifted at least once, according to our criterion, whereas there were 19 instances among the neurotics. Another check run on the author's own therapy cases in which oppositional trends were clearly evident indicated that in a group of 45 such cases, this phenomenon was present 32 times. Although there was no control group for this test, the data are consistent with the hypothesis, offering some indication of concurrent validity.

FACTORS RELATED TO SIZE

An individual may change the size of the reproduction without destroying its Gestalt quality and without other serious distortion. It would seem wise to consider both the changes in size and other types of deviation when refining the possible interpretative significance of changes in size. There are three useful measures of alterations in size: overall increase or decrease in size; isolated increase or decrease in size; progressive increase or decrease in size. Before commenting on these specific measures, a word is in order on expectancies concerning all of these measures.

Generally speaking, on the basis of the general experimental literature and clinical evidence on size estimation and distortions in the reproduction in size of stimuli, we should expect that anxiety and size deviation would be significantly correlated. However, there are many pitfalls in any attempt to establish such simple linear relationships between errors in size and anxiety. On the other hand, as the contracdictory and tortuous research concerning the measurement of anxiety has demonstrated, anxiety has many overt forms and some covert forms. Different indices attempting to measure "anxiety" are often poorly correlated or not correlated at all. Often the measure of anxiety has no specific attributes other than that it measures some aspect of anxiety. Different writers speak of basic anxiety, chronic anxiety, test- or situation-specific anxiety, induced anxiety, and so on. On the other hand, deviations in size may reflect a number of different, and even uncorrelated factors. There is the developmental factor (Davis et al. 1967; Piaget, 1950), the emotional factor (as we shall specify), and the factor of brain pathology. Great care is therefore needed in interpreting a simple correlational study of aspects of anxiety and aspects of size deviation.

When some form of anxiety is present, it may not necessarily manifest itself in the phenomenon of size deviation. Whether or not it does so, assuming that there is a tendency for these phenemona to be related, will depend upon other aspects of the individual's style and his defensive repertoire. Some anxious people act out, others inhibit, still others somatize their anxiety, and others may show a wide variety of derivatives even in the perceptual–motoric sphere. Sometimes, when anxiety does manifest itself in the perceptual–motoric sphere, the resultant is expressed in only one of the 9 figures, but a highly significant change in size may occur in that figure or a portion of it. Hence, while our measures of change in size have some value, their contribution becomes more significant when they are considered in relation to other aspects of the total test performance. We shall have more to say about this issue in the following chapter.

Overall Increase or Decrease in Size

DEFINITION

This factor refers to the increase or decrease in the reproduction by one-fourth the size of either the vertical or horizontal axis of the corresponding stimulus figure. There is an *overall increase* when 5 or more of the figures meet this criterion for increase in size; there is an *overall decrease* when 5 or more of the figures meet this criterion for decrease in size.

INTERPRETATION

An overall increase or decrease is frequently a means by which anxiety manifests itself in the test situation. Children over the age of 9 years more frequently tend to increase the size of their reproductions. However, children with very high anxiety may, compensatorily, decrease the size, especially if they are also suspicious and withdrawn. Increases in size are often accompanied by feelings of inadequacy and impotence. Decreases are more often associated with covert anxiety of an intense nature. Patients with markedly disturbed ego functions, especially those whose ego functions have become "fragmented" (Hutt & Gibby, 1957), may sometimes show the phenomenon of *micropsia,* that is, extremely small reproductions.

At the overt behavioral level, increase in size appears to be correlated with compensatory, outgoing, assertive modes of performance, whereas decrease in size is related to withdrawn, passive, and inhibited performance.

There is research evidence on this test factor on the HABGT. Byrd (1956), using an older criterion measure proposed by Hutt, found that overall change in size was significantly different for well-adjusted children and children needing psychotherapy (ages 10–15), and the difference was in the expected direction. Clawson (1959) used three measures of modification in size (following Hutt) and found the measures differentiated school and clinic children at the .001 level. Surprisingly, her children ranged in age from 7 to 12 years; but her more pronounced differences, in comparison with Byrd's, may have been a function, in part, of more significant differences between her two groups. She also found that decreased figure size was significantly associated with the behavioral phenomenon of being "withdrawn" ($p = .01$). In addition, constricted figure size was related to a Rorschach measure of constriction ($p = .001$). All of the findings were in the expected direction.

On the other hand, a study of adolescents (Taylor & Schenke, 1955) compared an agressive group with a passive group. The assignment to groups was made on the basis of responses to questionnaires by raters. The Bender protocols were scored using Peek and Quast's (1951) method. With respect to changes in size, the only positive finding ($p = .05$) was that aggressive individuals more frequently produced distortions in size than the other two groups. The differences in scoring methods, the nature of the criterion variables, and the methods of analysis may have had something to do with the generally negative results. In our view, meaningful results could not have been expected if, at the least, there were not significant differences in the anxiety levels of the groups. Another study (Gaveles & Millon, 1960) with college undergraduates compared the size deviations of four subgroups: high anxiety (as measured by the Taylor Manifest Anxiety Scale) and experimentally induced anxiety; high anxiety without induced anxiety; low anxiety with induced anxiety; and low anxiety without induced anxiety. It was found that the groups with induced anxiety produced significantly smaller Bender reproductions and the groups high in anxiety tended to be different in a similar manner from those low in anxiety.

Both Kai (1972) and Naches (1967) found that increased size in the drawings of young children reflect emotional disturbances and acting out tendencies. The work of Elliott (1968) as well as that of Kai supports the use of this factor, when there is a decrease of size, as an indicator of other types of emotional problems (involving withdrawal and inhibition).

In the author's own data, the significance of anxiety is more clearly shown. When the neurotic group ($N = 80$) is compared with the "normal" group ($N = 80$) in terms of overall increase or decrease in size on the HABGT (as defined), the results are significant in the expected direction at the .05 level. Moreover, when the subgroup of anxiety neurotics ($N = 42$) is compared on this factor with the total college group, the difference is significant at the .001 level.

Progressive Increase or Decrease in Size

DEFINITION

This factor refers to the increase or decrease in the size of the reproductions relative to the stimulus figures. *Progressive increase* is said to occur when there is a progressive increment in the size, by any measurable amount, over at least 6 figures. *Progressive decrease* occurs when the same criterion is met but there is a decrement on at least 6 figures.

INTERPRETATION

This factor is tentatively being retained although there is little research evidence to support it. Clawson's (1959) data are supportive but not definitive. Our own data have not lent themselves to an adequate statistical test. However, clinical experience continues to support the following hypotheses, which may, at this time, be taken to have low strength.

When a record clearly shows a tendency toward constant increase in size of the figures, it is likely to be associated with irritability, tendency toward loss of control, and acting out impulsively. Progressive decrease is likely to be associated with tendencies toward withdrawn, inhibited, and depressed reactions. Often psychosomatic complaints are present. In general, the phenomenon seems to be related to some type of low frustration tolerance and poor ego controls. Although research data are needed, we rely heavily upon our clinical impressions with respect to this factor.

Isolated Increase or Decrease in Size

DEFINITION

This factor refers to either an increase or a decrease in a portion of a figure or of a single total figure in relation to the other figures. The criterion that has been applied to changes in the sizes of parts of figures is that it is one-third larger or smaller than other parts of that figure. The criterion applied to a total figure is that it is about one-fourth larger or smaller than the other reproductions.

INTERPRETATION

It is felt that isolated changes in the size of parts of a figure or of a single total figure are clinically significant. Such meanings are likely to be highly idiosyncratic, although changes in some individual figures (insofar as size is concerned) may be more frequent than in other figures either because of their perceptual properties or because of their tendency to elicit symbolic associations (Sternberg & Levine, 1965; Story, 1960; Suczek & Klopfer, 1952; Tolor, 1960). Isolated changes in size may be regarded as "slips of the tongue" occurring in the perceptual–motoric area of behavior; although they may occur by chance, a much stronger hypothesis is that they are the result of some emotional disturbance and reflect an underlying personality process which is not easily and openly revealed by the individual.

In addition to the use one may make of the "general meanings" of the figures as adduced in research studies (limited as these may be), one should look for clues about the possible meaning of isolated shifts in size in terms of other "internal evidence." Of foremost importance in this regard are the associations that are obtained in the association phase of the test. These associations should be considered a beginning point if one wishes to explore fully the possible meanings of isolated size change. Further interview about this material can be helpful, as can other clinical data about the patient.

Isolated changes in size within figure A have been associated, frequently with comparative attitudes toward female figures (represented frequently by the circle) and male figures (represented frequently by the diamond). Similarly, such changes in figures 7 and 8 are often associated even more specifically with attitudes toward sexuality, and even more specifically toward phallic qualities (Sullivan & Welsh, 1947). In general, reproduction in size is associated, we believe, with withdrawal or other repressive maneuvers, while increase in size is associated with approach and compensatory defenses toward sexual stimuli. But we must caution against "wild" conclusions based on tiny bits of evidence. On the other hand, such shreds of evidence, considered as leads for hypotheses, can be extremely illuminating and should not be discounted.

For instance, a recent study by Brannigan and Benowitz (1975) found that among adolescents uneven size of the figures was clearly related to acting out, antisocial tendencies as rated by housemothers.

The reader is reminded of Mira's (1939–1940) important findings that have lead us to consider shifts in size in the vertical plane (especially if occurring on more than one figure) as indicative of conflicts in the area of relationship to authority figures, while shifts in size in the lateral or horizontal plane are considered as indicative of difficulties in forming or maintaining interpersonal relationships. The general relationship between constricted size of figures and constriction in other indices of personality functioning (Clawson, 1959), and between curves and emotionality (Breen 1953; North, 1953; Story, 1960) have already been noted.

FACTORS RELATED TO MOVEMENT AND DRAWING

Deviation in Direction of Movement

DEFINITION

This factor refers to deviation from the expected direction of movement in drawing the lines and curves in the test figures. The usual directions of movements fall into three classes: counterclockwise (especially for "closed" figures such as a circle, hexagon, etc.); from the top down; and from the inside of the figure to the outside. Examinees who draw with the left hand are a possible exception to these experiments.

INTERPRETATION

We have not included this or either of the two following factors in either the Psychopathology Scale or the Adience–Abience Scale. There are some supporting research findings that indicate these factors may have some value, but codification is inadequate and the infrequency of occurrence makes statistical treatment inadvisable at this time.

As will be noted on the *Record Form,* the examiner is requested to observe direction of movement as the examinee draws each figure, and to make appropriate notation of the direction. Direction of movement, as well as the end products in drawing, have been studied by several investigators (e.g., Mira, 1939–1940; Wolff, 1943). The significance of the fantasied movement response has also received clinical and research evaluation (e.g., Klopfer, Ainsworth, Klopfer, & Holt, 1954). There is some consensus that centrifugal movement, in comparison with centripetal movememt, represents personality trends toward assertion and autonomy; whereas centripetal movements indicate some degree of egocentrism and oppositional quality. Similarly, difficulty with movement in the vertical plane seems to be associated with interpersonal difficulties with authority figures, and difficulty in the horizontal plane may suggest difficulty in maintaining adequate, interpersonal relationships with peers. Mild counterclockwise movements are suggestive of active, overt oppositional trends, whereas clockwise direction of movement suggests passive, oppositional trends, egocentricity, and depression.

The author's clinical observations support these hypotheses. Particularly in the case of regular clockwise movements there is a strong tendency for oppositional and egocentric qualities to be present in the personality.

A study by Peek (1953) suggested that, in a limited test of this general hypothesis, psychiatric patients who drew the diagonal secant of figure 5 from the top down, rather than in the more usual manner, from the bottom up, tended to be more immature, depressive, and less well adjusted than the control population that was used. Peek felt that one could interpret the "inward" drawing of the secant as indicative of fear of being overwhelmed by external forces. This interpretation warrants further investigation. Clawson (1959) reported that the same phenomenon (she called it drawing the spike inward) differentiated school children from clinic children in the expected direction ($p = .05$): 66% of her well-adjusted group drew the spike outward, whereas only 30% of the heterogeneous clinic group did.

In a study of the drawing characteristics of 65 college students, Lieberman (1968) found that these subjects did not typically draw closed figures in a counterclockwise manner, nor did they always draw vertical features from the top down. It may be that college students are somewhat atypical; they may also be more oppositional than other groups. More data on this phenomenon could be very useful.

Inconsistency in Direction of Movement

DEFINITION

This factor refers to any shift from the previously established "typical" direction of movement. Such shifts in direction can usually be observed easily by the examiner, for they are often accompanied by other indications of some form of tension, both on the test and in behavior.

INTERPRETATION

Shifts of the kind we are referring to are usually sudden and unexpected. The examinee has already established his style on previous reproductions, then suddenly shifts on the next design or part of the design. Such inconsistencies tend to be indicative, we believe, of psychic blocking, oftentimes associated with the idiosyncratic and symbolic meaning of the design for the patient, and may be indicative of ongoing attempts to act out strongly conflictual trends in the personality. Sometimes such evidence may have a favorable connotation because the patient is actively struggling to work out a more reasonable solution to his conflicts.

Line Quality

DEFINITION

This factor refers to the quality of the lines used in making the reproductions. We identify 6 major types of abnormal line quality: excessively heavy lines; excessively heavy lines accompanied by poor coordination; excessively faint lines; excessively faint lines accompanied by poor coordination; poor corrdination; and sketching. Poor coordination is manifested by irregularities, unevenness in line quality, and tremulousness. We have used, as a rule of thumb, a definition of *coarse coordination* in which the irregularities in line quality exceed one-sixteenth of an inch. Sketching refers to retouching of a line, or of a joining. It should be distinguished from the type of art sketching that results in a reproduction that is well controlled and well executed. Rather, sketching, as we have defined, it, refers to productions that are inferior and sometimes result in distortion of the Gestalt.

INTERPRETATION

Based primarily upon clinical observations, line quality appeared to be important in a great many cases of diffuse brain damage, in diverse cases showing intense anxiety, and in cases showing high degrees of feelings of personal inadequacy. In a previous publication (Hutt & Briskin, 1960), specific hypotheses were offered concerning each of the types of deviations in line quality defined above. The specific hypotheses have not been borne out by any systematic research, although there is some supporting evidence. For example, coarse incoordination was shown by Mosher and Smith (1965) to differentiate organics from controls at the .01 level of significance. Heavy line pressure discriminated clinic from school children at the .10 groups of significance (Clawson, 1959). The relative heterogeneity of both groups as well as the relatively low-order power of this factor may have reduced the significance of these results. Peek and Quast (1951) have included tone of line quality in their scoring system, and Pascal and Suttell (1951) give fairly high weights to a sign they call tremors (both fine and coarse). On the other hand, "line tone" was not found to be differentiating among groups of aggressive individuals, passive individuals, and a control group (Taylor & Schenke, 1955). This negative finding is not surprising in view of a questionable rationale for expecting to find such differences and because of their definition of the three types of groups.

On the other hand, careful analysis of the records of hostile and aggressive children has demonstrated that line quality, particularly heavily reinforced lines, is a significant feature of such records (Brown, 1965; Handler & McIntosh, 1971).

Inconsistency in line quality may be even more important than the line quality itself, for it is probably indicative of disturbance stimulated by idiosyncratic reactions to the specific designs. Tremors, whether fine or coarse, suggest difficulty in motor control and are either indicative of a high level of anxiety or some neurological problem. Generally, heavy lines are an expression of anxiety being directed outwards, while faint lines are suggestive of anxiety that is being internalized or the expression of which is inhibited. Sketching is likely to be indicative of feelings of inadequacy with some attempts at compensation. All of these indicators should be considered suggestive, but should lead to more intense analyses of other concurrent indicators, either in test reproductions or in other clinical behavior. Used in this manner, they may offer important leads to significant understanding of the individual.

SOME OTHER FACTORS

Although we have tried to incorporate in our presentation of factors those test signs that have received clinical and research support from other workers, we have been biased in our selection by our own clinical experience, our own research, and our own rationale for test interpretation. Doubtless, other factors than those we have discussed may have great importance, and still others, or new integrations of factors, may finally turn out to be more sensitive and discriminating indicators than those we have thus far presented. In order to give some idea of the scope of creative suggestions that have been offered by others, we list below a sampling of some factors that are not included in our own listing.

Hain (1964) has found the following additional factors to be important in a total score designed to identify brain damage: "concretion," "unit line separation," "acute angle difficulty," and "added angles." (All receive high weighting.) In addition, "omission of elements," and absence of erasures" receive low weighting. Pascal and Suttell (1951) include such items as "workover," "asymmetry," and "guide lines" in their scoring scheme, but these are given relatively small weights. Guertin (1952) factor analyzed 41 test variables selected from Billingslea's work (Billingslea, 1948) and extracted five oblique factors: propensity to curvilinear movements; careless execution; poor reality contact; construction; and poor spatial contiguity. Although Clawson (1959) based her study on Hutt's suggested factors, she also analyzed some aspects of performance in her own way. For example, she scored for "scalloping," "dog ears," "the use of arcs instead of clear-cut angles," and "erasures." Kitay (1950) approached the problem of scoring by measuring size deviations by means of graph paper. Koppitz (1960, 1975a), whose work has been found to be so valuable in the analysis of children's Bender records from a maturational rather than a projective viewpoint, has offered a number of other innovations in her scoring scheme, originally presented in 1960. Since this approach is so fundamentally different from ours, the interested reader is referred to her research article.

Cross-cultural studies are also urgently needed. In addition to the works we have already cited, some useful findings may be found in studies by Fanibanda (1973), who suggests that cultural differences occur in elaborations, and by Money and Newcombe (1974), who indicate the usefulness of such studies.

9
Intensive Diagnosis: Inferential Analysis and Experimental-Clinical Procedures

The HABGT can provide a plethora of data—sometimes so complex and so rich that the clinician will have great difficulty in assimilating and integrating all of the material. Not only does the HABGT provide access to the subject's perceptual-motoric behavior, which is meaningful as a sample of that aspect of the subject's capacities, but the performance of such behavior can, and often does, "release" defended feelings and conflicts originating in early developmental experiences, sometimes stimulates associations to the symbolic meanings the figures evoke in the subject, and test responses can be investigated and evaluated in terms of idiosyncratic meanings and possibilities for modification and improvement. It is for such reasons that we developed procedures (the Elaboration and Association phases) and methods (now called microdiagnostic testing) to exploit fully the potentials of the HABGT.

In this chapter we shall discuss some of the special characteristics of the test figures, general problems in psychodiagnosis, and illustrate the Testing-the-Limits (microdiagnostic) methods. We shall reserve for a later chapter the utilization of such data in therapeutic understanding and management.

CHARACTERISTICS OF THE INDIVIDUAL FIGURES

An analysis of some of the properties of the individual test figures and of the test factors that are likely to be associated with them will provide the clinican with a basis for psychological evaluation of responses by the examinee.

160

Now we shall turn our attention to the separate Gestalt figures, commenting simultaneously on the other test factors as they are likely to emerge on these figures.

Figure A has several features to commend it as the initial figure in the test presentation. In the first place it is a relatively simple figure, requiring only a mental maturity, corresponding roughly to about 7–8 years of age for its successful reproduction. It is therefore useful to compare relative success on this figure with performance on the other simple and on the more complex figures (i.e., figures 1, 2, 3, and 4, on the one hand, and figures 6, 7, and 8 on the other). It can usually be assumed, for example, that consistently greater difficulty on the simple figures in comparison with the more difficult ones is due to intrapsychic difficulties rather than maturational problems.

Another feature concerning figure A is that it consists of two well-structured, closed, simple, and *tangential* figures. The tangential aspect makes the figure particularly useful in detecting difficulties in interpersonal cathexes (joining and closure factors). Still another feature is the presence of two figures that have well-nigh universal symbolic meanings: the circle represents the female object and the square represents the male object. (It is, of course, important to test the applicability of these symbolic meanings for a particular patient. The patient's responses during the association phase of the test furnish one basis for such verification.) It is possible to infer that relative increases in the size of one figure as compared with the other refer to problems in the patient's self-percept. Thus, for example, a patient who reproduces the square as greatly enlarged in proportion to the circle can be assumed to be attempting unconsciously to identify with a male role; the relative discrepancy in size is therefore indicative of difficulty in this identification, for otherwise both figures would receive equal emphasis. This type of hypothesis can be checked against the elaborations and the associations in the other two phases of the basic method of administration. Patients who wish unconsciously to see themselves as more masculine will be likely to exaggerate the square during the elaboration by some such method as placing the circle within the square or by producing a number of squares around the circle as a pivot.

Another feature of figure A is that it consists of a curved and a straight-line figure. From clinical and experimental evidence we know that difficulty in expressing aggressive drives is associated with difficulty in reproducing curved figures, whereas corresponding difficulty with passivity is associated with straight-line figure (Breen, 1953; North, 1953). We have already commented on the problem of placement of the first figure. We can also add that, since this is the first figure in the test, whatever transient factors are associated with initial adaptation to the test situation are likely to be projected into some aspect of the performance on this figure. Hence, careful examination of all of the features in the reproduction of this figure is recommended. Comparison with the subsequent figures may make it possible to deduce which features are associated with problems in initial adaptation and which are more probably characterological in nature.

Figure 1 consists of 12 equidistant dots. Because it is an unstructured figure (i.e., it has no clearly delineated boundary), it presents difficulties to some patients. Patients with organic problems find this figure more difficult than its inherent structure justifies (because of figure–ground perceptual problems associated with organic deficit). Patients with intense, diffuse anxiety also find the figure difficult for similar reasons. Patients with severe aspiration problems have difficulty in leaving this figure, as simple as it is; they spend a great deal of energy in filling in the dots or in emphasizing the circularity of the dots. To some patients with traumatic anxiety the dots are suggestive of bullets or pellets coming directly at them and, as a consequence, they may produce a very wavy line of dots. Some schizophrenic patients with high ideational and paranoid qualities elaborate the dots and may "extend" them into birds or symbolic figures or "doodles" (some anxious neurotics do the same thing). Finally, a word may be said concerning obsessive–compulsive patients who spend an inordinate amount of time completing this simple figure because of their perfectionistic needs and frequently count and recount the number of dots.

The relative placement of figures A and 1 also deserves some comment. It is interesting to note the directional orientation that the patient takes after completing figure A. Does he move to the right, or does he move to a position directly below figure A in beginning figure 1? Preferred direction of movement is a stylistic feature that we have already commented on in the preceding chapter. Preferred movements in the lateral or horizontal plane, for example, are likely to be associated with unresolved needs for interpersonal cathexes, while movements in the vertical plane are related to difficulties in dealing with authority figures. Some patients, moreover, draw the line of dots in such a way that it represents an arc (sometimes barely discernible) with themselves as the pivot—indicative of an egocentric or, possibly, narcissistic orientation. Others draw the line of dots with a slight clockwise rotation, which is indicative of depressive trends. These and other general characteristics of the drawing of this figure are worth noting for the rich harvest of hypotheses that they may offer.

Again, we wish to emphasize that the contrast in performance and in general behavior that may be noted for the first two figures—or the consistency that is evident—is important for still other hypotheses that may

be derived. Contrast may occur in size, in spacing, in directional orientation, in relative amount of time and energy expended in completing the
task, etc. One may lose sight of the sequential production of such phenomena if specific attention is not directed to this phase of the analysis.
As a consequence of this, only discrete hypothese that can be summated
in a score of deviations or distortions would remain.

Turning now to *figure 2,* we note that it consists of 10 angulated
columns of circles. Because there is a shift from the dots of figure 1 to the
circles of figure 2, we wish to attend particularly to the occurrence of
perseveration that may first be manifest on figure 2 (although another type
of perseveration may occur on figure 1). Some patients reproduce figure 2
with dots instead of circles, perseverating the dots of figure 1. This phenomenon is most characteristic of patients with severe ego impairment,
such as psychotics, but it may occur when transient anxiety is very intense. The open character of this figure (like that of figure 1) with no clear
indication of the boundary, is threatening to some patients. Organics and
those with severe problems in interpersonal relationships sometimes have
difficulty with this figure. When the figure is elongated in the lateral plane
but the number of columns of circles is correct, we can infer that the
problem is likely to be one of difficulty in interpersonal relations. When
perseveration of the dots of figure 1, or perseveration of the columns of
circles is present, some organic hypothesis is more likely.

Another feature of importance on this figure is any change in the
angulation of the columns of circles. In general, reduction in the acuteness of the angulation (or "increased angulation" as we have defined it)
corresponds to reduction in the affectivity of the patient, while increase in
acuteness corresponds to increase in affectivity. Sometimes, the patient
has difficulty in perceiving or in executing the angulation feature: for
example, when he reproduces the columns as perpendicular to the base of
the paper but rotates the whole figure in a counterclockwise manner to
achieve some semblance of angulation. This kind of difficulty is associated with the feelings of impotence experienced by some organics; occasionally it may be present in the production of psychopaths. Still another
phenomenon is the tendency to produce a figure with shifts in the angulation of the columns so that those at the left are produced with a relatively
correct angulation but, as the other columns are drawn, the position of the
columns tends to become more and more reversed, so that the whole
figure describes an arc with the patient at the center or point of origin. As
on figure 1, this phenomenon is indicative of egocentrism or narcissism.
Some patients manifest a progressive and regressive shift in the angulation of the successive columns, an indication of compensatory attempts to
maintain interpersonal cathexes.

Some patients draw the figure with a clockwise orientation or rotation, an indication of depressive trends. If depressive features in the personality result in clockwise rotation, this feature is usually present in all three of the first three figures and the hypothesis is thus strongly supported. Moreover, other test features may be associated with depression, such as light pressure in line movement and difficulty in completing any of the tasks. This combination of characteristics is usually associated with depression in a highly dependent and passive personality. When strong masochistic features are present, line pressure tends to be heavy. Another feature associated with masochism is the placement of dots within each of the circles. We have noted only some of the most important characteristics associated with the drawing of this figure. Many others are present and correlated hypotheses may be deduced.

Figure 3, the arrowhead constructed of dots, is another open figure. Some patients who have managed to maintain some degree of control with the previous open figures finally begin to break down on this figure. (Organics usually show their ego impairment before they have reached this figure.) For other patients the aggressive qualities of this figure, or its symbolic meaning to them, is threatening. For such patients we may expect that some compensatory effort will be made to reduce the apparent threat. This may be done by compressing the figure, thus destroying its essential Gestalt, or by reducing the angularity of the angles in the figure. Another fairly frequent characteristic of the reproduction of this figure in the case of regressed patients is a simplification of the figure (by reducing the number of dots or by reducing the number of component parts). Depressive trends are also frequently manifest on this figure in the form of rotational difficulties of a minor degree. Patients with strong anal fixations tend to be overly careful with this figure, counting the dots again and again, but sometimes losing the general Gestalt in the process because of their overconcern with minutiae. The specific associative meanings of this figure for the patient can frequently be easily inferred from the material in the elaboration and association phases of the test.

Figure 4, like figure A, presents two symbols that frequently are associated with sexual identification: the open square representing the male object and the curved figure representing the female object. It therefore has some of the same values as figure A. Confirmation of hypotheses dealing with identification can frequently be obtained by a comparison of the distortions on these two figures. Since figure 4 is more difficult than figure A, some problems usually emerge on this figure that have not been noted on figure A. The relative size of the curved portion of the figure in relation to the open square is particularly important in this respect. The tendency to flatten the curve or the tendency to produce an extra or excessive loop at the end of the curve is also important: the former is associated with emotional "flattening," the latter with impulsivity and poor emotional control.

Some patients have difficulty with the vertical sides of the open square, indicative of difficulty in authority relationships. This difficulty may be shown in a number of ways, such as sketching on the vertical sides, successive attempts to increase or extend these sides, or an increase in the dimensions of these sides. Other patients show fairly marked closure problems on this figure. Still others fragment the figure or separate the two components. The latter is associated with the severe ego impairment occurring in regressive states and in problems associated with organicity. The production on figure 4 should be compared with productions on other figures in which either straight lines or curved lines or both are present, in order to derive suitable hypotheses, and with the elaboration and association data for confirmation of these hypotheses and the development of new hypotheses to account for all of the data. A great variety of relevant inferences can be derived from this figure alone as well as from a comparison with the patient's productions on preceding figures.

Figure 5 is another open figure composed of dots. Several of the most pertinent phenomena associated with this figure will be discussed briefly. Rotation frequently occurs for the first time because of the perceptual valence of the secant, which forces some patients to rotate the entire figure; they are unable to resist the inertia created by the angulated secant and consequently rotate the entire figure. Another feature is the tendency to complete the circle by extending the circular portion of the figure. This phenomenon is usually associated with feelings of insecurity and dependence. Simplification may also occur as still another defensive maneuver. Obsessive–compulsive patients frequently count the dots over and over again, sometimes losing the Gestalt while trying to reproduce the number of dots accurately. The relative size of the secant should be examined for the deduction of any of a number of hypotheses, such as: paranoid features (elaboration or overextension of the size of the secant—because of its phallic characteristics); authority problems (decrease in vertical dimension of the total figure with foreshortening of the secant); passivity as a reaction formation to hostile wishes (decrease of the secant together with a wavy line quality). Simplification of the figure may be attempted by reducing markedly the total number of dots, by substituting a curved line for the semicircle of dots, or by using lines in place of dots for the entire figure (see Chapter 4).

Figure 6, coming as it does after a succession of previous figures and representing such a direct portrayal of emotionality, is another important figure in sequential and inferential analyses. Not only does the curvature present problems to some patients, but the intersection of two sets of curves in a nonsymmetrical manner aggravates the problem for many. Patients who are able to maintain a facade of appropriate affectivity but whose affective behavior is not spontaneous have great difficulty here. The various phenomena that may result are highly revealing. Are the curves flattened (reduction of the emotional value of the stimulus), are they spiked (difficulty in holding aggressive drives under check), or are they reduced in number or amplitude (affective withdrawal)? Again, are the two curves made to intersect at right angles or are the curves drawn with considerable evidence of motor incoordination (inability to handle with considerable evidence of motor incoordination (inability to handle the "hot" emotional meaning of this stimuli)? Some patients draw the two curves not as intersecting but as two tangential "U" curves—an important indication of marked fearfulness in interpersonal relations. Depressive features sometimes appear for the first time on this figure (mild clockwise rotation, light wavy lines, and similar features). Paranoid characteristics sometimes become evident (the elaboration of the curve as the profile of a face, or the insertion of a dot for an eye, as examples). Patients with markedly impulsive characteristics will frequently increase the size of the curves greatly and will use excessive line pressure. The highly anxious but intact patient may, on the other hand, diminish the size of the curves and draw them with light pressure and sketchy lines.

As is well known by now, *figure 7* offers the most clear-cut evidence of the presence of organicity in the patient (difficulty with overlapping) but it offers many other leads as well. With respect to the problem of intracranial damage it should be emphasized that overlapping difficulty may be evidenced in very many different ways. The most obvious of these is the failure to reproduce the overlapping Gestalt. There are also other, less obvious ways: sketching at the point of overlap of the two figures; severe rotation of the figures; marked difficulty with some of the angles (especially if none was noted on such figures as A and 4); simplification of either or both parts of the figure; overlap at an incorrect point; marked over-shooting in the closure at any of the apexes; substitution of curved for straight lines; and total destruction of the Gestalt.

The phallic quality of this Gestalt, and the threat it poses to some types of homosexuals, should not be overlooked. This type of reaction to the symbolic meaning of the stimulus figure can be checked against the reaction obtained with figure 8, discussed below. When the phallic quality is too threatening to the patient, he may defend against this in a number of ways, such as rounding off any of the upper or lower apexes of the figures, decreasing the length of the figures or increasing their width, or shortening the extreme sections of the figures. Sometimes patients with severe superego problems and guilt over fantasied sexual perversions or excesses separate the two figures or simplify them; in such cases the evidence of overt anxiety noted in this and other figures will help to differentiate this type of difficulty from that of organicity. Figure 7 also lends itself to rather clear manifestations of other types of anxieties and difficulties in interpersonal relations, evidenced by such phenomena as closure difficulties, crossing difficulties, variations in line quality, difficulties with angles, rotational problems, and the like.

Figure 8 is also reacted to, very frequently, in terms of its sexual, particularly its phallic, qualities (Sullivan & Welsh, 1947). One of the interesting findings is that individuals with conflict over homosexuality (and young adults or adolescents with conflict over masturbation) have difficulties with the extremities of this figure. The most common distortions involve: production of the two extremities in markedly different sizes; difficulties with the angles in the extremities; substitution of curved lines for the straight lines in the extreme portion of the figure; and excessive sketching.

Another feature to which special attention should be given is the production of the internal diamond. Difficulty with this portion of the figure may involve: reduction in size; misplacement in position (off center); or difficulty in closure or joining of either parts of the diamond or the diamond with the sides of the hexagon. Such difficulties are usually associated with conflict with the female sex and fearfulness in connection with intercourse. When such distortions occur it is instructive to note whether similar difficulties have been experienced in connection with the square (or diamond) in figure A. It will sometimes be noted that no significant distortions occur in figure A but they are quite marked in figure 8. There may be many reasons to account for this, but the two most common explanations are that figure 8 is the last in the test and reflects the cumulative anxieties that have been built up in the course of the examination, and that figure 8 seems to evoke more directly some of the conflicts related to sexual relationships. Confirmation of either of these (or other) explanations for this figure may often be obtained during the elaboration and association phases of the test.

THE DIAGNOSTIC PROCESS CONTRASTED WITH DIAGNOSTIC LABELING

In order to sue a diagnostic tool properly the interpreter must possess a number of basic attributes. It goes without saying that he must fully understand the tool that he is employing: its underlying rationale; its methods of standardization; its techniques of administration; its clinical and experimental findings; and its values and limitations in assessing the particular phenomena it is designed to test. However, having all of these attributes for a particular test or for a series of diagnostic techniques does not qualify the interpreter as a clinician. Without much more he is merely a psychometrist, although he may be a very good one and he may contribute significantly along this line. We should not underestimate the function and value of the psychometrician, but, by the same token, we should not confuse them with the function and value of the clinician.

The distinction between the psychometrician and the clinician is important for both theoretical and practical reasons. The former, according to our definition, has developed the appropriate knowledge and skills to use and interpret one or more instruments or techniques. He is not necessarily well versed in general psychology, much less in psychopathology or even the psychology of personality. He has not been trained to relate psychometric findings to other aspects of the clinical history or to other clinical data, nor to make decisions concerning the management of and therapy for the patient. He is familiar with and respects the research findings concerning reliability and validity of the measures he employs, but he is not in a professionally appropriate position to go beyond these confines of his knowledge. As we shall see, clinical diagnosis, or, as we prefer to term it, *psychodiagnosis,* characteristically involves much more. Psychodiagnosis includes the gathering and weighing of *all* relevant evidence concerning the patient, an analysis of the causative factors in the present condition, a description of the present condition in terms of the total syndrome which is evident, an evaluation of the dynamic characteristics of the present condition (under what conditions does a "cause" give rise to an "effect"), and prediction of those changes that may be expected from present and/or altered circumstances (Hutt & Gibby, 1957).

As we have indicated, the distinction between these two types of clinical workers is important for theoretical reasons. We are still in the stage of development concerning psychopathology in which we make the assumption that a given psychiatric syndrome constitutes a unique entity, separate and distinct from all other such entities. Some workers have begun to question this assumption and others have already rejected it. However, as long as the assumption is maintained, it is necessary to postulate that a given configuration of *behavioral characteristics* defines a particular clinical entity, with its own etiology, development, and final outcome. Thus, psychiatry arrived at the basic classification of "mental disorders" with the discovery that certain kinds of behaviors tended to belong to one set of etiologic conditions while others belonged to other conditions. This type of descriptive psychiatry had to assume a one-to-one relationship between behavioral configuration and underlying psychopathology. Almost all types of objective tests of personality make the same assumption—that there is a one-to-one relationship between measures of behavioral traits and psychiatric abnormality. Yet, clinical and research evidence has accumulated that challenges this fundamental assumption.

For one thing, it has been demonstrated that some patients who fall within one psychiatric category may later belong in other categories. For example, a group of patients originally diagnosed as manic-depressive were later found, in a follow-up study, to be more appropriately classified as manic-depressive in some cases, as schizophrenic in others, and as in still different categories in other cases, on the basis of the later development of their condition and their changing behavioral characteristics (Hoch & Rachlin, 1941). Increasing doubt has been cast on the essential homogeneity of schizophrenia as a distinct disease entity. Certainly, patients with simple and hebephrenic forms of this condition differ from others with paranoid and catatonic forms in certain important respects: amount of regression, susceptibility to treatment, spontaneous remission, etc. Similarly, many individuals who show, as a result of severe and acute trauma, reaction patterns that closely resemble essential psychoneurotic conditions differ significantly from the usual varieties of psychoneurotics. Clinical evidence gathered during the years of the Second World War amply substantiated these difference (Grinker & Spiegel, 1945). Finally, persons with neurotic character disorders are difficult to distinguish, on the basis of behavior syndromes alone, from other persons with classical neurotic disorders of the same type (Hutt & Gibby, 1957). All of these and related observations suggest that there is no one-to-one relationship between current psychiatric grouping and underlying psychopathology. Parenthetically, this is probably one of the important reasons that psychiatric criteria of psychopathology are relatively low in reliability.

If, then, there is no direct relationship between symptoms or behaviors and type of psychopathology, it follows that there cannot be a simple, unilateral relationship between a test sign or test measure and a psychiatric condition. On the contrary, a test sign or a test measure may acquire different meanings depending upon (1) the *constellation of which it is a part* and (2) the *conditions which give rise to it*. Qualification 1 may be tested statistically by evaluating the differential power of various configurations of signs. Indeed, this is the pattern which has been followed by a considerable portion of contemporary clinical research. Although this type of work has offered some promise, notably in some problem areas such as the differential diagnosis of brain pathology, the results have not been altogether encouraging. This outcome should not have been unexpected since configurations of behavioral measures can only (if done adequately) contribute to the accuracy of predicting configurations of behavior, i.e., psychiatric categories, and we have seen that psychiatric categories may be of limited value. The second qualification noted above, the condition that gives rise to the behavior, may, and on theoretical grounds should, give better results. For here we can begin to deal with *process phenomena* that have a certain independence of the resultant behavioral phenomena. Before we proceed to elaborate this point, let us note that we are not recommending abandonment of the use of configurational measures, for they do have important uses. Rather, we are emphasizing the value of process phenomena in differential diagnosis and the theoretical basis for their use.

By *process phenomena* we mean derivatives as directly related as possible to the underlying causative factors. We can further clarify this definition by comparing the usual behavior phenomena with process phenomena. An individual, for example, displays the behavioral trait of passivity. His passivity may be readily recognized as such, and techniques may be employed for measuring the intensity of this trait. But this behavioral trait in one person may mean something far different from what it means in another. In one case, it may be the direct expression of avoidance or withdrawal defenses. In another, it may signify the presence of some degree of conflict over dependency needs. In still another, it may represent a compromise reaction or a reaction formation to latent aggressive strivings. The accurate assessment of the trait, then, tells us little or nothing about the underlying processes that have given rise to the behavior. The trait may be conceived of as the indirect result of varying underlying process phenomena. Passivity may thus occur as the end product of various conflicting drives and their "resolution" in terms of the ego's resources in dealing with them in the context of a given cultural setting.

The same argument may be made concerning all such traits—which are more accurately described as *surface traits* (Hutt, Isaacson, & Blum, 1966). Traits are usually conceived of as more or less persistent behavioral tendencies. Most present-day objective tests of personality measure such surface traits, and evidence concerning them has considerable value in predicting the likely, overt, behavioral phenomena that an individual may manifest. However, to deal adequately with the person who has these traits, or even to understand him, we need to know something of the conditions which give rise to them. And to do this we have to understand, measure, and deal with the primary process phenomena which produce them (Carr, 1960).

Process phenomena, then, refer to the dynamics of the behavioral resultant. They are rooted in the latent tendencies that each individual possesses—in the drives what motivate his behavior. Rarely do drives manifest themselves directly in observable behavior, even in the most primitive of people. It may be said that the more civilized an individual is, the more indirect is the expression of primary drives. Civilization imposes the requirement that drives be socialized: they must be inhibited, delayed, and integrated in socially appropriate ways. Psychopathology, for different reasons, defensive in character, also requires that only the most indirect expression of drives be permitted. But in both types of instances, the overt behavior can only offer obtuse cluse to the processes that give rise to them. It might be added that it is easier to infer the drives which motivate behavior in the case of a "normal," civilized individual than in the case of a psychopathologic individual; their expression in behavior is more direct in the former instance.

Projective tests, and clinicians employing projective hypotheses, probe for the underlying processes that give rise to a given form of behavior. When a person is asked to respond to a relatively unstructured stimulus, we assume that in the process of organizing his response to this situation, he will display some derivatives of the underlying drives, that he will project these drives into the "test" situation. If we obtain a number of samples of such projective behavior, we are then able to infer the presence and intensity of such drives. Note that we said *infer,* for projective behavior is still overt behavior and merely gives us greater access to underlying phenomena, not direct measures of them. There are two conditions, then, for effective use of projective behavior: a sufficient sample of such behavior under varying conditions, and an inference concerning the sample with respect to the kind of process which gave rise to it.

Now we are in a position to begin to understand the role of the clinician. He will wish to employ, like the psychometrician, those techniques and measures that will enable him to assess, with an appropriate degree of reliability and validity, the presence and intensity of the important traits that the patient manifests. But he will go one step further: he will try to relate these findings and the findings of the case history to the intrapsychic conditions that give rise to them. In this latter step he will employ, among other things, devices like projective tests in order to gain access to process phenomena. To do this he will need more than good instruments for eliciting projective behavior. He will need to know how to go about making certain kinds of inferences from the results of such "tests," and, if he is scientifically trained, he will carefully weigh the significance of the evidence, look for corroborating and constrasting findings, and integrate all of this data into the most parsimonious explanation he can offer for the problems that have been raised.

To play the role of the clinician appropriately, and not just to *play at* the role of clinician, the individual will have acquired certain kinds of training and be able to use this training effectively. In the first place, he will have secured training in general psychology so that he has sophistication about the findings relative to behavior in general. Among other things, he will know the following: something about the principles of scientific method; basic information concerning biological mechanisms; what has been learned concerning behavioral development, including sensory processes and perception, and patterning of behavior; the values and limitations of current theories of personality; the present state of knowledge concerning psychopathology; and theories and techniques relating to therapeutic process. Of these, perhaps of greatest importance for the clinician is his knowledge of personality theory and psychopathology, for without this he cannot make appropriate inferences about his observations and test findings now can he check his intial hypotheses about a patient against other plausible, perhaps more plausible, hypotheses. With these assets in his training, he can, if he is not too rigidly bound in his *initial* speculations about a patient, begin to think through the possible implications of his data (Hutt, 1968).

The last point probably needs elaboration if its meaning is to be clearly conveyed to the reader. There are probably two great limitations in the work of a clinician that may interfere considerably with his effectiveness. One of these is an insensitivity to relevant data. This may come from inadequate knowledge about behavior, especially about psychopathologic behavior, or it may come from an inability to use function appropriately as an observer. Both of these may be improved by training, although there may be serious limitations as to what training can accomplish with some types of personality. The other limitation, also related to both training and personality, concerns the "freedom to speculate wisely" about a patient. The data, once they have been gathered, must be examined in such a variety of ways as to maximize whatever significance they must have. The clinician must be able to entertain relevant hypotheses about the patient, even when the evidence is at first quite tentative, check these hypotheses against all relevant findings, and reject or confirm the hypotheses on the basis of the evidence. Scientific training too often overemphasizes the checking of hypotheses and underemphasizes the ability to develop creative and frankly speculative hypotheses. Both types of creative thinking are essential in developing and checking hypotheses about a patient.

Projective tests offer access to data related to underlying process phenomena, and these data may then be manipulated in various ways to germinate and corroborate inferences concerning psychopathologic behavior. They are less useful in defining specific psychiatric syndromes that have been derived from an examination of clusters of overt behavior. The latter task may well be left to good history and case analysis procedures or to more exactly defined, objective tests of personality. Critics of projective tests who have pointed out that validation studies of such tests have not had great success are essentially correct. The criticism is valid but it overlooks another, at least equally important point. The designation of a particular psychopathologic syndrome tells us very little about the meaning of a particular patient's behavior.

Here, again, we must emphasize our contention that a psychiatric label has little significance when we are dealing with an individual patient. It defines the broad category of people who have the same designated, overt behavioral features, but it does not warrant the assumption that *all* the people with that label have the same conflicts, the same drives, or even necessarily the same psychopathology. To acquire knowledge about these matters requires more appropriate assessment of the nature of the drives, conflicts, ego resources, and other specific characteristics of the psychopathology. This is the clinician's tasks: describing or measuring the character structure of the individual, not merely designating the behavioral syndrome that is present. And this is the task with which the therapist must deal if he is to have meaningful data to manage effectively his interpersonal relationship with the patient. One might highlight this argument by stating that a psychiatric label offers information as to the general category of patients to which the individual belongs and is most useful for administrative reasons, while a psychodiagnostic evaluation of the patient offers information as to the specific features of the dynamic processes which a particular patient possesses and is useful in the appropriate management of the patient.

The HABGT is particularly useful in gaining access to underlying process phenomena. It can be used, as some studies have done, to derive scores based on clusters of perceptual errors in order to define psychiatric categories or severity of psychopathology (Bender, 1938; Gobetz, 1953; Pascal & Suttell 1951). As we have indicated, such a use is of limited value, and there may be other and more efficient ways of securing such results. Or the HABGT may be used to get at underlying process phenomena that give rise to the resultant behavior. Because the ways in which an individual perceives, organizes, and executes responses to a task of this kind maximizes the projective aspects of his behavior, this test offers leads to projective hypotheses about the patient.

We shall now elaborate on this aspect of psychodiagnosis and then present a sample of a projective analysis of a test protocol to concretize the discussion.

When a person is asked to examine a simple Gestalt design, he may or may not perceive it accurately. Whether or not he does depends, first, upon the biological maturation of the organism. Without such maturation the organism is unable to perceive mature Gestalten (Wertheimer, 1923). If, in a particular instance, the individual is able to perceive some of the more mature Gestalt forms (more mature as determined on the basis of normative data), but is unable to perceive accurately some of the less mature Gestalten, we have prima facie evidence that some personality disturbance, and not inadequacy in general maturation, is responsible.

Now, assuming that discrepancies of the kind suggested above do appear, what can be inferred? There are several patterns of perceptual distortion, each of which is related to different kinds of defenses. If, for some idiosyncratic reason, the Gestalt is perceived as threatening to the individual, it may be defended against by *over-adient* or *over-abient* behavior. (See Chapter 6). Abient behavior represents an attempt to withdraw from the perceptual stimulus. In extreme instances, the individual may "black out" the stimulus (or part of it) and not "see" it at all. Some cases of hysterical blindness manifest this kind of defense. Or he may see the stimulus as smaller then it is in reality. Such cases of micropsia represent this kind of defense. Or he may perceive some parts of the stimulus as relatively smaller than other parts. Some cases of withdrawal and repressive responses to curved portions of stimuli represent this kind of defense against the symbolic meaning of curved lines to some patients. On the other hand, he may show an over-adient response, probably a more mature and active type of defense, by increasing the perceptual size of the stimulus or of part of it. In such instances, the patient is able to deal more directly with the stimulus than when he "withdraws" by decreasing size, but he also makes some compensatory efforts in dealing with it.

In addition to gross distortion in size, another type of general defense pattern may be employed. The patient may show the type of distortion which we have called *retrogression*. In such instances, the patient substitutes a more primitive Gestalt for a more mature Gestalt, such as the substitution of a circular form for a diamond, or a substitution of loops for dots, or of nonoverlapping characteristics for overlapping characteristics.

Still another type of distortion is represented by perceptual rotation in which the figure is perceived as it its axis has been rotated to some degree. There are various hypotheses related to different degrees of rotation and to direction of rotation, but, in general, rotation appears to represent feelings of impotency in reacting to the stimulus and to the psychological characteristics that it represents.

These three examples of perceptual distortion may suffice at this point to indicate the projective possibilities of ascertaining relatively pure examples of defensive behavior. As we shall see, there are many other types and subtypes of perceptual distortion, many of which have been studied experimentally and clinically.

However, the HABGT involves not only perceptual but also motoric behavior. Here we can utilize examples of aberrant motor behavior as leads to underlying needs, defenses, and conflicts. For example, a very simple indication of anxiety is the inability to make a smooth, even, motor movement, resulting in incoordination and impulsive motor behavior. Another example is the tendency to exaggerate or to decrease movements in either the horizontal or vertical planes, tendencies that are related to conflict in dealing with close interpersonal relations and authority figures, respectively (Mira, 1939–1940, 1943). Still another is the difficult in executing relatively simple motor responses involving the crossing of lines or the closing of figures, difficulties related to fear of or inability to maintain emotional cathexes with other people (Clawson, 1959; Story, 1960). Each of these behaviors may, of course, be the result of disturbances in the perceptual as well as the motoric sphere.

Finally, the HABGT involves the planning, organizing, and revising of plans in the successive phases of the *basic* method: the copy phase, the elaboration phase, and the association phase. The arrangement on the page (or pages) of successive drawings, the use of space, the use of margins, the ability or inability to modify or to correct discrepancies—these and many other features involving planning and organizing of successive responses give us projective evidence of characteristic personality styles employed by different patients. For example, the crowding of many drawings into a small corner of one page, or the need to separate each drawing from every other drawing, or the inability to shift the placement of the figure in accordance with the reality features of the drawing and the space available represent different kinds of needs and defenses that may be present in different psychiatric syndromes, yet these syndromes have basic underlying features common to all or to some.

One feature of process diagnosis involved the *experimental modification* of test procedures so as to provide a better basis for inferring the factor or factors that help to explain the test behavior. This can be especially important in an individual case. We have indicated that any test phenomenon, no matter how bizarre, can usually be due to more than a single unitary antecedent or cause. The test phenomenon may clearly suggest organic brain damage, or mental retardation, or simply immature perceptual-motoric development. Although this analysis may prove to be true in most cases, the clinician may have reason to be suspicious of the usual conclusion in a given case. In such an instance he may explore the possibility of other explanatory factors by questioning the individual in order to uncover, if possible, what led to the specific test behavior, or by modifying the conditions of the test so as to expose the underlying cause or causes. I have called this procedure Testing-the-Limits (Hutt & Shor, 1946), but it is clearly an experimental–clinical method.

Suppose an individual produced the drawings that are shown in Plate 3. These drawings are taken from a record of a 13-year-old boy who had been referred for study because of delinquency and very inferior school work. The examiner had correctly noted that on design 1 (see Plate 1) the production clearly showed marked evidence of *perseveration* and some degree of *clockwise rotation*. On design 7 the drawings indicated *difficulty with overlapping, difficulty with angulation,* and *closure difficulty*. These and other findings led the examiner to suggest that there was the possibil-

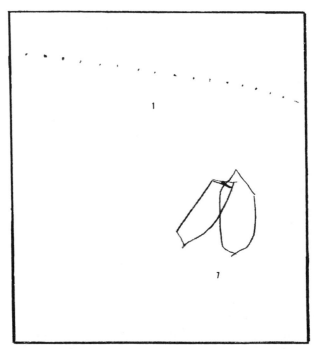

Plate 3. Two Productions on HABGT of a Boy Suspected of Having Organic Brain Damage or Mental Retardation, or Both

ity of organic brain damage or mental retardation, or both. Yet there were inconsistencies in the record that suggested that some other explanation might account for the test behavior. Almost nothing was known about this boy's educational, social, and physical background; he had arrived in his present school only some 9 months before, and no school or medical records were available. The present writer, who was consulting on this case, asked why such information was unavailable and was told that the parents were uncooperative and the boy was uncommunicative! I suggested that we employ a clinical–experimental procedure to investigate some of the factors that might account for the abnormal test phenomena.

The boy was recalled for further examination and another attempt was made to establish better rapport—with some degree of success. Then the examiner presented the test card (for design 1) alongside the test production that the boy had offered on the initial test. He was asked: "Can you tell me whether these two are exactly the same?" When he responded that they were not, he was asked: "And how are they different?" He replied that his design had too many dots. He was asked: "Is there anything else that is different in your drawing?" And the boy stated

that his drawing was "not straight." The examiner then gave the boy a
new sheet of paper and told him: "This time, I'd like you to copy the
drawing on the card to that yours is exactly like that one." In Plate 4, it
will be seen that the boy's first new effort was much better than his
original reproduction. Since the product was still inaccurate, the boy was
again asked whether it was exactly correct, and when he noted that it was
not, he was asked to try again. His second new effort resulted in a very
fine reproduction, without any indication of psychopathological significance.

The same type of procedure was followed for design 7. Again it took
two additional trials before a good production was achieved. It was also
obvious from observation of the boy's behavior that he needed a great
deal of encouragement and urging in order for him to exert sufficient effort
to complete satisfactory drawings. It was clear that he did not suffer from
any gross perceptual-motoric abnormality and that he had not had much
previous experience in performing with great care on tasks such as these.

Subsequent interviews with the boy and his parents revealed that he
had attended school for only short periods during his previous educational

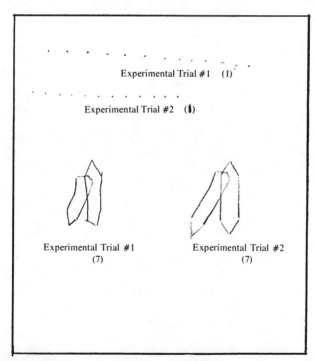

Plate 4.   Clinical–Experimental Trials on HABGT for the Drawings Reproduced
in Plate 2

career, that his parents, who were illiterate and not very involved with their child, offered almost no motivation for schooling, and that the family had suffered from severe financial difficulties, was of very low socioeconomic status, and was, in other respects, seriously "disadvantaged." We shall not attempt to elucidate the picture further except to indicate that this boy, who had suffered from such deprivation, was apparently of about average intelligence but had a very low aspiration level, very limited educational skills, and little interest in coping with the very complex situation into which he had been moved when the family came to live in this new area. The "apparent" pathological indicators on the first HABGT were, rather than evidence of pathology, manifestations of his low level of involvement in the tasks he was given and indicative of his practice of doing things in the easiest way available to him. Perseveration and the slight rotation design 1 essentially resulted from a lack of adequate effort and involvement in the task. The difficulties on design 7 reflected the same factors, this design presenting an even more difficult task and requiring even greater attention and careful effort. The clinical–experimental procedures were instrumental in eliminating some of the tentative formulations suggested earlier, and they led to exploration and elucidation of some of the relevant factors.

10
Illustrative Cases: Intensive Diagnosis

We now present two cases, those of an adult and a child, to illustrate scoring on the objective scales, inferential analysis, and integration of the data. In actual clinical work the findings on these cases would be supplemented with case history and other types of data. First, however, we shall discuss principles of inferential analysis.

INFERENTIAL ANALYSIS

Inferential analysis depends, in the first instance, on the presence of discrete phenomena that already have a substantial body of data for validation purposes. However, this type of analysis goes beyond the simple statement of a correlational relationship between each phenomenon and each "trait." It assumes, on the contrary, that the successive productions of a given sequence of events are uniquely determined by the interaction of multidetermined events over a span of time so that the final product on the test represents the idiosyncratic resultant of the *given constellation of events operating over time.* Moreover, it involves the postulation of not one but several alternate hypotheses during the process of developing inferences, until the analysis of sequential findings tends to confirm one or several of these hypotheses and simultaneously reject others. To illustrate in a general way what we mean by these latter two phases in sequential inference we may refer once again, as we did previously, to the problem of passivity.

Suppose that our test results indicate that, as one of the plausible hypotheses, the patient in question shows passivity. We may have come to this inference on the basis of such evidence as: light line drawings, reduction of the Gestalten in the vertical plane, increased size of the figures involving curved lines, and difficulty with intersecting figures. Assuming that passivity is indeed present, we are now confronted with questions as: "Is the passivity a reaction formation to pronounced aggressive drives?" "Is the passitivity part of a feminine orientation on the part of the patient?" "Is the passivity part of a general withdrawal of cathexes or of some other type of withdrawal?" At this point we have to examine the test data before and especially after those points at which the passive phenomena appeared. We may then find that the patient responds only to certain figures by passive withdrawal, that during the elaboration phase of the test, when he is offered greater freedom, passive characteristics do not occur, and that during the association phase he offers a number of marked but covert responses (symbolic) of aggression, like "hitting," "tearing," "cutting," and "disintegrating." In the light of the total response repertoire, and particularly in the light of successive sequences during which passivity occurs or fails to occur, we may be led to some final inference concerning the meaning, intensity, and etiology of the phenomenon of passivity.

General Stylistic Qualities

There are many ways in which to start the process of inferential analysis. One might begin with the first figure on the test, "speculate" concerning the specific features of the reproduction of this figure (or, more precisely, list the separate hypotheses that all of the features of the reproduction might suggest), and then move on in sequence to each of the subsequent figures, following this, in turn, with a similar type of analysis of the material from the elaboration and association phases. However, this type of procedure fails to take into account the general stylistic qualities of the total set of drawings, and we believe it is generally desirable to begin with this feature of the test. The major argument for this proposal is that the general style of the patient, as revealed in the overall organization and arrangement of the drawings on the page (and the repetition or modification of this style in the various phases of the test) reveals the most general and pervasive qualities of the patient's personality at the time of the test, and thereby offers some important and convenient parameters within which to organize the several separate and successive inferences from each of the drawings.

Let us contrast one aspect of "style" in two patients in order to make this point more meaningful. Suppose that we had the records of two adult patients, one of which showed a crowding of the nine figures within the confines of the upper one-third a single page, while the other showed a "distribution" of the figures over three pages. We could infer from the first patient's record a reaction of extreme withdrawal, perhaps suspiciousness, as well as marked anxiety in the face of a relatively nonthreatening test situation. Similarly, we could infer from the other record, a reaction of an extratensive individual, perhaps manic in quality, perhaps egocentric and the like, with relatively little overt anxiety or suspiciousness. Having offered such general hypotheses about each patient, we could then go on to test them, add to them, or modify them in the light of the several features of each of the separate drawings.

We shall begin, then, with features concerning the general style of the patient's drawings. The following suggestions may be applied separately to the drawings obtained from each phase of the test (or each method). When these several and separate analyses have been made from the data obtained in each phase, they may then be integrated into the most parsimonious set of explanations and predictions for the entire set of drawings.

The first question that confronts us is how much *space* the patient used for all the drawings. Was it excessive, constricted, or normal (in terms of the criteria listed in Chapter 4)? The amount of space used tells us something concerning the patient's self-percept vis-a-vis the rest of the world. Furthermore, the ways in which he uses space as he moves through the total test tells us how adaptable he is with respect to this general orientation. It is highly useful in analyzing this portion of the data to try to emphathize with the patient's actual performance so that, in addition to the hypotheses we have offered in Chapters 4 and 8 concerning the use of space, we can derive tentative, alternative hypotheses concerning the specific ways in which this particular patient used space as he proceeded through the successive portions of the test.

Next, having extricated all of the possible inferences we can from the patient's use of space, we may turn our attention to the problem of *sequence*. Here, we start again with the criteria listed in the previous chapter, noting all of the hypotheses that the data suggest concerning sequence. These are noted, first, without regard to whether or not they appear to be in conflict with the hypotheses derived from the analysis of space. Moreover, any idiosyncratic features of the sequence are noted and hypotheses are developed. An example of this would be a generally orderly sequence with an outstanding exception, say, on figure 6 (the sinusiodal curves), in which a marked change in sequence appears, followed by an orderly sequence for the remaining figures. One would want to consider the possible difficulties that figure 6 might impose upon this or any patient, and the possible reaction to the previous figure in the light of what is known about these figures (see later discussion in this chapter). Having formed these two general sets of hypotheses, from the use of space and from sequence, it would be well, next, to attempt to reconcile them, being sure not to discard any hypothesis that cannot clearly be rejected. In this process, hypotheses of a higher, more integrated order might appear, or additional, alternative hypotheses, not deducible from either space or sequence alone, might be formed.

The next step in the general analysis of style concerns the *placement of the first figure*. Here again, as with the problem of the use of space, the patient's initial stylistic adaptation to his life space can be inferred (see Chapter 4). Does he, for example, place his first figure (i.e., himself) in the middle of the page, suggesting a highly egocentric orientation with respect to the world? Does he squeeze the first figure into the upper left-hand corner of the page, suggesting extreme withdrawal and fearfulness? Of course, the nature of the reproduction of the first figure (figure A) will enter into the speculative hypotheses that may be offered, but we shall leave until later the discussion of the separate figures. Once again, having made whatever hypotheses seem plausible on the basis of this stylistic feature, we attempt to integrate these with the previous hypotheses we have derived.

Next, we note whether any *collision or near collision phenomena* are present. Such data are indicative of loss of anticipatory controls and are most frequently associated with either marked anxiety (basic or transitional) or with intracranial damage and possible loss in psychological or motor control. In either case, there is an impairment of ego functions, and we carefully note the adaptation made during and following the figures on which collision tendencies occur. For instance, collision tendencies involving curved figures differ from those involving straight-line figures: the former are more likely to be associated with difficulty in expressive aggressive drives; the latter are more likely to be associated with passive drives. As another example, collision involving more complex figures, such as 7 and 8, but not simple figures like 3 and 4, are more likely to relate to loss in cognitive rather than emotional factors. We also examine the drawings to determine whether the patient is aware of or attempts to correct his collision phenomena. Such behavior indicates at least marginal awareness of the perceptual–motoric problem and, when corrected placement occurs after collision, is indicative of modifiability of response pattern—a highly useful finding in terms of therapeutic management and prognosis.

Another general stylistic feature refers to the *use of the margin*. We have already noted the most probable hypotheses associated with this phenomenon (see Chapter 8). We can offer a number of hypotheses based on the general use of the margin and others based on the use of the margin for some of the individual figures alone. If, by this point in our analysis of a particular record, consistent hypotheses have been derived from the several sources of data concerning general style, we can be reasonably certain that these are strong hypotheses. Further indication of their strength may be derived from subsequent analyses of the separate figures, and then again from analysis of the data obtained during the elaboration phase of the test.

One other general source of hypotheses derived from stylistic features is that of *rotation of the test paper and the test cards.* Hypotheses related to egocentricity and/or rigidity are based on rotations of 90 degrees to about 180 degrees, while those related to oppositional qualities are based on rotation of 180 degrees or more.

All of the inferences derived thus far are based upon the overt behavior shown by the patient during the test and in his responses. To the extent that the behavior has obvious meaning to the patient, as, for example, when he rotates the cards despite the structuring of the test in opposition to such placement, or when he places his first figure in the center of the page, we can assume that the phenomena in question are at the conscious or preconscious level. To the extent that the behavior has only latent meaning, such as, for example, when the sequence is changed because a particular figure has some symbolic threat for the patient, we can assume that unconscious factors are operating. Not only can we therefore make a rough categorization of the level of meaning of the behavior to the patient (from conscious to unconscious), but by virtue of our general knowledge of phychopathology and the operation of defenses, we can begin to infer some specific types of dynamics (nature and severity of conflict) for the patient. Such dynamic inferences, especially as they are reinforced or confirmed in the light of evidence associated with the distortions on the several figures and with data from the elaborations and associations, are powerful tools for predicting the nature and significance of unconscious processes for the patient. When these are integrated with the overt behavior of the patient they enable us to extend our clinical analysis to cover a wider varity of contingencies than when they are limited to only one source of data (see Chapter 9).

Elaboration and Association Phases

If the clinician has been following our suggestions for developing inferences from the responses to the copy phase of the test he will have developed many explanations and hunches concerning the patient, he will have revised and extended some of these, and he will have rejected others in the light of a more parsimonious explanation that became available. Further, utilizing his knowledge concerning personality theory and psychopathology, he will have developed a general personality conceptualization concerning the specific patient. On the basis of such leads a number of second-order inferences can then be developed. However, if data are available from the elaboration and association phases of the test, it would be advisable to examine these data before attempting to integrate these second-order hypotheses.

We have already discussed the rationale for the procedures of the elaboration and association phases of the test in Chapter 3. At this point we wish merely to emphasize certain features of these rationales.

In the first place, the motoric activity involved in the process of elaborating the Gestalt figures (especially since ego controls are relaxed somewhat by the instruction to "modify the figures . . . so as to make them more pleasing") tends to produce both exaggeration of underlying and relatively more unconscious processes, and associations and material (traumatic) related to the anal and oedipal phases of development (the periods of "socialization"). Consistencies in distortions first found in the copy phase and later exaggerated in the elaboration phase are therefore of special interest. Also of interest are new types of distortions that occur only on the elaboration phase. These consistencies and new types of evidence can be evaluated more completely in terms of the associations given by the patient to both the copy phase and the elaboration phase material. Although we have stressed the capacity of these procedure to elicit material from anal and phallic phases, other phases of development may be projected in these materials—for example, such obvious "oral" associations to figure 6 as "a fountain" or "sucking movements."

Sometimes patients will reveal "sudden insights" concerning material they have produced during the elaboration phase. They will verbalize with surprise that they didn't know just what they were doing, or they were just "doodling," but now it is very clear that the figure means "such and such." Often, they will insist that no other explanation is possible; i.e., because of the intensity of the projection, they will have "lost distance" from their productions and can entertain no alternative explanations. Sometimes they will exclaim that the association is something they had forgotten or had never thought about before. Such kinds of verbal behavior are important evidence of the intrinsic validity of the productions—although, of course, any clinician will realize that sometimes the most apparently valid recollections are but screen memories.

In analyzing the elaboration data, it is suggested that the general rules offered for developing hypotheses in connection with the copy phase data be followed. First, it is desirable to analyze the general stylistic features of the total set of elaboration productions, and then it is advisable to analyze the separate productions in the sequence in which they were offered. Also, the same general procedures should be followed for entertaining apparently contradictory hypotheses until the evidence forces a selection or integration of the explanations. Only after the elaboration material has been analyzed in this manner is it desirable to compare the implications of the elaboration with the copy phase hypotheses in detail.

Now we present an adult HABGT record to illustrate our analysis.

STEPHEN—A CASE OF SEVERE INTERNAL TURMOIL

This is the case of a 26-year-old man who felt that his only problems were those created by his and nagging and inconsiderate wife. He did not profess to see any need for psychotherapy for himself, but came for consultation because he felt that his marital problems were serious. He was quite successful in his career as a consulting engineer. However, he recognized that his associates kept at a distance from him and sometimes complained that he was rigid and spiteful. After the HABGT had been administered he was asked to comment on his performance and his reactions during the test. He felt he had done well, but could not understand why he had "changed" some of the figures. He said he had tried to draw them veridically, yet felt "compelled" to modify them as he did; he was fully aware of the differences between his drawings and those on the test cards. Further discussion of the test and his personal situation convinced him that he had significant intrapersonal problems and he requested therapy for himself.

Inferential Analysis

We shall comment only briefly on the major aspects of his test performance in order to highlight some of the personality characteristics that they suggested.

On the copy phase (Plate 5), one notes his need to compartmentalize completely all of his drawings by enclosing them in "boxes." He boxed in each figure after he had completed it. Figure A is accurate except that he enlarges the diamond; some closure difficulty is noted. Figure 1 is constricted in size. Figure 2 is also constricted (horizontally) and shows some highly unusual and idiosyncratic characteristics. It is composed of two sections, and contains ellipses in the middle row instead of circles. Thus far, we note that this is the performance of a highly compulsive, highly repressed, and overly controlling individual. The unusual features of figure 2, especially the loss of angulation in the columns, with a shift in their orientation toward himself as the focus, suggest that he is very willful, highly egocentric, and possibly paranoidal in orientation. Spacing between the figures throughout the record tends to be constricted.

Figure 3 is elongated in the horizontal dimension, and the dots are filled in heavily; we would infer that he reacts in the interpersonal sphere

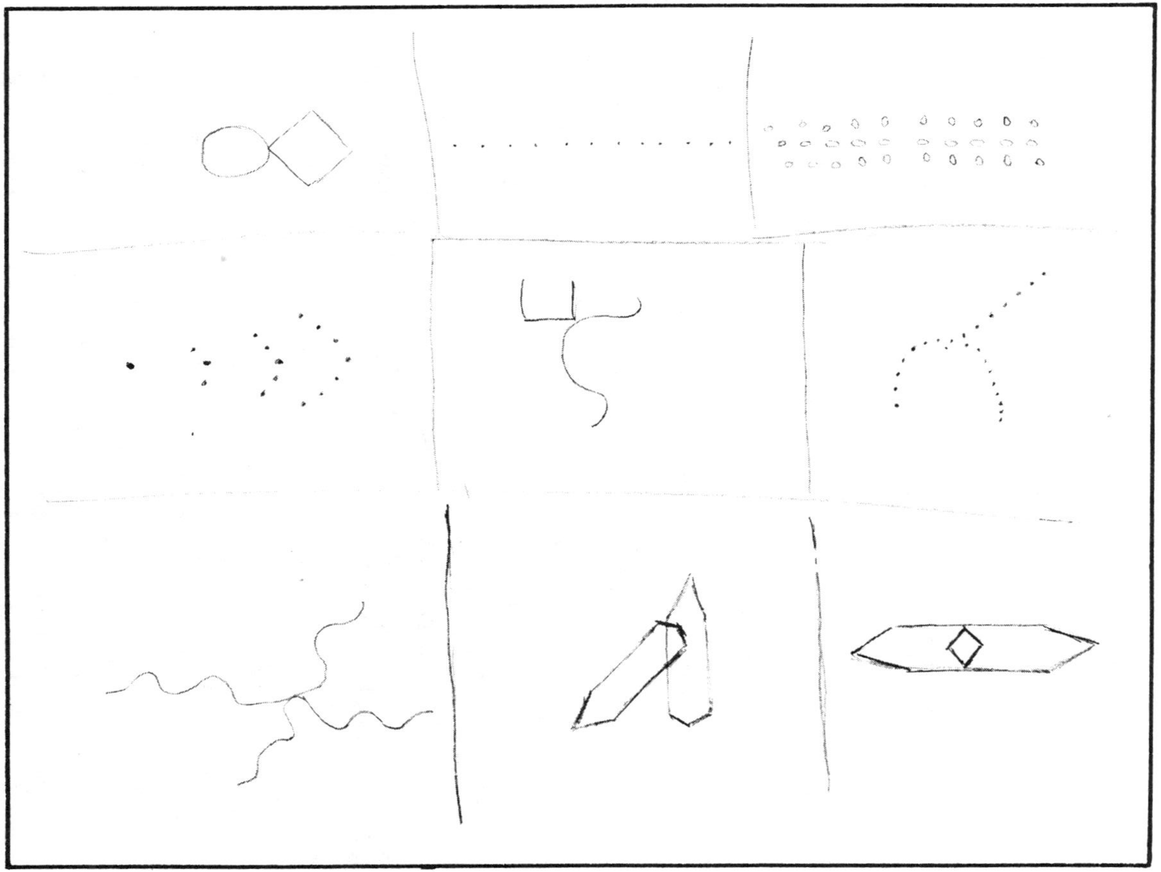

Plate 5. Stephen—Copy Phase

by overassertion and aggression. Figure 4 contains a number of distortions. There is a slight "gap" between the figures, the open square is compressed, and the curved portion is exaggerated and off focus. One would suspect that he is a highly tense individual who is overly defensive and has some problems in terms of sexual identity.

Figure 5 is rotated slightly in a clockwise direction. He sketches the curved portion of the figure before filling in the dots. Figure 6 is drawn as two asymptotic curves, rotated slightly in a clockwise direction, and the curves are uneven in amplitude. By now we have indications of depressive features in the personality and indications of poor affective control with a tendency to turn anger inward (which may be a source of his depression). He simplifies figure 7 (perhaps to avoid the difficult overlapping problem) and does obvious sketching and redrawing. Figure 8 is also sketched and shows redrawing. The closure difficulties on figures 7 and 8 plus the "hallmark" on figure 8 of sexual conflict (intensely drawn internal diamond, and difficulties with the "phallic" ends of the hexagon), suggest how impotent this individual feels as "a man" and how much he must overcompensate.

The obsessive and compulsive features of this record are conspicuous. In the light of this, his distortions take on added significance.

Turning now to the elaboration (Plate 6) and association phases, we note first that his compulsive style is quite evident; he still finds it necessary to compartmentalize each figure. (Note: only 6 of the figures were given for the elaboration phase.) With the exception of figure 2 and 4, he simply tries to reproduce, rather than elaborate, the drawings. Figure 2 is "tied together" with straight lines; figure 4 is elaborated into what looks like a "Valentine presentation." Moreover, on figure 4 the open squares are made even smaller and the curved portion even larger.

His associations are quite revealing. He gives two associations to stimulus card A: "A ball that hangs on the end of a chain, knocking down a building;" and, "An error in a computer program. Each symbol represents an action. It should have an arrow." No associations are given to his elaboration. The possible meanings of the associations are quite apparent. They will become even more clear as we examine his other associations. His associations to the stimulus of figure 2 are "Webbing in a building;" and "Military formation or a disarranged pegboard." His association to his elaboration of this figure is: "Edge of tapestry. Woven material. Woven fabric or frame of a picture." We should comment on the obviously ambivalent characteristics of these associations: militaristic and aggressive, on the one hand, and feminine and soft, on the other.

His association to card 4 is: "A vessel poised on the edge of a table" (note the projection of his self-precarious identity), while his associations to his elaborations are: "My mother; an asymmetrical figure; a design, a

Plate 6. Stephen—Elaborations

nonobject.'' The possible meanings of these associations were explored in his therapeutic sessions and clearly indicated how tied he was emotionally to his mother, yet how much he "hated" her.

On card 6 he associated: "Looks like uncombed hair; grotesque tree limbs." On figure 7 (to the card only) he responded: "Two geometrical symbols; parts of a plane intersecting, as in teaching parallelograms." On figure 8, he offered his associations to the elaboration: "Kerchief of a Boy Scout's ring; like a totem belt you buy in a souvenir store; pieces of costume jewelry."

We could profitably spend considerable time in dealing with these associations. Suffice it to say that his confused sexual identity, his intense narcissistic attitudes, and his repressed rage seem strongly suggested.

Thus far we have evaluated this man's performance in terms of stylistic qualities, types of distortions, and associations to the test reproductions. Now, we shall evaluate him in terms, first of his Psychopathology Score, and then in terms of a Configurational analysis. These objective indices will help us to confirm the severity of his psychopathology and offer clues to its nature.

Findings on the Psychopathology Scale

As we see, Stephen obtains a Psychopathology Scale score of 51.5 (see Table 10.1). This score places him close to the mean of outpatient neurotics (see Table 4.2, Chapter 4). Moreover, his score is more than 3 SDs *above* the mean of "normals." His score is also significantly lower than the means obtained for psychotics. Moreover, with the possible exception of moderate scores on Rotation and Overlapping, he shows none of the serious indications of psychotic or organic patients; i.e., he shows no destruction of any of the Gestalts. Thus, we have confirmation that, although he shows severe emotional problems, ego functions and personality integration are reasonably intact.

Table 10.1
Psychopathology Scale Findings: Case K, Stephen

Test Factor	Scale Value	Test Factor	Scale Value
1. Sequence	4.0	10. Perc. Rotation	4.0
2. Positon 1st Fig.	1.0	11. Retrogression	1.0
3. Space	10.0	12. Simplification	1.0
4. Collision	1.0	13. Fragmentation	1.0
5. Shift of Paper	1.0	14. Overlapping	5.5
6. Closure Diff.	10.0	15. Elaboration	1.0
7. Crossing Diff.	1.0	16. Perseveration	1.0
8. Curvature Diff.	4.0	17. Redrawing	1.0
9. Angulation	2.0		
Total scaled score: 51.5			

Findings on Configuration Analysis

In Table 10.2 we present the scores on the Configuration for Essential Psychoneurotics (refer to Table 5.4, Chapter 5).

Stephen's Configuration Score of 6–8 places him within or above the Marginal Scores for neurotics (4–7) and, possibly, just within the range of Critical Scores (8 or above), if we count his score on compartmentalization. This is the record of an individual with highly idiosyncratic characteristics and who most closely fits the configuration of neurotics, rather than that of more severe psychopathology. Thus, again, we find confirmation of our Inferential Analysis.

Our analysis has revealed that Stephen has quite serious emotional problems, that he is sufficiently "intact" to be able to function reasonably well in most situations, and that he is most disturbed in terms of interpersonal and sexual relationships. In addition to his narcissism, there is evidence to suggest that he denies a great deal, that he is somewhat paranoidal, and that he has considerable, repressed anger. He is obviously intelligent and is highly compulsive. There is some ego–alien characteristics in that he is dimly aware that many of his problems are "internal," but at the same time he is likely to project many of his problems to others rather than to accept them as his own.

This man did enter psychotherapy and made very good, but slow and painful, progress. Gradually, he became less "defended" and was able to experience his internal conflicts and feelings. His suspiciousness of others (his paranoidal tendencies) were brought into focal awareness and were finally resolved. In the end, he became quite sensitive to the sources and nature of his conflicts and was not only able to make a much better

Table 10.2
Scores on Configuration: Essential
Psychoneurosis

PS #	Test Factor	Weight
1	Irregular sequence	0
7	Crossing difficulty	0
8	Curvature difficulty	0
9	Angulation difficulty	0
*	Isolated changes in size	2
*	Inconsistent lines	1
*	Constriction in size, severe	2
*	Excessive use of margin†	0–2
*	Inconsistent movement	1
	Stephen's Score = 6–8	

† (not margin, but compartmentalization)

interpersonal adjustment, but was able to become more creative and productive in his work.

THE CASE OF DAVID—AN APPARENTLY BENIGN RECORD

This case is presented for historical reasons. Note should be taken of the fact that the analysis, and the scoring on which it is based, were completed in 1951 with the definitions and normative data available at the time.

The HABGT record of this 25-year-old male is presented in Plate 7. The record was obtained as part of a psychological evaluation and was then given to the present author with only the information summarized in the next paragraph. The interpretation is quoted essentially as it was presented and published in the volume by Shneidman, Joel, and Little (Hutt, 1951). Following the summary, we shall comment briefly on the problems that this record presents and on the clinical and therapeutic findings that were later made available and summarized in the volume by Shneidman et al. (1951).

It shall not be our purpose to discuss the types of qualifications one must bear in mind in discussing this record, qualifications arising from a situation in which the interpreter is in ignorance of such things as the nature of the setting in which this examination was administered, the sequence of tests, the therapy preceding the test, if any, the nature of the interpersonal relation, and the like. This interpreter had at his disposal the test record (photographic reproductions) and some very brief notes on methods of work (both of which are included with this record of interpretation). The only other information available were these limited identification data: age, 25 years; sex, male; marital status, single; education, high school; handedness, left; no gross physical limitations.

Inferential Analysis

Our first "general" inspection of the test protocol reveals the following: the drawings are arranged in "correct" sequence from A, the introductory design, to 8, the last design, and the patient "lines" his drawings up along the left margin until he has reached the bottom of the sheet, then proceeds by "completing the available space," introducing design 7 to the right of and under design 2, and follows this, again in sequence and in the vertical plane, with the last design. We note further that design A is attempted in a locus slightly to the right of the next six designs that follow it. Our first hunches then are: this individual has strong orderly i.e.,

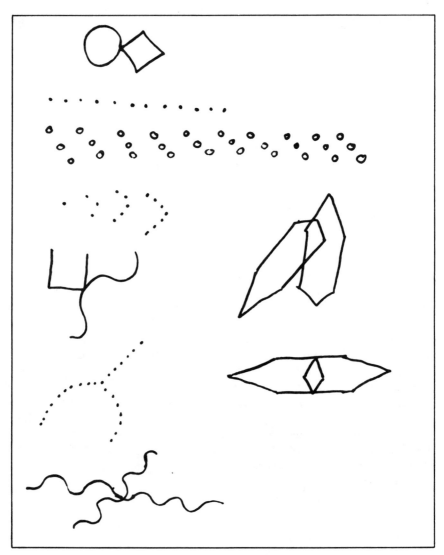

Plate 7.   David—An Apparently Benign Record

compulsive needs, tending toward a sort of compulsive ritual, but tries to
deny them (the aberrant position of A plus the examiner's comment on
this design, "Draws fast, without hesitation"), and he is oppressed with
some (probably) generalized feelings of anxiety and (more specifically)
personal inadequacy (clings to the left margin and is "constrained" to use
all of the space available to him on this one sheet). We raise the question
for consideration, at once, "How strong and from what source is this

anxiety and what is his defense?" We can speculate, from his use of space, that he attempts in some way to "bind" his anxiety, i.e., he cannot tolerate it for long or in large amounts, and that one of the features of this young adult's functioning is the need of control. Taken together, the compulsivity, the "binding" of anxiety, and the need of control offer the first general inference: the superego is very strict.

Permit us to interrupt the formal analysis at this point to review some features of our method of interpretation, since what we have attempted to demonstrate thus far is characteristic of our approach to the analysis of this test. We examined two main features of the test record: spatial arrangement (sequence) and use of the total space area. We correlated extreme orderliness of sequence with compulsivity in functioning (based on the normative findings from our clinical samples from young adults) and the fairly extreme use of the margin with anxiety (again a normative clinical finding). These are considered *tentative* formulations at this point, to be confirmed, modified or rejected in the light of subsequent analysis. We also noted that the "locus" of figure A was slightly deviant from the others (in the use of the margin), considered the examiner's comment regarding subject's haste in drawing, and offered the implication: "but tries to deny them," i.e., his needs for control. Next, utilizing our general knowledge of pathology (or, better, personality dynamics), we tried to speculate concerning the meaning of these clinical manifestations and offered the *inference:* "the superego is very strict." This, in microcosm, is our method of analyzing traits, needs, defenses, symptoms and function. The test is a sample of the nonverbal, perceptual-motor behavior of the individual. As such it has intrinsic validity as a behavioral representation of the patient's adaptation at the moment. We utilize our normative data as cues to interpretation for this particular sample of this particular individual. Some of the cues may appear to be contradictory; others may supplement and confirm each other. The clinical task is to make meaning not only of the cues but their interrelationships and, based on the frame of reference for all humans from a similar population (i.e., the personality dynamics of young, American, ostensibly white, high school graduate adults, in this case), to predict the underlying kind of personality that could be responsible for this total production.

Returning now to the test record, we examine figure A more carefully. The size is slightly smaller than the original. The horizontal axis of the figure is rotated slightly in a clockwise direction. These suggest: fear (self-critical attitude) and depressive reaction, respectively. Both figures are of proportionate size (no specific, exaggerated reaction to either male or female sex symbol), but, perhaps, the moderate rotation of the horizontal axis of the total figure is due to a specific reaction (dread of, hostility toward or lack of identification with, the male parent or surrogate). The latter possibility, or a derivative of it, is supported by the difficulty in "joining" the two figures (exaggerated, redrawn, overemphasized junction of the figures). This point is the more likely to be significant in view of the patient's speed in drawing and in view of the apparently impulsive, concave sides of the square.

Figure 1, the twelve dots, is also drawn fast, with "no checking back on number of dots," the examiner notes. The number of dots is correct (confirms the patient's need for exactness, i.e., his compulsive trend), but the line of dots is wavy, the dots are filled in, and they are somewhat uneven in size and intensity. Here again, we find the apparent dilemma proposed above: the patient is compulsive but attempts to deny it. For a person who arranges his drawings on the page so methodically this "carelessness" in the alignment and size of the dots is striking. Perhaps he perceives the task of figure 1 as too simple to require careful effort. His tendency toward "haste" on all of the drawings suggests: impulsivity *or* a derogatory attitude toward the test *or* inner tension that is flowing over. The fact that the dots are heavily (and unevenly) filled in suggests that it is the last alternative which fits best. General, tentative inference: high aspiration level in a tense individual unable to accept simple experiences as nonchallenging. It is also worth noting that the dots tend to follow a downward trend: depressive reaction.

Figure 2, the ten diagonal columns of circles, offers further evidence of the marked variability that begins to appear to be characteristic of this patient. The examiner notes, "Checks number of rows (i.e., columns) about two-thirds through." We note that the angles of the columns of dots differ, becoming more obtuse (from the vertical) with a correction toward the end. The whole figure is exaggerated in the lateral plane. Together, these findings suggest a strong need to relate to people, but difficulty in establishing such relationships. The orientation of the first column is correct, so the variation in "angulation" is not a simple perceptual difficulty. The patient gets the number of columns correct, but varies both angulation and spacing. We have evidence, then, for the presence of considerable internal tension with an attempt at denial of its existence. How can we explain the apparent contradiction of the need for order and control with the speed and variability of performance? His compulsive defenses do not function effectively enough. In addition to the postulation of his impulsivity, we must add some mechanism that permits him to react so emotionally, i.e., so violently. This is especially necessary in view of "collision tendency" (figures 1 and 2). We therefore think of "acting-out," a mechanism in which ego controls are cut off (cease to function temporarily) and regressive impulsivity breaks through. If this is indeed the case, we can argue that superego demands can be side-stepped, guilt is temporarily overome only to return in increasing intensity once the ego is later able to survey the transgression. This would thereby satisfy the patient's masochistic needs (to expiate his guilt) and thus serve a doubly useful purpose. Another possibility, which we should like to consider, is that of psychotic episodes, but the evidence for this in the record is lacking (there is no indication of a full-fledged psychotic process in the record), so we abandon this for the more parsimonious explanation already given.

Figure 3 is elongated laterally, a further indication of the patient's attempt to relate to others. The dissociation of the parts of the "arrow-head" supports the possibility of the "acting-out" mechanism offered above. The downward orientation of the figure again suggests depressive reaction. The correct number of dots and the intensity of the dots indicate: orderliness (i.e., compulsive trend) and inner tension. The Gestalt is accurate, although, again, in the segment consisting of five dots, the "postmark" of impulsivity is revealed. The increase in the horizontal dimension of the figure is accompanied by a decrease in the vertical dimension; is he fearful of authority figures?

In figure 4, the patient has increased the vertical sides of the open square; (there are no notes by the examiner); this is deduced from the "breaks" occurring in both vertical lines. His reaction to authority figures can now be inferred more completely: he is hostile to such figures, unable to express his hostility directly, and reacts either symbolically or impulsively. In line with the "acting-out" hypothesis, the former is more likely. The curved portion of this figure is enlarged, flattened out in the middle, and reveals an impulsive flourish at the upper end. Now we may speculate that his major identification is with a female figure, but she is perceived as more masculine (i.e., dominant, aggressive) than feminine and is reacted to openly with antagonism. It is interesting that the upper portion of the curved figure extends well above its position on the stimulus card, and is at least as high up as the vertical lines. Here we may conjecture that his mother (or surrogate) was stronger psychologically than his father, or at least seemed so to him, and that he would like to use his mother (or women) to defy his father (or men).

The depressive coloring in the patient's attempt at figure 5 is striking (clockwise orientation of the total figure). He has difficulty with the projecting line of dots, attaching it about midway on the circumference of the "semicircle" of dots, although it is off-center on the stimulus. Despite this, other features of the drawing are precisely accurate: the number of dots in the "semicircle," the number of dots in the projection, and the position between the seventh and eighth dot of the circumference for the point of union. Here is, indeed, compulsive attention to detail, despite which, the figure in toto is distorted. If we accept the premise that this figure "stands for" the mother surrogate, we may then infer that his vehemence against this symbol can be, and is, expressed in an open-structured figure, while he cannot so distort it in the simpler, more conventional symbolism of figure A. Again, this would support the premise of a symbolic acting-out of his conflict with his mother (and with women), although conventionally he is deferent, obedient and conformist.

Figure 6, the sinusoidal curves, taxes him to the utmost. Affect is strong (amplitude of curves), but is expressed unevenly (uneven wave lengths). Marked difficulty occurs at the crossing. (E's notes support this.) The excessive loop at the top of the vertical curve plus the fact that this curve was drawn first, from the top down, express the patient's suppressed hostility to male, parental symbols. The Gestalt is accurate, but the difficulty with this figure is apparent in the drawing. One would expect this patient to show some apathy in his typical behavior, but react on occasion with outbursts, probably of a sexual, or, better, sexual-symbolic, character.

On figure 7, the right-hand figure is rotated slightly in a clockwise direction and all of the joinings show "closure difficulty." There is an exaggeration of the lower section of the left-hand figure. The Gestalt is accurate. We infer: depressive reactions; difficulty in maintaining interpersonal relations; feelings of sexual inadequacy (possibly feelings of impotence).

The same closure difficulty is noted on figure 8, on which E says, "Draws small inside diamond first, then encloses." The figure is increased in size laterally and the ends are exaggerated. Inferences: difficulty in interpersonal relations; major identification with female figures; sexual impotency (or fear thereof).

One final observation: the spacing between successive figures is constricted. This fits in with our conception of him as essentially anal in fixation and generally suppressive of conscious hostility feelings.

From all of the above, we may attempt to etch out the personality as it functions on this psychological task, and offer some predictions to be considered in the light of other data.

We would suspect that this individual tries to give the impression of a sophisticated, but conforming, individual. He has unusually high aspirations, but feels limited and inadequate, although ordinarily denying this to others and attempting to deny it to himself. He is subject to marked inner turmoil, but attempts to conceal this, too, from others and himself. His ambition and drive toward achievement, and in general his compulsive controls offer some compensation, but they are not enough. He suffers from melancholy and intense feelings of frustration. He finds it increasingly difficult to work effectively. At the root of his difficulty lies an identification with a dominant, and to him, unrewarding mother-figure, toward whom he reacts with some hostility, but toward whom he is very attracted sexually. For some reason (the record is not indicative) he is also fearful (and unable to express it) toward the father-figure. We may speculate that the father is perceived as strong but ineffectual in relation to the mother (for some reason) and that he has guilt over his attraction to the mother, who is objective, strong, just, but unobtainable. With this nucleus in this type of oedipal conflict as a base, his development was attended by deep guilt reactions stirred by a strict superego development. A relatively strong ego enabled him to move along for a time until late adolescent and young adult situational factors decreased the effectiveness of ego functions, at least for a time. It is suggested that then either Don Juan behavior or symbolic acting-out occurred (possibly both), and guilt increased until the prevalent masochistic pattern was reestablished. One would suspect that depressive reactions, possibly suicidual preoccupation, began as the cycle became tighter and as the vocational-occupational sublimations became less effective with decreased efficiency in total functioning. The Don Juan hypothesis is in line with the speculation that he tried to act out his needs for masculine competence in the fact of increasing feelings of sexual inadequacy and guilt. the anchorage of good, intense relationships with peers is lacking, although wished for.

Superficially, this young man may give the impression of control and fair effectiveness. If our speculations concerning the nature of his difficulties are substantially correct, we may suggest that he will be able to make very effective use of analytically oriented therapy, providing this is both intensive and fairly extensive.

Additional Data

The above analysis of a record attempts to present an illustration of inferential analysis. We can evaluate it in terms of effectiveness against the extensive clinical and treatment findings which Shneidman et al. (1951) subsequently presented in the same volume.

Insofar as basic dynamics are concerned, the HABGT analysis comes remarkably close to the findings of the man's therapist; not only are the statements of the nature of the conflicts and their attempted resolution the same or very similar, but even the rhetorical phrasing of the problem in the HABGT report and in the report of the therapist is very similar, almost identical.

It might also be pointed out that the report of the psychology staff of the hospital where this man was under study and treatment, based upon a battery of tests and interviews, also arrived at findings essentially similar to those of the analysis based on the HABGT.

Specifically, the psychiatric history indicated that this man, a patient in a neuropsychiatric hospital, was admitted with the following symptoms: insomnia, palpitation, night sweats, trembling when people observed him, and feelings of inadequacy. His difficulties were reported as having begun some six months after he entered the Navy, in which he was assigned to the medical corps. Since his discharge his concentration had become quite poor and his symptoms had increased progressively.

At the hospital his first diagnosis was psychoneurosis, anxiety type, acute and severe. Later, psychiatric consultation suggested that he was most likely an obsessive–compulsive, but the diagnosis was "between obsessive–compulsive neurosis, anxiety–hysteria, and schizophrenia." The discharge diagnosis was that of anxiety reaction.

Following discharge from the hospital, the patient was seen in therapy at a mental hygeiene clinic. The patient terminated therapy, which had been conducted by a psychiatric case worker under close psychiatric consultation. The closing note on this case may be of interest. "The material obtained seemed to indicate more and more clearly that his defenses were crumbling and that he was either close to a psychotic break or actually psychotic. . . . Diagnosis: schizophrenic reaction, paranoid type."

We cannot take the space to review the specific dynamic findings of the therapist, which confirmed those of the HABGT, but the interested reader may study these for himself in the fairly exhaustive summary that Shneidman presents (Shneidman et al. 1951).

Addendum

This patient's Psychopathology Scale (Original Scale) score is presented in Table 10.3. An examination of these scores indicates that there is little scorable pathology on this scale. This is an excellent example of

Table 10.3
Psychopathology Scale Findings: David (Original Scale)

Test Factor	Scale Value	Test Factor	Scale Value
1. Sequence	1.0	10. Perc. Rotation	1.0
2. Position 1st Fig.	3.25	11. Retrogression	1.0
3. Space, I	1.0	12. Simplification	1.0
4. Collision	2.5	13. Fragmentation	1.0
5. Shift of Paper	1.0	14. Overlapping	1.0
6. Closure Diff.	5.5	15. Elaboration	1.0
7. Crossing Diff.	4.0	16. Perseveration	1.0
8. Curvature Diff.	4.0	17. Redrawing	1.0
9. Angulation	2.0		

Total scaled score: 32.25

the limitations of any objective scale, not only this one. There are many instances in which a low Psychopathology score is not suggestive of the severe disturbance that may be present. Casual inspection of such scores might lead to the inaccurate conclusion that there is no pathology. The same conclusion might be reached by a casual inspection of the actual or test behavior. One of the major reasons for such possibilities is that the pathology may be disguised by compensatory processes. Many disturbances involve an insidious process that is not easily detectable. *Low scores on objective scales do not necessarily mean, however, that there is an absence of pathology.* High scores are more likely to be indicative of such pathology. The advantage of a careful, detailed inferential analysis, as this case illustrates, is that the trained clinician is much more apt to pick up subtle signs and, especially, contradictions in the record, which finally lead to a more accurate appraisal.

11
Clinical and Therapeutic Use of the HABGT

In this chapter we shall present some additional research findings related to the projective uses of the HABGT and then present illustrative methods and examples of clinical and therapeutic uses of this procedure. I should like to emphasize, first, that it is the *idiosyncratic* responses of subjects to the HABGT figures and elaborations of these figures that are of paramount interest. Although research studies may find that, for example, some test designs tend to produce certain common associations, or that certain test measures may define ego strength or aggressive traits, such findings are, by their nature, nomothetic in character; i.e., they may apply to a class of individuals. Such data are of value but they are far less important than the unique and particularized associations the figures or their elaborations have for a given individual. For example it would not be surprising to find that for groups of individuals, associations to elongated figures, like figure 8, are frequently related to sexual interests or conflicts, and that responses to circular figures, like a portion of figure A, are frequently associated with the vagina or with female sexuality, but of greater and more meaningful significance is *what a figure means to a particular person.* Such meanings can only be confirmed by *investigating such associations in a particular case,* and exploring the specific connotations the figure and associations have for that person.

Another preliminary consideration should be emphasized. As we have indicated previously, there are many memory traces that each individual carries that were derived during early formative periods. During these periods, when cognitive, and particularly when verbal skills were also in their formative period, much of experience, particularly highly affective and traumatic experience, is encoded in motoric and perceptual behavior. Consequently, when an individual performs acts that are largely determined by perceptual-motoric behavior, and especially when that subject is asked to "elaborate" or modify the drawings as he wishes so as to make them "more pleasing," the resulting associations tend to "release" such bound-up memories, or at least release derivatives of such experience. I shall cite an unusual experience I encountered in psychotherapy to illustrate this point. Later in this chapter, I shall offer a striking example of *particularized associations* evoked by elaborations to an HABGT figure.

A young, graduate student who was in psychotherapy with me kept referring to a puzzling experience he had—sometimes in dreams and sometimes while awake. He would see "clearly defined lines in the sky." He was able to describe these *parallel lines* quite clearly, and he always experienced tension when the phenomenon occurred. After much therapeutic investigation, we were able to formulate the hypothesis that, *in his case,* these lines represented electrical wires or cables strung on poles and were viewed *from below* as lines in the sky. The hypothesis seemed a strong one, but it was still puzzling as to what such lines might really represent in *his experience,* and why they continued to produce tension in him over the years. Finally, on a visit this patient made to his mother, in a distant city, he learned that his mother would take him in a carriage to the food market and that she would leave him, lying in his carriage, out on the street in front of the store, while she completed her shopping. She was also able to recall that, on occasion, when she stopped outside of the store, to speak with a friend, she and the neighbor would notice how restless he became while they engaged in reminsicing about things. His mother told him that she frequently went shopping *just before his meal time,* and that there were occasions when she delayed feeding him far beyond his usual feeding time.

It turned out that his mother placed his carriage next to a pole on which were strung several parallel lines of electric and telephone wires. She chose this spot because it was visible from inside the store and the pole provided an anchorage for the carriage. Visits to this food store were made two, sometimes three, times per week and occured for many months.

These experiences occurred when our patient was about 1-year-old or slightly more. Our investigation seemed to indicate that he was experiencing *physiological tension* due to hunger pangs, and that he expressed this tension, in part, by *vigorous motor activity*. The possible veracity of this interpretation was strengthened by supplementary data that indicated that these frustrating experiences were reinforced by other delays in immediate gratification during infancy and early childhood (his mother was a "very busy woman" with four other children), and by fairly severe restrictions in his movements and other motor activities (he was a "sickly" child and often admonished to "stay quiet" and not to engage in vigorous physical activity). Although one may question the plausibility of this explanation, it seemed to "fit" and our discussions did lead to less motoric tension and elimination of the associated muscular tension. Most important, however, is the illustration of memory traces that seem to be associated with early perceptual-motoric experiences.

STUDIES ON PROJECTIVE ASPECTS OF PERCEPTUAL-MOTORIC BEHAVIOR

There have been relatively few research studies on projective properties of perceptual-motoric behavior. In addition to the studies that have been evaluated by Tolor and Brannigan (1980) and those evaluated in an earlier work by Tolor and Schulberg (1963), we have already reported on other relevant studies as they apply to the factors in our objective scales for the HABGT. At this point, we shall cite a few of the more important research reports and their findings. As we pointed out in our earlier edition of this work (Hutt, 1977), research on projective possibilities of the BG and the HABGT is difficult because of the criterion problem; i.e., it is difficult to obtain appropriate and measurable samples of many aspects of personality functioning. In addition, the development of sophisticated research hypotheses and appropriate research designs is also far more difficult than, for example, the measurement of "personality traits." In short, to evaluate personality processes the psychologist faces a difficult research problem. Hence, it is not surprising that there is relatively little research in this area and that what there is often lacks adequate rationale or appropriate research design.

In 1952, Suczek and Klopfer investigated the symbolic value of the Wertheimer figures that comprise the Bender-Gestalt Test. These figures were presented to a group of college students for their associations. The assumption was that people tend to perceive these designs in characteristic ways. Their findings suggested that their assumption was correct and led them to advance tentative hypotheses regarding the symbolic value of each test figure. Hammer (1955) made specific tests of these prior findings as they dealt with the psychosexual values of certain designs and attempted to isolate indices of phallic sensitization, castration feelings, and reactions to castration feelings. The experimental group was composed of men who were to undergo sterilization under the eugenic laws of the state of Virginia. Men who were to undergo surgery other than sterilization were used as a control group. The testing was carried out on the day of surgery. Hammer found support in his data for Suczek and Klopfer's hypotheses. He was also able to isolate test factors that were significant in distinguishing the experimental from the control group. The majority of these factors involved distortions of the elongated or phallic elements in the test figures.

Another study investigated the possible utility of those determinants proposed by Hutt (in the "Tentative Guide") as indicative of psycho-pathology (Byrd, 1956). It is significant that, unlike Billingslea, this inves-tigator tested the determinants as defined and scored by Hutt. In all, 15 determinants were evaluted. The experimental and control groups con-sisted of 200 children each, ranging in age from 8 to 15 years. Each group was further subdivided into 4 subgroups on the basis of age. The contrast-ing subgroups consisted of 50 "well-adjusted" and 50 "maladjusted" children each. The "maladjusted" children were selected on the basis of clinical study and diagnosis as in need of psychotherapy. One difference in method of administration of the figures from that proposed by Hutt (but favored by Bender) was that the children were required to make all of their drawings on a single sheet of paper (see Chapter 3 on Administra-tion). Byrd found that his data " . . . support the validity that the major-ity of test factors selected from Hutt are signs of personality adjustment." Further, he found that these factors operated in the *direction* predicted by Hutt. Bryd acknowledged that his study was essentially a test of the "sign" approach, and not an adequate test of the full projective potential when combinations of factors and their interactions were considered. He stated: "Evaluation of a record involves far more than a listing of signs. The total test performance must be considered." It might be added that the methods of defining and scoring the determinants used in this study were arrived at from a study of adult records and their direct applicability to children, especially in the younger age range, had not been proposed.

Clawson (1959) also investigated the utility of some of the factors proposed by Hutt in differentiating emotional disturbance. Again, her study was confined to children, ranging in age from 7 to 12 years. The experimental group consisted of 40 boys and 40 girls who were clients of the Wichita Guidance Center and whose problems could be described clinically "as maladjustive behavior associated with emotional distur-bances." The control group, matched individually on the basis of age, sex, and I.Q., and matched on a group basis on socioeconomic status, consisted of a like number of children judged by their teachers to be "normally developing children typical of the age group." Because Claw-son's study was sophisticated both with respect to conceptualization and with respect to design, it will be dealt with at some length.

She utilized three kinds of statistical tests to validate test factors: comparisons of clinic and school populations in terms of frequency of occurrence of the pathologic factor; chi square tests between test factors and behavioral symptoms for clinic cases; and chi square comparisons between test factors and Rorschach indicators. Of 48 chi squares that were tested, 19 were significant at the .01 level. The probability of obtaining this number of significant statistics is less than .001. Specific test factors that differentiated clinic from school children (3 at the .001 level, and 1 at the .01 level) were regression, closure, joining difficulty, and erasures. Gestalt factors that were significantly related to behavior indicators (all but one at the .01 level or better, and 1 at the .05 level) were expansive organization (on the Bender) with acting out (in behavior), compressed organization with withdrawn behavior, decreased figure size with withdrawn behavior, incorrect number of units with reading problems, and horizontal page placement with acting out. Similarly, Gestalt factors that were significantly related to Rorschach indicators (at the .01 level or better) were constricted size with constriction (on the Rorschach), figure joinings with interpersonal aggression, and uneven figure size with aggressive responses. In addition, it was demonstrated that "use of white space" was significantly related to aggression and that orderly sequence was associated with good adjustment while poor sequence was associated with maladjustment. She concluded: "The results of this study reveal the presence of meaningful diagnostic signs in children's BVMGT records beyond a simple ability to reproduce designs of differing complexity. Of the 13 variables which differentiated the two groups significantly, the data supported five hypotheses of interpretive significance and demonstrated three significant relationships between the BVMGT and the Rorschach. It is believed that Hutt's hypotheses about the *significance of deviations with adults* [italics mine] have been established, in part, with children."

A number of studies have been concerned with the projective properties of specific types of distortions or work methods on the Gestalt reproductions or with the associations to specific test figures. In examining some of the more relevant studies, it should be remembered that *no single indicator is likely to have high validity in assessing personality characteristics.* Any sign may be produced by quite a variety of conditions—such as the age or sex of the subject, recent traumatic experiences, prior cultural conditioning, learned methods of drawing, and various psychological conditions. Any proposed "sign" should therefore be interpreted as a *likely hypothesis* whose probable meaning needs to be checked against other concurrent evidence as well as against *the accumulation of other signs having similar probable import.* Even the most valid of "signs" would be likely to have relatively low reliability (as well as validity) if taken entirely by themselves and should not be used by itself to make predictions in individual cases. In an individual case, only the concurrent contribution of a number of signs, *without the occurrence of contraindicative evidence,* would be highly meaningful.

One of these earlier studies investigated the types of differences found among aggressive, passive, and a control group of preadolescent and adolescent children (Taylor & Schenke, 1955). Aggression and passivity were judged on the basis of a questionnaire checked by two raters. The control group was selected on the basis of intermediate scores on the ratings. A study such as this raises a number of basic questions: how valid are the ratings of aggression and passivity; was either the "aggressive" or the "passive" group homogeneous in other personality characteristics or degree of maladjustment; what type of aggression and what type of passivity were being rated; and what types of related personality characteristics (and Bender-Gestalt factors) were expected to be related? None of these questions is dealt with in this research. It was found that aggressive children distorted the size of the drawings more often than did the passive children. Other Bender-Gestalt factors that were studied (such as the sequence of placement of the drawings on the page, and direction in drawing the secant on figure 5) did not significantly differentiate the groups. However, in terms of considerations of basic research design and appropriate rationale for specified hypotheses, a study such as this must be considered inconclusive.

Other studies have dealt with specific types of distortions as indicators of emotional disturbance or of specific personality conflicts. Distortions involving an increase in the size of the figures have been investigated by a number of workers. For instance, Elliot (1968) found that this factor significantly distinguished between psychiatric patients and normal school pupils of comparable age. Naches found (1967) that large size of the reproductions was correlated with acting out behavior in youngsters. Kai (1972) was able to show that kindergarten children with emotional problems revealed significant differences on this characteristic from those without such problems. A related study by Brannigan and Benowitz (1975) found that the best "Bender-Gestalt" indicators of antisocial acting out tendencies in adolescents were uneven figure size and exaggerated curvature. It should be noted that even when individual test factors are shown to differentiate significantly between different psychiatric conditions or between psychiatric and nonpsychiatric conditions in groups of subjects, the presence of such a factor in an individual case *does not necessarily signify that this is an adequate or sufficient explanation in that case.* The same test factor may occur due to other causes. *It is always necessary to test and evaluate the relevance of other possible explanations of that test factor in a given instance.*

Goldfried and Ingling (1964) conducted an elaborate evaluation of the possible symbolic meanings of the HABGT test figures by, among other things, asking subjects (40 college men and 40 college women) to rate the designs in terms of critical verbal concepts and, using the semantic differential method, to evaluate the designs in terms of symbolic meanings attributed to them by Hutt and Briskin (1960). They found that design 5 had attributed to it: interpersonal relations, dependency, and "man" for both sexes, designs 1 was related to "Dependency," design 4 offered some support for the hypothesis of "mother surrogate" as well as "dependency" in males and "Vagina" "dependency," and "Interpersonal relations" in females, design 7 was associated with "man" for both sexes and with "penis" and "anger" for women, and design 8 was associated with sexuality and with sexual intercourse, in particular. Although the authors did not feel that their findings strongly supported Hutt and Briskin's hypotheses, their data, as actually reported, seem to support, in fact, the contention that many, if not all, of the test figures do provoke symbolic associations as predicated. In fact, if one allows for some of the methodological limitations of the study, despite its otherwise excellent design, such support seems even more strongly indicated.

Another study by White (1976) reveals both the potential for research on projective aspects of HABGT behavior as well as the limitations of some kinds of research in this area. Using the MMPI as the criterion measure, White found that, as postulated by Hutt, depressives had significantly more "constriction" in their records than did nondepressives. A major problem with studies such as this is that a *single sign of depression* (namely "constriction"), is evaluated *without simultaneously* considering other depressive indicators or other nondepressive indicators. The obviously inadequate assumption is that any *single sign,* taken out of context with respect to supporting and nonsupporting evidence, can be tested adequately. Such an assumption defies the whole conception of our projective approach, namely: that it is the total configuration that must be evaluated in terms of the patterning of the relevant elements!

In contrast to the above studies, consider one done on the basis of sophisticated theory and rationale (Story, 1960). This investigator was interested in the possible *projective differences* on the HABGT between a group of 30 alcoholics and a control group of 30 nonalcoholic, nonpsychiatric individuals, similar with respect to age and socioeconomic status. The groups were also controlled for educational background. Story begins his report by asserting: "Psychological research in the area of alcohol addictions has been very deficient with respect to the most rudimentary projective aspects of the Bender-Gestalt test." He is also careful to specify, when contrasting his research procedure with that of others he reviewed, " . . . it is first necessary to grasp the *method of test administration employed,* for it differs considerably from the procedure used in the studies reviewed above." Story used the cards and the specific methods of administration proposed by Hutt, including the method of "elaborations" and "associations" (see Chapter 3). He then derived several hypotheses from personality theory and theory of psychopathology *concerning expected dynamics* common to the alcoholic syndrome. He finally selected determinants from the HABGT which Hutt had proposed *as related to these dynamics*.

As an example of the manner in which Story developed these hypotheses, the following may be indicative:

A low tolerance for frustration and corresponding avoidance of stress are among the most frequently observed behavior patterns of alcoholics. Characteristically, this behavior is to be seen in withdrawal or escape from the demands of interpersonal activities rooted in a deep-seated and pervasive anxiety about interpersonal relations in general. Briefly, rather than endure the satisfactions of unsatisfactory cathexes, the alcoholic chooses to flee from them. We hypothesize that this psychological blocking in the face of interpersonal demands should be evident in the response behavior to certain designs having intersecting, overlapping, or joined lines; e.g., designs A, 4, 6, and 7. On the revised design 6, for example, where the stimulus may be perceived as either two intersecting sinusoidal lines or two separate, nonintersecting, yet still touching sinusoidal lines, we hypothesize that alcoholics will perceive and reproduce these lines in the latter fashion; i.e., as nonintersecting, significantly more often than the control subjects.

As an aside, Story's use of the "revised designs," by which he means the Hutt adaptation of the designs (rather than the Bender designs), makes possible the testing of this particular hypothesis—the Bender designs might not lend themselves to a test of this hypothesis because of their possibly quite different stimulus value. It is also important to note that the expected "response behavior" is predicated on clinical observations already summarized in Hutt and Briskin's published volume on the test, and is not based on armchair or abstract symbolic theorizing.

Story also formulated other hypotheses in a similar fashion. In essence, these were as follows.

1.   In their elaboration of design 7, alcoholics will tend to reproduce it as nonoverlapping hexagons.

2.   In elaborating design 2, alcoholics will either change the columns of circles to the vertical plane, use solid straight lines, or reverse the direction in angulation of the circles.

3.   Alcoholics will count the dots on design 5, aloud or with a finger or pencil.

4.   Alcoholics will rotate the upright hexagon in design 7 more than 5 but less than 20 degrees to the left.

The reader will note, especially after he has had an opportunity to read the material in Chapter 4 on specific test factors and their interpretation, how Story wisely selected and adapted test factors *and* test behavior in order to test the relevant hypotheses.

The findings in this particular research study support each of the proffered hypotheses at significant statistical levels. An additional unpredicted finding was that the alcoholics tended to elaborate figure 6 (the sinusoidal curves) as waves, ripples, rivers, torrents, lakes, etc., significantly more ($p < .005$) than the control group, a rather striking and suggestive finding in the case of alcoholics.

Another line of investigation has been concerned with the projective interpretation of *directionality of lines*. I have been impressed with findings from Mira's work, as well as that of Werner (1957), that the characteristic direction in which adults tended to draw lines (as, for example, from the outside inward, or from the top to the bottom) is indicative of some rather basic and generalized attitudinal orientation toward the world (see Chapter 4). In general, the hypothesis was advanced that movement toward the self reflected an egocentric orientation, and that movement away from the self represented both an attitude of greater involvement with the "world" and a more assertive orientation. Similar hypotheses have been proposed and explored in research in connection with drawings, particularly the drawings of children (Alschuler & Hattwick, 1947). Two studies were specifically related to the question of directionality of movement as a possible indicator of egocentric personality orientation. Both used a single phenomenal indicator of direction of movement, i.e., the direction of movement in drawing the diagonal line of dots that forms part of figure 5. Naturally, any test based on this single phenomenon furnishes an attenuated measure of the possible general directionality that an individual may employ in his drawings, and thus may be expected to yield meager results at best. Nevertheless, surprisingly "good" results have been obtained.

Peek (1953) investigated the relationship between direction of movement on the diagonal of figure 5 and specific aspects of the clinical condition of 75 adults. A control consisted of randomly selected hospitalized, neuropsychiatric patients, similar in diagnosis, treatment at the hospital, and measure of improvement, but not selected with respect to directionality of drawing of the diagonal or "spike" on figure 5. The patient's clinical condition was rated on a check list of 40 items—again, not the most valid of indicators of these conditions. Nineteen significant differences (significant at the .05 level or better) were obtained. The results confirmed Hutt's hypothesis that direction of movement from the outside inward was indicative of egocentric personality makeup. Other related findings showed the experimental group to be more dependent, to be more reactive to frustration, and to have more bodily complaints—again, tending to confirm the general traits of egocentricity. Although Peek indicates that the practical utility of this finding is limited by the considerable variability found within the two groups, I am more impressed with the theoretical significance of his findings, especially in view of the limitations of the design noted above.

Clawson, in the study already referred to (1959), tested the power of the same phenomenon, direction in drawing the "spike" on figure 5, with her school children. She found that this single factor discriminated the "maladjusted" from the "adjusted" group at the .05 level.

Findings such as these suggest the potential value of appropriately designed scores, based on a *number* of indicators of a presumably significant characteristic, both for research and for clinical purposes.

MICRODIAGNOSIS AND CLINICAL PRACTICE

We have discussed previously some aspects of the process I have called *microdiagnosis*. This process involves the minute investigation, *in a particular case,* of the nature of the subject's performance (the nature of any impairment and the specific "routes" taken by the subject in the performance), and of the conditions under which the subject can improve his performance. Thus, for example, if the subject has difficulty with the overlapping figure 7, the questions one may ask are: is the difficulty due to the complexity of the task; is it primarly due to the figure-ground problem that figure 7 presents; is the subject's difficulty due to organic brain damage; or, is the subject's difficulty due to the sexual symbolism this figure poses? Other questions, of course, may be pertinent in a given case. Moreover, the examiner may wish to investigate: whether the subject can improve the performance and, if so, under what conditions: what factors in the performance (i.e., routes) led to the subject's difficulty with this figure?

These are the kinds of questions every clinician must pose and attempt to answer both for better diagnostic understanding and for leads to rehabilitation/psychotherapy. I have spelled out, elsewhere, some of the specific issues that are involved in this problem (Hutt, 1980). Too often some clincians are content simply to examine the subject's performance and score and/or evaluate them rather than to employ experimental-clinical methods to investigate the nature of the performance.

In the example of the subject's poor performance on figure 7, the examiner may first examine the subject's performance on "easier" figures to note whether figure-ground problems (such as figures 5 and 6 also present) cause the difficulty, or whether the subject has increasingly greater difficulty on all of the more difficult figures compared with the easier figures. However, certain other "experimental" procedures may be indicated. The examiner may provide the subject, for example, with two eliptical or two circular and overlapping designs (hand-drawn by the examiner and then presented to the subject) and ask the subject to copy these. This will help to determine whether simpler overlapping figures present the subject with similar problems in execution. The examiner may, utilizing the *elaboration* and *association* phases of the test, note whether the subject responds to the symbolic meaning of the figures and determine, by questioning, whether this may have contributed to the impaired performance. The examiner may ask the subject whether he is able to determine whether his reproduction and the stimulus are alike, and if not, what the difference may be. The examiner may ask the subject to attempt to improve his performance by asking him to try to make a more accurate reproduction. These are but a few of the ways in which the examiner can attempt to determine what led to the subject's failure on the figure and to attempt to determine whether and under what conditions the examiner can improve the performance.

Our major point, however, is to emphasize that the examiner's task is not simply to rate or score, but to investigate the situation *experimentally*.

THERAPEUTIC USES OF THE HABGT

When the clinician has administered all three phases of the HABGT (Copy, Elaboration, and Association), there are available for analysis (by *both* the clinician and the patient) a considerable amount of possibly meaningful data: test protocols and associations; behavior of the patient; spontaneous verbalizations by the patient. Moreover, utilization by the clinician of the objective scales and the inferential process of analysis provides rich leads for intensive diagnosis. Some additional procedures, such as microdiagnostic methods, may make the analysis more complete and confirming. The subject's *experience* in taking the test and spontaneous reactions to this experience may, by themselves, lead to therapeutic movement or to bases for planning therapeutic tactics and strategy (Hutt, 1977). We shall now illustrate how such spontaneous reactions by the subject and the utilization of additional clinical procedures may enrich and amplify therapeutic gains.

Our first example involves a 26-year-old male whom the writer saw in his consultative capacity at the University Medical Hospital of the University of Michigan. He had been brought to the hospital for observation and evaluation after he had been charged with attempted rape of a female college student. This attempt had taken place in broad daylight on the steps of a neighborhood church. The patient was extremely resistant, refusing to participate in psychiatric interviews and unwilling to discuss the alleged incident or circumstances surrounding it. He was then referred to the writer for diagnostic evaluation.

I explained to this patient that he had every right to refuse to participate in hospital procedures but that I hoped that by getting to know him a little, I might be of some assistance. He remained obdurate and impassive. I explained that if he would take a simple "drawing test," I might be able to understand him better and that this might help him to deal with the pending charges. I pointed out that he need not say anything while doing this task, unless he wished to do so, but at least we could observe how he functioned and that this might be of help. I also took pains to point out that I was not interested in "how well he could draw" but only in observing "how he went about it." He agreed to take this procedure and completed the Copy Phase and the Elaboration Phase without making any verbal comments. I, then, placed design A alongside his elaboration of that design and asked him what *either* the design or his modification might look like or remind him of. Plate 8 shows his (Mike's) elaboration of figure A.)

It should be noted that Mike first drew the figure at the left (1), *erased the left-hand portion of the internal X, and then drew the external portion of the square (2).* I was struck by the *possibility* (purely speculative) that this might represent a *cross,* lying on its side—possibly because I knew that Mike was alleged to have attempted rape *on the steps of a church.* Of course I said nothing about this but, instead, waited to see what Mike might say.

He stared at his elaboration and said nothing for a while. Then, without prompting, he began: "Damn that cross. . . . I erased that (sic). Then it looks like a circle and a box. No! It looks like a bridge table in a fish pond."

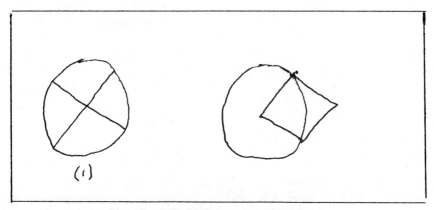

Plate 8.   Mike's Elaboration of Design A

I stop Mike's narration at this point (Mike didn't) to indicate that his associations thus far are clearly idiosyncratic and that his second association is *extremely unusual;* i.e., I'd never heard one like that before. If Mike had said nothing else, he would already have provided significant leads for further therapeutic exploration. But Mike didn't stop at this point. Instead, like a torrent rushing down a hill, he continued. "We were playing poker—the other kids and I. (He was speaking almost as if in a trance, reliving the emotional experience.) My father *always* said playing cards was a sin. My father rushed in, grabbed the bridge table, and threw it through the French doors into the fish pond."

Without any prompting on my part, Mike continued to talk about that, for him, highly traumatic experience, how his father was overly moralistic and brutal, and how he had wanted to escape from his "hated home." He also spoke of his brother, a priest, who had always been a "good son" according to his father, and with whom Mike had never gotten along. He continued with his story—finally indicating that he didn't know why, but he had attempted to rape "this girl" on the steps of his brother's church (!), but was apprehended in the attempt.

There is much more to this story. Our point, however, is that the perceptual-motoric activity stimulated by the HABGT figures seemed to provoke the release of early memories, and led to a moving cathartic experience for Mike. (Mike's other elaborations on the HABGT were not as dramatic as that on figure A, but were also revealing.)

It is not often that the HABGT provides such a rich lode for therapeutic exploration. However, it often does stimulate the recovery of early memories and often leads to self-revelatory behavior, as our next illustration will show.

Our next illustration highlights the values of the Elaboration and Association phases of the HABGT for both diagnostic and therapeutic purposes. This young, married female adult had been in psychotherapy with a psychiatrist for a number of years. Although she appeared to have made good progress in improving her self-percept, her initial complaints of nervous twitchings of the right shoulder and head had remained constant during her psychotherapy. The psychiatrist referred her to me "for emotional evaluation of her adjustment and to offer suggestions for more effective psychotherapy." She was an attractive and highly intelligent woman who felt that her marriage "was satisfactory" but "not particularly rewarding." She had favorable attitudes toward her therapist but, like him, felt "stymied" in not being able to relieve her "nervous twitching."

She quickly established a very favorable relationship with me and was "open" and cooperative during the psychodiagnostic evaluation. Part of this evaluation involved the administration of the HABGT. On the

Copy phase, her drawings were "precise" and accurate, placed in orderly sequence, well-spaced, and showed no significant distortions. She was given only four of the designs on the Elaboration phase (see Plate 9). She drew these elaborations quickly and apparently enjoyed doing them (figures A, 4, 5, 6, and 7). She offered no spontaneous verbalizations during this process.

When confronted with each of the test designs and her elaborations of them, she began by saying, "These look awfully childish. I suppose I am showing some regression." However, she did not block in offering her associations. Her associations to the original designs were "descriptive"

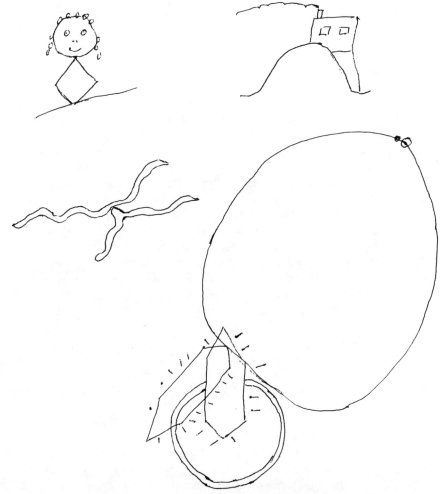

Plate 9.   The Revealing Elaborations of Marilyn

and nonrevealing. On the other hand, her association to her elaborations were quite another matter. (For didactic purposes we are not presenting either her Copy phase drawings or her associations to the test designs.) Her association to the elaboration of figure A was: "This looks like a little, happy girl, probably looking for and expecting affection." (Later she added that she had had a happy childhood and was the "apple of her father's eye." To figure 4 she associated: "This is the happy house where the child lived." On figure 5, she associated: "A gold necklace with a diamond near the clasp." On figure 6: "Two sinuous snakes in the Garden of Eden." Finally, on figure 7: "This is also a necklace with two immense diamond pendants."

The reader will easily recognize, I believe, that these associations are not only highly unusual for a grown, married woman, but suggest infantile wishes for affection, attention, and sensual gratification. However, such speculations need to be checked with the patient's further associations and elaborations. We proceeded with this task, and found that, unknown to her therapist (with whom she had not revealed such wishes), she had an active fantasy life in which she was the seducer of men, tantalizing them with her sexual attractions, and *often frustrating them*. We spent two additional sessions discussing her associations to the HABGT and these and other fantasies. She saw some connection between her "twitchings" and: her desire for special attention; her fear of exposing these wishes; her (dimly) perceived sexual-aggressive wishes; and some aspects of her oedipal problems. All of this was self-actualized and motivated.

This patient expressed the strong desire to continue with this writer in further psychotherapy. After discussion with her and her therapist, all of us agreed that this might be a wise decision. She entered into therapy with the writer and spent the better part of a year working out many aspects of her oedipal problems—even becoming an effective speaker in public without any recurrence of the nervous twitchings—which were now understood as a consequence of her exhibitionistic-sexual wishes and, therefore, a neurotic method of satisfying these wishes. Both her marital experience and her career goals were very significantly improved.

This case illustrates the values of the HABGT in releasing subconscious wishes and conflicts and in utilizing these experiences in formulating a more precise psychodynamic evaluation as well as in promoting "movement" in psychotherapy. From the viewpoint of general therapeutic strategy, it assists in evaluating ego strength (her Copy productions revealed a relatively low Psychopathology Scale score, for instance), and in suggesting the "sector" or focus for therapy that is immediately available for exploration (the precise nature of her sexual wishes and their superego constraints). The present illustration also suggests how the HABGT can be a *facilitator* of therapeutic movement.

The reader who wishes to examine other examples of HABGT proto-cols is referred to the volume by Hutt and Gibby (1970). This work con-tains many examples of the HABGT records of patients with organic brain damage, psychoneuroses, psychoses, and mental retardation. The protocols are scored for psychopathology and for adience-abience, and clinical descriptions are provided. Illustrations of projective analyses of test records are also included.

SOME GENERAL PRINCIPLES IN THERAPEUTIC USE OF THE HABGT

Based, primarily, on our own therapeutic use of the HABGT over the years and our psychodynamic orientation toward therapy (Hutt, 1977), we may formulate a few guiding principles in utilizing the HABGT for therapeutic purposes.

1. *The patient's over-all reactions to the test.* After the test ad-ministration has been completed, whether Copy Phase only or other phases as well, *ask the patient what his reactions to the test are.* Apart from the specific spontaneous verbalizations and specific associations to test figures and elaborations, the subject's feelings, attitudes, and mar-ginal thoughts about the test may be quite helpful. Some subjects are astounded by their own reactions/behavior to the test. One reaction by a well-defended patient was: "I see that I didn't change any of the designs. I don't know why I was scared to do so." Another patient, the Dean of a well-known university who came for diagnosis/therapy because he was having considerable difficulty in "thinking clearly" and "working effec-tively," said, after inspecting his productions on the HABGT: "I didn't know I was that tight. Why did I crowd my drawings together so closely? Why did I make the drawings so big? They're all out of proportion. I guess there are some things in me (sic), and not so much in the real world, that are bothering me." Still another subject, a college professor of psychol-ogy, who published frequently but whose research was on "safe" prob-lems on which he prided himself because of their "clean methodology," said, after looking at his drawings on the Copy phase: "I note that I lined these figures up precisely, so that the center of each figure is precisely centered beneath the center of the preceding figure." When I asked him why he supposed he worked that way, he responded: "I suppose I have to have perfect control. But I notice that in my anxiety to line-up the figures, I also changed some of their properties!" This individual was motivated to seek personal psychotherapy (although he had previously disdained

doing so), and was able to become much more creative in his research activities.

The over-all reactions to the tests of younger subjects, especially of adolescents, can be even more rewarding. Frequently, such individuals will first focus their attention on their difficulties in "drawing" as a first defensive manoeuver, but then quickly continue with highly, self-reveltory remarks.

2. *Significant changes in sequence, form, or size.* The principle that applies to this type of feature in the test protocol involves *two procedures. The first is: to ask the subject whether he sees any differences between his drawings and those on the test card.* The second is: *when the subject has not spontaneously pointed out or commented on discrepancies,* or *has not spontaneously commented on unusual shifts in sequences, to ask him: "I wonder why you changed that figure,"* or, *"I wonder why you shifted your placement on that figure?"* If one can, it is usually wise to allow the subject to find and comment on such factors spontaneously. But, if they are not offered spontaneously, the examiner may "wonder" out loud what led the subject to do what he did.

Highly defensive, and especially, highly suspicious subjects may resist such challenges. In such instances, the examiner may seek a more appropriate time to ask about them later—perhaps, when the therapeutic alliance has been more firmly established. Frequently, however, since the focus of the questioning seems to be on the "test" and not on "the subject", the subject will offer some meaningful comment that may be explored at that or at a more propitious time.

3. *Therapeutic utilization of associations.* The principle here is to *explore* with the subject any *blockings* or any *apparently unusual associations.* In the first place, as we have emphasized previously, the apparently innocuous nature of the HABGT task tends to "throw" the subject off guard. The test figures have no clearly recognizable meanings and are not reacted to, in themselves, as paricularly threatening. This is one of the reasons why some clninicians like to use this procedure as a buffer test when other tests are also administered. Nevertheless, various types of "blocking" do occur, either in the Copy or in the Elaboration phase, precisely because the figures have symbolic-associative meanings for that patient, or the reproduction and elaboration of them (and the dissonance created by exposing, side by side, the test design and its elaboration during the Association phase) provoke repressed or marginal memories.

It is often useful, after the test proper has been completed, to ask the subject to associate further to unusual associations given during the Association phase, or to discuss these associations in terms of their particular meanings. It may seem surprising that not only patients with considerable self-awareness, but patients with characterological problems, respond to these approaches with meaningful associations. Individuals with characterological problems frequently develop massive distortions in psychological reactions due to persistent and severe traumatic experience during the largely nonverbal periods of life. Such individuals respond first to the perceptual-motoric behavior and then to feelings and vague thoughts associated with them.

Not only may the subject's initial associations to the HABGT be explored more fully directly after the test has been completed, but these associations may be recalled by the subject during the course of therapy, or the therapist may be reminded of them and call them to the subject's attention at such times. In this respect, associations evoked by perceptual-motoric activity are similar to dream material. They, too, are a "royal road to the unconscious." They, too, can be usefully integrated with other therapeutic data as therapy progresses.

4. *Therapeutic use of microdiagnosis.* This principle involves *the exploration of routes by means of which the subject can be assisted.* Following the completion of the administration of the HABGT, and perhaps much later in the course of psychotherapy, the clinician may attempt to determine what factors block the subject's maximal performance or growth. For example, if the subject has had difficulty with figure 7 or with figure 8, but neither the subject nor the clinician know why, various experimental-clinical procedures may be followed.

Suppose it seems clear that the difficulty with figures 7 and 8 are not due to either inadequate oerceptual-motoric development or drawing skills, but some emotional problem is suspected. At the same time, the subject has not associated any material with these figures that suggests sexual conflict. The examiner may suspect that there may be, however, some severely repressed sexual conflict or some more general problem in interpersonal relationships. A number of *ad hoc* procedures may then be employed, at the appropriate time, to test out such possibilities.

If, for example, the subject had difficulty with the designated figures because of some "apparently" phallic quality of the figures, the examiner may present the subject with similar figures but with these features eliminated. Thus, figure 7 may be presented as two overlapping rectangles or two overlapping ellipses. Figure 8 may be similarly altered before presentation to the subject for redrawing and associating. In the case of figure 8, it may be that the internal diamond is psychologically disturbing to the subject because it evokes marginal thoughts related to the vagina or to the anus. The examiner may modify the figure, based on relevant hypotheses, present it to the subject, and obtain associations to the altered figure and its elaboration (if this is also done).

Other types of problems may similarly be approached from an experimental-clinical orientation. Suppose that the subject has suffered from some mild form of OBS and has shown some of the classic characteristics of such patients. In a particular case, let us say that there is difficulty with perceptual rotation and fragmentation. The microdiagnostic-therapeutic problem is to determine, then, whether and under what conditions his performance can be improved. Does the performance improve if only and simply he is asked to take his time and try to improve the drawing so as to make it more closely resemble the test figures? In other words, can this or other *motivational* assitance help? Or, can the subject improve his performance if *specific difficulties* in his performance are pointed out? Or, can he learn to correct the problem by making use of other resources that are available? The specific difficulties for a particular patient may involve: motoric control; more persistence in defining the figure-ground problem; overcoming the feeling of impotence that the task first provokes; or, using some guides and practice to perform the task in a different manner than would have been the case before the impairment occurred.

Our major point is that the HABGT lends itself to experimental manipulation if it is viewed not only as a test but as a sample of perceptual-motoric behavior. If the clinician and the subject approach the HABGT situation as one that may be helpful in exploring the "whys" of behavior, and the "hows" such behavior may be improved or compensated for, the situation can become a "therapeutic experience." The therapist can act as "guide" and the patient as the "learner" who seeks to improve his behavior in terms of his own, immediate goals. Both can learn and find the experience a mutually profitable one.

References

Aaronson, B. S. (1957). The Porteus Mazez and the Bender-Gestalt recall. *Journal of Clinical Psychology, 13,* 186–187.

Adams, J., & Canter, A. (1969). Performance characteristics of school children an the BIP Bender test. *Journal of Consulting Psychology, 33,* 508.

Adams, J., Kenny, T. K., & Canter, A. (1973). The efficacy of the Canter Background Interference Procedure in identifying children with cerebral dysfunction. *Journal of Consulting and Clinical Psychology, 40,* 498.

Allen, R. M. (1968). Visual perceptual maturation and the Bender Gestalt Test quality, *Training School Bulletin, 64,* 131–133.

Allen, R. M. (1968). Experimental variation of the mode of reproduction of the Bender-Gestalt stimuli by mental retardates. *Journal of Clinical Psychology, 24,* 199–202.

Allen, R. M., & Frank, G. H. (1963). Experimental variation of the mode of reproduction of the Bender-Gestalt stimuli. *Journal of Clinical Psychology, 19,* 212–214.

Allport, G. W. (1937). *Personality: Psychological interpretation.* New York: Holt, Rinehart & Winston.

Alschuler, R. H., & Hattwick, L. B. W. (1947). *Painting and personality: A study of young children.* Vols. 1 & 2. Chicago: University of Chicago Press.

Ames, L. B. (1974). Calibration of aging. *Journal of Personality Assessment, 38,* 527–529.

Armstrong, R. G. (1965). A re-evaluation of copied and recalled Bender-Gestalt reproductions. *Journal of Projective Techniques and Personality Assessment, 29,* 134–139.

Armstrong, R. G., & Hauck, P. A. (1960). Correlates of Bender-Gestalt scores in children. *Journal of Psychological Studies, 11,* 153–158.

Barker, B. J. (1949). A note on the development of the Western Reserve Hapto-Kinesthetic Gestalt Test. *Journal of Clinical Psychology, 5,* 179–180.

Becker, J. T., & Sabatino, D. A. (1971). Reliability of individual tests on perception administered utilizing group techniques. *Journal of Clinical Psychology, 27,* 86–88.

Bender, L. (1938). *A visual motor test and its clinical use.* American Orthopsychiatric Association Research Monographs, No. 3. New York: American Orthopsychiatric Association.

Bender, L. (1946). Instructions for use of the Visual Motor Gestalt test. New York: American Orthopsychiatric Association.

Bender, L., Curran, F. J., & Schilder, P. (1938). Organization of memory traces in the Korsakoff syndrome. *Archives of Neurology and Psychiatry, 39,* 482–487.

Bernstein, I. H. (1963). A comparison of schizophrenics and nonschizophrenics on two methods of administration of the Bender-Gestalt Test. *Perceptual and Motor Skills, 16,* 757–763.

Billingslea, F. Y. (1948). The Bender-Gestalt: an objective scoring method and validating data. *Journal of Clinical Psychology, 4,* 1–27.

Billingslea, F. Y. (1963). The Bender-Gestalt: a review and a perspective. *Psychological Bulletin, 60,* 233–251.

Bilu, U., & Weiss, A. (1974). A configurational analysis of the Bender-Gestalt Test. *Israel Annals of Psychiatry and Related Disciplines, 12,* 37–52.

Black, F. W. (1973). Reversal and rotation errors by normal and retarded readers. *Perceptual and Motor Skills, 36,* 895–898.

Blum, R. H., & Nims, J. (1953). Two clinical uses of the Bender Visual-Motor Gestalt Test. *United States Armed Forces Medical Journal, 4,* 1592–1599.

Boake, C., & Adams, R. L. (1982). Clinical utility of the Background Interference Procedure for the Bender-Gestalt Test. *Journal of Clinical Psychology, 38,* 627–631.

Brannigan, G. G., & Benowitz, M. L. (1975). Bender Gestalt signs and antisocial acting out tendencies in adolescents. *Psychology in the Schools, 12,* 15–17.

Bravo, L. (1973). Psychological tests in the diagnosis of infantile minimal cerebral dysfunction. *Revista Latinoamericana de Pscolgia, 5,* 131–141.

Bravo, V. L. (1972). The conservation, stimulation, and development of superior ability. Paper presented to the California Association of School Psychologists.

Breen, H. (1953). The differential diagnostic technique as a measure of hostility. Unpublished doctoral dissertation, University of Western Ontario, Canada.

Brown, F. (1965). The Bender Gestalt and acting out. In L. E. Abt (Ed.). *Acting out: theoretical and clinical aspects.* New York: Grune & Stratton.

Brown, W. R., & McGuire, J. M. (1976). Current assessment pratices. *Professional Psychology, 7,* 475–484.

Bruhn, A. R., & Reed, M. R. (1975). Simulation of brain adage on the Bender-Gestalt Test by college students. *Journal of Personality Assessment, 39,* 244–255.

Butler, O. T., Coursey, R. D., & Gatz, M. (1976). Comparison for the Bender

Gestalt Test for both black and white brain-damaged patients using two scoring systems. *Journal of Consulting and Clinical Psychology. 2.* 280–285.

Byrd, E. (1956). The clinical validity of the Bender-Gestalt Test with children. *Journal of Projective Techniques, 20,* 127–136.

Canter, A. (1963). A background interference procedure for graphomotor tests in the study of deficits. *Perceptual and Motor Skills, 16,* 914.

Canter, A. (1966). A background interference procedure to increase sensitivity of the Bender-Gestalt Test to organic brain disorder. *Journal of Consulting Psychology, 30,* 91–97.

Canter, A. (1968). BIP Bender test for the detection of organic brain disorder: Modified scoring method and replication. *Journal of Consulting and Clinical Psychology, 32,* 522–526.

Canter, A. (1971). A comparison of the background interference effect in schizophrenic, nonschizophrenic, and organic patients. *Journal of Clinical Psychology, 27,* 473–474.

Canter, A. (1976). *The Canter Background Interference Procedure for the Bender Gestalt Test: manual for administration.* Nashville, Tennessee: Counselor Recordings and Tests.

Carr, A. C. (Ed.) (1960). *The prediction of overt behavior through the use of projective techniques.* Springfield, Illinois: Charles C. Thomas.

Caskey, W. E., Jr., & Larson, G. L. (1977). Two modes of administration of the Bender Visual-Motor Gestalt Test to kindergarten children. *Perceptual and Motor Skills, 45,* 1003–1006.

Chorost, S. B., Spivack, G., & Levine, M. (1959). Bender-Gestalt rotations and EEG abnormalities in children. *Journal of Consulting Psychology, 23,* 559.

Clawson, A. (1959). The Bender Visual Motor Gestalt Test as an index of emotional disturbance in children, *Journal of Projective Techniques, 23,* 198–206.

Credidio, S. G. (1975). A construct validity study of a measure of perceptual approach-avoidance. Unpublished doctoral dissertation, University of Detroit.

Crenshaw, D, Bohn, S., Hoffman, M., Matthews, J., & Offenbach, S. The use of projective methods in research. *Journal of Projective Techniques and Personality Assessment, 32,* 3–9.

Culbertson, F. M., & Gunn, R. C. (1966). Comparison of the Bender Gestalt Test and Frostig Test in several clinic groups of children. *Journal of Clinical Psychology, 22,* 439.

Davis, D., Cromwell, R. L., & Held, J. M. (1967). Size estimation in emotionally disturbed children and schizophrenic adults. *Journal of Abnormal Psychology, 5,* 395–401.

Dibner, A. S., & Korn, E. J. (1969). Group administration of the Bender-Gestalt test to predict early school performance. *Journal of Clinical Psychology, 25,* 265–268.

Dinmore, D. G. (1972). Developmental Bender Gestalt performance as a function of the educational setting and sex of young Negro children. Unpublished doctoral dissertation, University of Pennsylvania.

Donnelly, E. F., & Murphy, D. L. (1974). Primary affective disorder: Bender-

Gestalt sequence as an indicator of impulse control. *Perceptual and Motor Skills, 38*, 1079–1082.

Drever, J. (1967). Early learning and the perception of space. *American Journal of Psychology, 5*, 395–401.

Elliot, J. A. (1968). A validation study of the Koppitz and Pascal and Suttell systems with eleven through fourteen year old children. Unpublished doctoral thesis, University of Michigan.

Fabian, A. A. (1945). Vertical rotation in visual-motor performance: Its relationship to reading reversals. *Journal of Educational Psychology, 36*, 129–154.

Fabian, A. A. (1951). Clinical and experimental studies of school children who are retarded in reading. *Quarterly Journal of Child Behavior, 3*, 129–154.

Fanibanda, D. K. (1973). Cultural influence on Hutt's adaptation of the Bender-Gestalt: a pilot study. *Journal of Personality Assessment, 37*, 531–536.

Flint, F. S. (1965). A validational and developmental study of some interpretations of the Bender-Gestalt Test. Unpublished doctoral dissertation, New York University.

Freed, E. X., & Hastings, K. C. (1965). A further note on the stimulus factor in Bender-Gestalt test rotations. *Journal of Clinical Psychology, 21*, 64.

Friedman, A. F., Wakefield, J. A., Sasek, J., & Schroeder, D. (1977). A new scoring system for the Spraings Multiple Choice Bender Gestalt Test. *Journal of Clinical Psychology, 33*, 205–207.

Fuller, J. B., & Chagnon, G. (1960). Factors influencing rotation in the Bender-Gestalt performance of children. *Journal of Projective Techniques, 26*, 36–46.

Gardner, R. W., & Long, R. I. (1960). Cognitive controls as determinants of learning and remembering. *Psychologia, 3*, 165–171.

Garron, D. C., & Cheifetz, D. I. (1960). Comment on Bender-Gestalt discernment of organic pathology. *Psychological Bulletin, 63*, 197–200.

Gavales, D., & Millon, T. (1960). Comparison of reproduction and recall size deviations in the Bender-Gestalt as a measure of anxiety. *Journal of Clinical Psychology, 16*, 278–300.

Gesell, A., Ilg, F. L., & Bullis, G. (1949). *Vision: Its development in the child.* New York: Harper.

Gilmore, G., Chandy, J., & Anderson, T. (1975). The Bender-Gestalt and the Mexican-American student: a report. *Psychology in the Schools, 12*, 172–175.

Gobetz, W. (1953). A quantification, standardization, and validation of the Bender Gestalt test on normal and neurotic adults. *Psychological Monographs, 67* (6, Whole No. 356).

Goldberg, L. R. (1959). The effectiveness of clinicians' judgments: the diagnosis of organic brain damage from the Bender-Gestalt Test. *Journal of Consulting Psychology, 23*, 25–33.

Goldfried, M. R., & Ingling, J. H. (1964). The connotative and symbolic meaning of the Bender-Gestalt. *Journal of Projective Techniques and Personality Assessment, 28*, 185–191.

Goodstein, L. D., Spielberger, C. D., Williams, J. E., & Dahlstrom, W. G. (1959).

The effects of serial position and design difficulty on recall of the Bender-Gestalt designs. *Journal of Consulting Psychology, 23,* 25–33.

Gordon, M. (1982). Central placement of Bender figure in clinic-referred and non-referred children. *Perceptual and Motor Skills, 54,* 1241–1242.

Greene, R., & Clark, F. K. (1973). Predicting reading readiness with the Bender-Gestalt Test in minority students. Unpublished findings.

Griffith, R. M., & Taylor, V. H. (1960). Incidence of Bender-Gestalt figure rotations. *Journal of Consulting Psychology, 24,* 189–190.

Griffith, R. M., & Taylor, V. H. (1961). Bender-Gestalt figure rotations: a stimulus factor. *Journal of Consulting Psychology, 25,* 89–90.

Grinker, R. R., & Spiegel, J. P. (1945). *Men under stress.* Philadelhia: Blakiston.

Guertin, W. H. (1952). A factor analysis of the Bender-Gestalt Test of patients. *Journal of Clinical Psychology, 8,* 362–367.

Guertin, W. H. (1954). A factor analysis of curvilinear distortions on the Bender-Gestalt. *Journal of Clinical Psychology, 10,* 12–17. (a)

Guertin, W. H. (1954). A transposed factor analysis of schizophrenic performance on the Bender-Gestalt. *Journal of Clinical Psychology, 10,* 225–228. (b)

Guertin, W. H. (1954). A transposed factor analysis of the Bender-Gestalts of brain disease cases. *Journal of Clinical Psychology, 10,* 366–369. (c)

Guertin, W. H. (1955). A transposed factor analysis of the Bender-Gestalts of paranoid schizophrenics. *Journal of Clinical Psychology, 11,* 73–76.

Guertin, W. H., & Davis, H. C. (1963). Similarities of meanings of elements and figures of the Bender-Gestalt. *Journal of Projective Techniques, 27,* 68–72.

Guilford, J. P. (1959). *Personality.* New York: McGraw Hill.

Hain, J. D. (1964). The Bender-Gestalt Test: a scoring method for identifying brain damage. *Journal of Consulting Psychology, 28,* 473–478.

Hammer, E. F. (1955). An experimental study of symbolism on the Bender-Gestalt. *Journal of Projective Techniques, 18,* 335–345.

Handler, L., & McIntosh, J. Predicting aggression and withdrawal in children with the Draw-a-Person and Bender-Gestalt. *Journal of Personality Assessment, 35,* 331–337.

Hannah, L. D. (1958). Causative factors in the production of rotations on the Bender-Gestalt designs. *Journal of Consulting Psychology, 22,* 398–399.

Hanvik, L. J., & Andersen, A. L. (1950). The effect of focal brain lesions on recall and the production of rotations in the Bender Gestalt test. *Journal of Consulting Psychology, 14,* 197–198.

Harris, J. G. (1957). Size estimation of pictures of thematic content for schizophrenics and normal subjects. *Journal of Personality, 257,* 651–657.

Hasazki, J. E., Allen, R. M., & Wohlford, P. (1971). Effects of mode of administration on Bender-Gestalt performance of familial retardates. *Journal of Clinical Psychology, 27,* 360–362.

Heaton, R. K., Baade, L. E., & Johnson, K. I. (1978). Neurological test results associated with psychiatric disorders in adults. *Psychological Bulletin, 85,* 141–162.

Hebb, D. O. (1949). *The organization of behavior.* New York: Wiley.

Helson, H. (1953). Perception and personality—a critique of recent experimental literature. USAF School of Aviation Medicine, Project 21, July.

Hoch, P., & Rachlin, H. L. (1941). An evaluation of manic-depressive psychosis in the light of follow-up studies. *American Journal of Psychiatry, 97,* 831–843.

Holland, T. R., & Wadsworth, H. M. (1979). Comparison and contribution of recall and Background Interference Procedures for the Bender-Gestalt test with brain-damaged and schizophrenic patients. *Journal of Personality Assessment, 43,* 123–127.

Howard, J. (1970). The group Bender Gestalt test as a screening procedure for the identification of children with a lag in visual perceptual development. *Journal of School Psychology, 8,* 64–65.

Hunt, J. McV. (1961). *Intelligence and experience.* New York: Macmillan.

Hutt, M. L. (1945). *A tentative guide for the administration and interpretation of the Bender-Gestalt Test.* U.S. Army, Adjutant General's School (Restricted). (a)

Hutt, M. L. (1945). The use of projective methods of personality measurement in army medical installations. *Journal of Clinical Psychology, 1,* 134–140. (b)

Hutt, M. L. (1951). The Bender Gestalt drawings. In E. S. Shneidman, W. Joel, K. B. Little (Eds.). *Thematic test analysis.* New York: Grune & Stratton.

Hutt, M. L. (1953). Revised Bender Visual-Motor Test. In A. Weider (Ed.). *Contributions toward medical psychology.* Vol. II. New York: Ronald Press.

Hutt, M. L. (1960). The Revised Bender Gestalt Test. In A. C. Carr (Ed.). *The prediction of overt behavior through the use of projective techniques.* Springfield, Illinois: Charles C. Thomas.

Hutt, M. L. (1963). The Bender-Gestalt Test. In D. Rosenthal (Ed.). *The Genain quadruplets: a study of heredity and environment in schizophrenia.* New York: Basic Books.

Hutt, M. L. (1968). The projective use of the Bender-Gestalt Test. In A. I. Rabin (Ed.). *Projective techniques in personality assessment.* New York: Springer.

Hutt, M. L. (1969). *The Hutt adaptation of the Bender-Gestalt Test.* 2nd ed. New York: Grune & Stratton. (a)

Hutt, M. L. (1969). The potentiality of a measure of adience-abience in predicting inner psychological adaptability. Paper presented at American Psychological Association, Washington, D.C., (Sept.). (b)

Hutt, M. L. (1976a). The significance of perceptual adience-abience in child development. In D. V. S. Sankar, (Ed.). *Mental health in children.* Vol. II. Westbury, New York: PJD Publications.

Hutt, M. L. (1976b). The significance of perceptual adience-abience in child development. In D. V. S. Sankar (Ed.). *Mental Health in children,* Vol. II. Westbury, New York: PJD Publications.

Hutt, M. L. (1977). *The Hutt adaptation of the Bender-Gestalt Test,* 3rd ed. New York: Grune & Stratton.

Hutt, M. L. (1980). Microdiagnosis and the misuse of scores and standards. *Psychological Reports, 50,* 239–255.

Hutt, M. L. (1983). Can a "squiggles" test be that revealing? *Contemporary, 28,* 391–392.

Hutt, M. L., & Briskin, G. J. (1960). *The Hutt adaptation of the Bender-Gestalt Test*. New York: Grune & Stratton.

Hutt, M. L., & Dates, B. G. (1977). Reliabilities and Interrelationships of two HABGT scales in a male delinquent population. *Journal of Personality Assessment, 41*, 353–357.

Hutt, M. L., Dates, B. G., & Reid, D. M. (1977). The predictive ability of HABGT scales for a male delinquent population. *Journal of Personality Assessment, 41*, 492–496.

Hutt, M. L., & Feuerefile, D. (1963). The clinical measnings and predictions of a measure of perceptual adience-abience. Paper presented at American Psychological Association, Annual Meeting, Philadelphia.

Hutt, M. L., & Gibby, R. G. (1957). *Patterns of abnormal behavior*. Boston: Allyn & Bacon.

Hutt, M. L., & Gibby, R. G. (1970). *An atlas for the Hutt adaptation of the Bender-Gestalt Test*. New York: Grune & Stratton.

Hutt, M. L., & Gibby, R. G. (1976). *The mentally retarded child: development, education, and treatment*, 3rd ed. Boston: Allyn & Bacon.

Hutt, M. L., Isaacson, R. L., & Blum, M. L. (1966). *Psychology: the science of interpersonal behavior*. New York: Harper & Row.

Hutt, M. L., & Miller, L. J. (1975). Further studies of a measure of adience-abience: reliability. *Journal of Personality Assessment, 39*, 123–128.

Hutt, M. L., & Miller, L. J. (1976). Interrelationships of psychopathology and adience-abience. *Journal of Personality Assessment, 40*, 135–139.

Hutt, M. L. & Monheit, S. (1985). The effectiveness of the Hutt Adaptation of the Bender-Gestalt Test Configuration in differentiating emotionally disturbed adolescents. *Psychological Reports,* in press.

Hutt, M. L., & Shor, J. (1946). Rationale for routine Rorschach "testing-the-limits". *Rorschach Research Exchange, 10*, 70–76.

Johnson, J. H. (1973). Bender-Gestalt constriction as an indicator of depression in psychiatric patients. *Journal of Personality Assessment, 37*, 70–76.

Jung, C. G. (1939). *The integration of the personality*. New York: Holt, Rinehart, & Winston.

Kachorek, J. (1969). Relationships between measures of adience-abience and field independence-dependence. Unpublished master's thesis University of Detroit.

Kai, T. (1972). An examination of the Koppitz Bender Gestalt Test (II): the correlation between each item of emotional indicators (EI) and the emotional problems in younger children. *Memoirs of the Faculty of Education, Kumamoto University, 20*, section 2.

Keller, J. E. (1955). The use of the Bender-Gestalt maturation level scoring system with mentally handicapped children. *American Journal of Orthopsychiatry, 25*, 563–573.

Keogh, B. K., & Smith, C. E. (1961). Group techniques and proposed scorring system foe the Bender-Gestalt with children. *Journal of Clinical Psychology, 17*, 172–175.

Kitay, J. I. (1950). The Bender-Gestalt as a projective technique. *Journal of Clinical Psychology, 6*, 170–174.

Klopfer, B. (1942). *The Rorschach technique.* Yonkers, New York: World Book Co.

Klopfer, B., Ainsworth, M. D., Klopfer, W. G., & Holt, R. R. (1954). *Developments in the Rorschach technique.* Yonkers, New York: World Book Co.

Koffka, K. (1931). *The growth of the mind.* New York: Harcourt-Brace.

Koppitz, E. M. (1958). The Bender-Gestalt Test and learning difficulties in young children. *Journal of Clinical Psychology, 14,* 292–295.

Koppitz, E. M. (1960). The Bender-Gestalt Test for children: a normative study. *Journal of Clinical Psychology, 16,* 432–435.

Koppitz, E. M. (1963). *The Bender-Gestalt Test for young children.* New York. Grune & Stratton.

Koppitz, E. M. (1965). Use of the Bender Gestalt Test in elementary school. *Skolepskyologi, 2,* 193–200.

Koppitz, E. M. (1975). *The Bender Gestalt Test for young children.* Vol. II. *Research and application,* 1963–1973. New York: Grune & Stratton. (a)

Koppitz, E. M. (1975). The Bender Gestalt Test and Visual Aural Digit Span and reading achievement. *Journal of Learning Disabilities, 8,* 154–157. (b)

Korchin, S. J., & Basowitz, H. (1954). The tachistoscopic Bender-Gestalt Test. *American Psychologist, 9,* 408, (Abstract).

Korim, H. (1974). Comparison of psychometric measures in psychiatric patients using heroin and other drugs. *Journal of Abnormal Psychology, 83,* 208–213.

Korner, I. N. (1962). Test report evaluation. *Journal of Clinical Psychology, 28,* 194–197.

Kramer, E., & Fenwick, J. (1966). Differential diagnosis with the Bender-Gestalt Test. *Journal of Projective Techniques and Personality Assessment, 30,* 59–61.

Krop, D., & Smith, C. R. (1969). Effect of special education on the Bender-Gestalt performance of the mentally retarded. *American Journal of Mental Deficiency, 73,* 693–699.

Labentz, E., Likenhoker, F., & Aaron, P. G. (1976). Recognition and reproduction of Bender Gestalt figures: a developmental study of the lag between perception and performance. *Psychology in the Schools, 13,* 128–133.

Lackman, F. M. (1960). Perceptual-motor development in children in reading ability. *Journal of Consulting Psychology, 24,* 427–431.

Lacks, P. (1984). *Bender Gestalt screening for brain dysfunction.* New York: John Wiley & Sons.

Lacks, P., Colbert, J., Harrow, M., & Levine, J. (1970). Further evidence concerning the diagnostic accuracy of the Halstead organic test battery. *Journal of Clinical Psychology, 26,* 480–481.

Lacks, P., & Newport, K. (1980). A comparison of scoring systems and level of scorer experience on the Bender Gestalt Test. *Journal of Personality Assessment, 44,* 351–357.

Landis, B., Baxter, J., Patterson, R. H., & Tauber, C. (1974). Bender-Gestalt evaluation of brain dysfunction following open heart surgery. *Journal of Personality Assessment, 38,* 556–562.

Landmark, M. & Grinde, T. (1964). *Children's Bender drawings from 1938–1962.* Copenhagen, Denmark: Nord Psykology, 1964 (Monograph).

Lapointe, R. E. (1974). The use of psychological tests by Ontario psychologists. *Ontario Psychologist, 6,* 75–82.

Lieberman, L. P. Drawing norms for Bender-Gestalt figures. *Journal of Clinical Psychology, 24,* 458–463.

Lindsay, J. (1954). The Bender-Gestalt Test and psychoneurotics. *Journal of Mental Science, 100,* 980–982.

Lubin, B., Wallis, R. R., & Paine, C. (1971). Patterns of psychological test usage in the United States: 1935–1939. *Professional Psychology, 2,* 70–74.

Lyle, O., & Quast, W. (1976). The Bender Gestalt: use of clinical jusgment versus recall scores in prediction of Huntington's disease. *Journal of Consulting and Clinical Psychology, 2,* 229–232.

Mark, J. C., & Morrow, R. S. (1955). The use of the Bender-Gestalt Test in the study of brain damage. *American Psychologist, 10,* 323.

Marley, M. L. (1982). *Organic pathology and the Bender Gestalt Test.* New York: Grune & Stratton.

McCann, R., & Plunkett, R. P. (1984). Improving the concurrent validity of the Bender Gestalt Test. *Perceptual and Motor Skills, 58,* 947–950.

McCarthy, D. P. (1975). The feasibility of a group Bender-Gestalt Test for pre-school and primary school-aged children. *Journal of School Psychology, 23,* 370–374.

McConnell, O. L. (1967). Koppitz' Bender-Gestalt scores in relation to organic and emotional problems in children. *Journal of Clinical Psychology, 23,* 370–374.

McConville, M. G. (1970). Perceptual adience-abience and social field dependence: an attempt at construct validation. Unpublished master's thesis, University of Windsor, Canada.

McPherson, M. W., & Pepin, L. A. (1955). Consistency of reproduction of Bender-Gestalt designs. *Journal of Clinical Psychology, 11,* 163–166.

Meyer, R. (1973). Altruism among male juvenile delinquents related to offense committed and parents' cultural status. Unpublished doctoral dissertation, University of Detroit.

Miller, L. J., & Hutt, M. L. (1975). Psychopathology Scale of the Hutt Adaptation of the Bender-Gestalt Test: reliability. *Journal of Personality Assessment, 2,* 129–131.

Mills, H. D. (1965). The research use of projective techniques: a seventeen year survey. *Journal of Personality Techniques and Personality Assessment, 29,* 513–515.

Mira, E. (1939–1940). Myokinetic psychodiagnosis: a new technique in exploring the conotative trends of personality. *Proceedings of the Royal Society of Medicine.*

Mira, E. (1943). *Psychiatry in war.* New York: Norton.

Molodnosky, L. B. (1972). The Bender Gestalt and the Frostig as predictors of first-grade reading achievement among economically deprived children. *Psychology in the Schools, 9,* 25–30.

Money, J., & Newcombe, P. (1974). Ability test and cultural heritage: the Draw-a-Person and Bender tests in aboriginal Australia. *Journal of Learning Disabilities, 7,* 197–303.

Monheit, S. (1983). The Bender-Gestalt Test as a discriminator of normal, severely disturbed, and delinquent male adolescents. Unpublished doctoral dissertation, University of San Francisco.

Mosher, D. L., & Smith, J. P. (1965). The usefulness of two scoring sustems for the Bender Gestalt Test for identifying brain damage. *Journal of Consulting Psychology, 29,* 530–536.

Naches, A. M. (1967). The Bender Gestalt Test and acting out behavior in children. Unpublished doctoral dissertation, Colorado State College.

Newcomer, P., & Hamill, D. Visual perception of motor impaired children: Implications for assessment. *Exceptional Children, 39,* 335–337.

Niebuhr, H., Jr., & Cohen, D. The effect of psychopathology on vusual discrimination. *Journal of Abnormal and Social Psychology, 53,* 173–176.

North, S. (1953). The diagnostic efficiency of a drawing technique. Unpublished doctoral dissertation, University of Western Ontario, Canada.

Olin, T. D., & Reznikoff, M. (1957). Quantification of the Bender-Gestalt recall: a pilot study. *Journal of Projective Techniques, 21,* 265–277.

Olin, T. D., & Reznikoff, M. (1958). A comparison of copied and recalled reprodcutions of the Bender-Gestalt designs. *Journal of Projective Techniques, 22,* 320–327.

Pardue, A. M. (1975). Bender-Gestalt Test and background interference procedure in discernment of organic brain damage. *Perceptual and Motor Skills, 40,* 103–109.

Parker, J. W. (1954). Tactual-kinesthetic perception as a technique for diagnosing brain damage. (1954). *Journal of Consulting Psychology, 30,* 91–97.

Pascal, G. R. (1950). Quantification of the Bender-Gestalt: A preliminary report. *American Journal of Orthopsychiatry, 20,* 418–423.

Pascal, G. R., & Suttell, B. J. (1951). *The Bender-Gestalt Test: Its quantification and validity for adults.* New York: Grune & Stratton.

Peek, R. M. (1953). Directionality of lines in the Bender-Gestalt Test. *Journal of Consulting Psychology, 17,* 213–216.

Peek, R. M., & Olson, G. W. (1955). The Bender-Gestalt recall as an index of intellectual functioning. *Journal of Clinical Psychology, 11,* 185–188.

Peek, R. M., & Quast, W. (1951). *A scoring system for the Bender-Gestalt Test.* Hastings, Minn.: Roland M. Peek.

Petrie, A. (1967). *Individuality in pain and suffering.* Chicago: University of Chicago Press.

Piaget, J. (1953). *The psychology of intelligence.* London: Routledge, Kegan Paul, 1950.

Postman, L. (1953). On the problem of perceptual defense. *Psychological Review, 6,* 198–206.

Rapaport, D. (1951). *Organization and pathology of though.* New York: Columbia University Press.

Research Report No. 43. (1964). *Identification and vocational training of the institutionalized deaf-retarded patient. The diagnostic study.* Lansing, Mich.: Department of Mental Health.

Reznikoff, M., & Olin, T. D. (1957). Recall of the Bender-Gestalt designs by organic and schizophrenic patients: A comparative study. *Journal of Clinical Psychology, 13,* 183–186.

Rock, I. (1974). The perception of disoriented figures. *Scientific American, 230,* 78–85.

Rogers, D. L., & Swenson, W. M. (1975). Bender-Gestalt recall as a measure of memory versus distractibility. *Perceptual and Motor Skills, 40,* 919–922.

Rosenberg, L. A., & Rosenberg, A. M. (1965). The effect of tachistoscopic presentation on the Hutt-Briskin Bender-Gestalt scoring system. *Journal of Clinical Psychology, 21,* 314–316.

Ross, N., & Schilder, P. (1934). Tachistoscopic experiments on the perception of the human figure. *Journal of Genetic Psychology, 10,* 152.

Ruckhaber, C. J., (1964). A technique for group administration of the Bender Gestalt Test. *Psychology in the Schools, 1,* 53–56.

Sabatino, D. A., & Ysseldyke, J. E. (1972). Effect of extraneous "background" on visual-perceptual performance of readers and non-readers. *Perceptual and Motor Skills, 35,* 323–328.

Schachtel, E. G. (1959). *Metamorphosis: On the development of affect, perception, attention, and memory.* New York: Basic Books.

Schilder, P. (1934). Space, time and perception. *Psyche, 14,* 124.

Schilder, P. Preface, (1938). *In* L. Bender, *A visual motor Gestalt test and its clinical use.* American Orthopsychiatry Association Research Monograph, Number 3. New York: American Orthopsychiatric Association.

Schneirla, T. C. (1959). An evolutionary and developmental theory of biphasic processes underlying approach and withdrawal. In M. R. Jones (Ed.), *Nebraska symposium on motivation.* Lincoln, Nebraska: University of Nebraska Press.

Schulberg, H. C., & Tolor, A. (1961). The use of the Bender-Gestalt Test in clinical practice. *Journal of Projective Techniques, 25,* 347–351.

Schwartz, M. L., & Dennerll, R. D. (1969). Immediate visual memory as a function of epileptic seizures. *Cortex, 5,* 69–74.

Segall, M. H., Campbell, D. T., & Herskovitz, M. J. (1966). *The influence of culture on visual perception.* Indianapolis: Bobbs Merrill.

Sĕpic, J. (1972). *Detection of simulators with Bender-Gestalt Test.* Psihölöske razprave: IV Kongres psihologov Serj. Ljubljana, Yugoslavia: University of Ljubljana Press, 502.

Shapiro, D. (1965). *Neurotic styles.* New York: Basic Books.

Shapiro, M. B., Post, F., Löfving, B., & Inglis, J. (1965). Memory function in psychiatric patients over sixty: Some methodological and diagnostic implications. *Journal of Mental Science, 102,* 233–246.

Shneidman, E. S., Joel, W. & Little, K. B. (Eds.) (1951). *Thematic test analysis.* New York: Grune & Stratton.

Sipola, E. M. (1984). Bender Gestalt, In Corsini, R. (Ed.). *Encyclopedia of Psychology.* Vol. I. New York: Wiley & Sons.

Smith, D. C., & Martin R. A. (1967). Use of learning cues with the Bender Visual Motor Gestalt Test in screening children for neurological impairment. *Journal of Consulting Psychology, 31,* 205–209.

Snortum, J. R. (1965). Performance of different diagnostic groups on the tachistoscopic and copy phases of the Bender-Gestalt. *Journal of Consulting Psychology, 4*, 345–351.

Solley, C. M., & Murphy, G. (1960). *Development of the perceptual world.* New York: Basic Books.

Song, A. Y., & Song, R. H. (1969). The Bender-Gestalt Test with Background Interference Procedure on mental retardates. *Journal of Clinical Psychology, 25*, 69–71.

Sonoda, T. (1968). The Bender Gestalt Test for young children: A review of verification studies made on the Koppitz scoring system. *Kumamoto Shodai Ronshu, 27*, 1–24.

Sonoda, T. A. (1973). A study of the development of visual–motor perception. *Kumamoto Shodai Ronshu, 37*, 1–9.

Spraings, V. (1966). The Spraings Multiple Choice Bender-Gestalt Test. Olympia, Washington, Sherwood Press.

Sternberg, D., & Levine, A. (1965). An indicator of suicidal ideation on the Bender Visual Motor Gestalt Test. *Journal of Projective Techniques and Personality Assessment, 29*, 377–379.

Stewart, H. F., Jr. (1957). A note on recall patterns using the Bender-Gestalt with psychotic and non-psychotic patients. *Journal of Clinical Psychology, 13*, 95–97.

Stewart, H. F., Jr., & Cunningham, S. (1958). A note on scoring recalled figures of the Bender-Gestalt Test using psychotics, non-psychotics, and controls. *Journal of Clinical Psychology, 14*, 207–208.

Stoer, L., Corotto, L. V., & Curnutt, R. H. (1965). The role of visual perception in reproduction of Bender-Gestalt designs. *Journal of Projective Techniques and Personality Assessment, 29*, 473–478.

Story, R. I. (1960). The revised Bender-Gestalt test and male alcoholics. *Journal of Projective Techniques, 24*, 186–193.

Suczek, R. F., & Klopfer, W. G. (1952). Interpretation of the Bender-Gestalt Test: The associative value of the figures. *American Journal of Orthopsychiatry, 22*, 62–75.

Sullivan, H. S. (1953). *The interpersonal theory of psychiatry.* New York: Norton.

Sullivan, J. J., & Welsh, G. S. (1947). Results with the Bender Visual Motor Test. In E. L. Phillips et al. (Eds.), *Intelligence and personality factors associated with poliomyelitis among school age children.* Monographs of the Society for Research in Child Development, 12, No. 2.

Sundberg, N. D. (1961). The practice of psychological testing in clinical services in the United States. *American Psychologist, 16*, 79–83.

Suttell, B. J. & Pascal, G. R. (1952). "Regression" in schizophrenia as determined by performance on the Bender-Gestalt Test. *Journal of Abnormal and Social Psychology, 47*, 653–657.

Taylor, H. D., & Thweatt, R. C. (1972). Cross-cultural developmental performance of Navajo children on the Bender-Gestalt Test. *Perceptual and Motor Skills, 35*, 307–309.

Taylor, J. R., & Schenke, L. W. (1955). The Bender-Gestalt Test as a measure of aggression in children. *Proceedings of the Iowa Academy of Sciences, 62,* 426–432.

Terman, L. M. & Merrill, M. A. (1960). *The Stanford-Binet Intelligence Scale: Manual for the third revision.* Boston: Haughton Mifflin.

Tiedman, R. (June 1971). A comparison of seven-year-olds around the world. Lecture, San Jose State College.

Tolor, A. (1956). A comparison of the Bender-Gestalt Test and the digit-symbol span as a measure of recall. *Journal of Consulting Psychology, 20,* 305–309.

Tolor, A. (1958). Further studies on the Bender-Gestalt Test and the digit-span test as a measure of recall. *Journal of Clinical Psychology, 14,* 14–18.

Tolor, A. (1960). The "meaning" of the Bender-Gestalt Test designs: A study in the use of the semantic differential. *Journal of Projective Techniques, 24,* 433–438.

Tolor, A. (1968). The graphomotor techniques. *Journal of Projective Techniques and Personality Assessment, 32,* 222–228.

Tolor, A., & Brannigan, G. G. (1980). *Research and clinical applications of the Bender-Gestalt Test.* Springfield, Illnois: Charles C. Thomas.

Tolor, A., & Schulberg, H. (1963). *An evaluation of the Bender-Gestalt Test.* Springfield, Ill.: Charles C Thomas.

Tripp, C. A. (1957). Some graphomotor features of the Bender Gestalt Visual Motor Gestalt Test in relation to delinquent and non-delinquent white adolescent males. Unpublished doctoral dissertation, New York University.

VandenBos, G. (1973). An investigation of several methods of teaching experiential focusing. Unpublished doctoral dissertation, University of Detroit.

Verms, S. K. (1974). Some perceptuo-motor disturbances on the Bender Gestalt test as effected by changes in orientation of the paper. *Journal of Clinical Psychology, 1,* 61–63.

VonBékésy, G. (1967). *Sensory inhibition.* Princeton N.J.: Princeton University Press.

Weiss, A. A. (1971). Incidence of rotation of Bender-Gestalt figures in three age groups of normal Israeli school children. *Perceptual and Motor Skills, 32,* 691–694.

Weiss, A. A. (1971). The influence of sheet position on placement of Bender-Gestalt figures. *Israel Annals of Psychiatry and Related Disciplines, 9,* 63–67. (b)

Werner, H. (1957). *Comparative psychology of development.* New York: International Universities Press.

Wertheimer, M. (1923). Studies in the theory of Gestalt psychology. *Psychologische Forschung, 4,* 301–350.

White, R. B. (1976). Variations of Bender-Gestalt constructions and depression in adult psychiatric patients. *Perceptual and Motor Skills, 42,* 221–222.

Wiener, G. (1966). The Bender Gestalt Test as a predictor of minimal neurological deficit in children eight to ten years of age. *Journal of Nervous and Mental Diseases, 43,* 175–180.

Witkin, H. A., Dyk, R. B., Faterson, H. F., Goodenough, D. R., & Karp, S. A. (1967). *Psychological differentiation.* Princeton, N.J.: Princeton University Press.

Wolff, W. (1943). *The expression of personality: Experimental depth psychology.* New York: Harper & Row.

Wurst, E. (1974). Factors in visual perception. *Zeitschrift fur Experimentelle ubd Angevandte Psychologie, 21,* 491–498.

Yulis, S. (1970). Performance of normal and organic brain-damaged subjects on the Canter Background Interference Test as a function drive. *Journal of Consulting Psychology, 34,* 184–188.

Author Index

Subject Index